Milo L. Brekke
Merton P. Strommen
Dorothy L. Williams

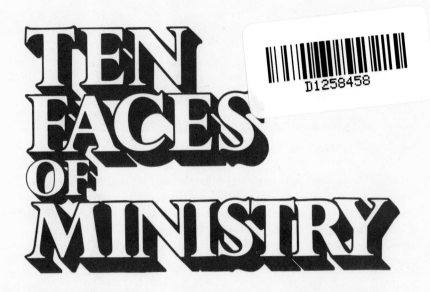

TEN FACES OF MINISTRY

Perspectives on Pastoral and Congregational
Effectiveness Based on a Survey
of 5000 Lutherans

AUGSBURG Publishing House • Minneapolis

TEN FACES OF MINISTRY

MANUFACTURED IN THE UNITED STATES OF AMERICA

Contents

Preface

The preparation of a book such as this presents two distinct challenges. The first is to do the research with the care and attention to quality demanded by the disciplines of social scientists, and to organize, study, and interpret the results according to those same standards. The second is to communicate those results.

The point of our work, then, was not to acquire information for its own sake, but to inform, to clarify, and to support ministry. That work could be considered complete only when the results were communicated to those who can make the most practical and effective use of the information. We were committed to that audience before we began.

To meet the second challenge (translation of research results into general readability) is more complex and difficult than might at first appear; the whole process involved, essentially, writing the book twice, in two different "languages." Research results emerge, at birth, in the form of numbers, statistics, and symbols. The first writing task was to attach verbal meanings to the symbols and to see, understand, and describe the relationships of those meanings to one another. The second writing task was to set those meanings and relationships into a new form that would communicate them to parish pastors, seminary educators, lay people, and all the other audiences for whose benefit we originally undertook the research. Beyond that, we also took seriously the request that we try to spell out some of the implications of what we had learned for the variety of people in those audiences.

A persistent conflict continued, therefore, throughout the writing process. Our tendency to communicate research in the language natural to and respected by researchers was in conflict with our commitment to make our findings and observations meaningful to people not trained in research. By and large, we believe that the nonresearcher audience has appropriately won. Social scientists will look in vain for our work to outline methodology, present evidence, and validate conclusions in the pre-

4

scribed ways. Responsible answers to all those typical research questions exist, but not in this book.

In both fields—in the doing of the research and in the writing—we have been aided by a whole host of people to whom we are very grateful.

We want first to express our appreciation to the members of Aid Association for Lutherans. Their financial support and gift of computer time made not only the research but the writing possible. We appreciate also the personal involvement of two members of the AAL management staff, William Selle and Paul Picard, who offered both critical appraisal and support of the project from its earliest days.

At the outset of the project, an advisory council was formed, including representatives of seminary education from the three Lutheran church bodies involved—the American Lutheran Church, Lutheran Church in America, and the Lutheran Church–Missouri Synod. The council members were Charles S. Anderson, Arthur Arnold, Reuben Baerwald, John Damm, Samuel Golterman, Allen Nauss, Carl Reuss, Robert Roth, Lloyd Sheneman, Walter Wietzke, and Walter Wolbrecht. These people gave generously of their time to attend meetings, wrestle with decisions, and offer wise advice and counsel.

Five thousand members of three Lutheran church bodies contributed an irreplaceable resource when they gave several hours of their time to completing the long questionnaire about ministry that formed the basis for our discoveries. To them and to the project representatives in each congregation, who took on the necessary administrative tasks, we give our sincere thanks.

In the later stages of the analysis of research data, we were greatly helped by the data processing facilities and staff of Lutheran Brotherhood Fraternal Benefit Society in Minneapolis, available as part of a larger grant of computer time extended to Search Institute over a number of years. Two Search Institute staff members, Ernest Thompson and Jerilyn Cornelius, spent many long days preparing and processing the data.

Two people gave help at special times. As Marvin A. Johnson shared experiences and findings from the LCA Growth in Ministry Project, he provided insights and encouragement for the shape of the book. William Streng, in inviting me to lead a Wartburg Seminary continuing education seminar on "Authenticity in Ministry" afforded an experience which gave impetus to the early development of these findings into a form meaningful to pastors.

We want to acknowledge the considerable contributions made to the successful completion of the research by two team members who were not involved in the writing. Daniel Aleshire's research insights and sensi-

tivity to seminary students' needs were a constant and dependable resource. Mary Kay O'Brien's faithful and skillful work as administrative
assistant for the project was invaluable.

The following persons who, in addition to some members of the
advisory council, served on an instrument development panel helped
immensely in naming, describing, and interpreting both the characteristics
and areas of ministry: Walter Buschmann, Wesley Fuerst, Roland Hop-
mann, Randolph Nelson, Daniel Simundson, Paul Sponheim, Jeffrey
Jerde, and Barbara Vogt.

Two people offered a number of important suggestions regarding interpretation and presentation of data. Roland Martinson made significant
contributions to our reflections on the implications of the research, particularly as related to seminary educators and seminarians. David Schuller
made several presentations to groups of pastors incorporating early parts
of the manuscript in his material. His communication to us of the pastors'
reactions and his own interpretative insights led to important modifications and additions to the manuscript.

We are grateful for the help of the editorial staff of Augsburg Publishing House, which offered incisive early critical review of the manuscript.
Shelby Andress also provided a number of helpful suggestions on form
and terminology, based on her readings of an early manuscript.

Several typists cheerfully carried the manuscript through what eventually became six revisions. Their efficiency, their patience in the face
of revision upon revision, and the unsought gift of their expressed interest
in the subject matter went far to redeem many a long day of writing.
The members of that blest crew were Betsy Schwebke, Jean Wachs, Carla
Dahl, Ellen Hanson, and Carolyn Rask.

Several members of the clergy read and lent advice at various points
in the manuscript's preparation: Harald Grindal, Maynard Nelson, Harlan
Norum, John Westby, Peter Strommen, Timothy Strommen, and George
Weinman. Lay people who discussed portions of the book and offered
reactions from their special perspective are Jean Hanson, Robert Engman,
Juanita Carpenter, Valerie Westby, Kay Nelson, Irene Strommen, and
Jean Erlandson.

We are also grateful to the readers whose careful scrutiny of the nearly-
completed book spurred us on to our final revisions—Allen Nauss, John
Damm, David Schuller, Wayne Stumme, Burnice Fjellman, Walter Wag-
ner, Lloyd Sheneman, Daniel Simundson, Leland Elhard and Frederick
Meuser.

Finally, we are indebted to C. Thomas Spitz, Arnold Mickelson, and
George Harkness, and, over the years, to the members of the Steering
Committee of the Division of Campus Ministry and Educational Services,

but especially to Reuben Baerwald, who, on behalf of the Lutheran Council in the USA, as supervisor of the project, offered us encouragement, counsel, and support throughout both the many years of the project and the writing of the book.

MILO L. BREKKE
Search Institute
(formerly Youth Research Center)

Partners in Ministry:
An Introduction

"*Ministry:* an act of service or aid; a vocation; a profession." The meanings are clear and universally understood. But for people involved in Christian ministry, or in preparing students for that ministry, or for people whose lives that ministry affects, the simplistic clarity of a dictionary definition does not suffice. More needs to be known.

What are the boundaries of the whole territory of ministry? What is its scope? What are the shapes and contours of the image each of us carries in our minds as we speak of ministry? Is my own personal concept of ministry too narrow or too broad? How does it differ from yours? What is our collective, corporate image of ministry in the Lutheran church? How can we make it visible?

Ministry is like no other profession. One who practices it touches people at the peaks and valleys of their lives—at times when they celebrate their greatest joys, and at times when they struggle with the depths of pain and loss. A minister deals with ultimate values, constantly turning people's attention to that which is basic, fundamental, and essential in life. A minister is a leader, facilitator, guide, confidant, encourager, exhorter, and friend to all kinds of people in all kinds of conditions. Ministers occupy a peculiar and sensitive position; they are persons both more powerful and less powerful than others with similar education and social status. People feel free both to admire them extravagantly and criticize them severely. A minister occupies a very public position, yet often shares people's most private thoughts and concerns. Ministry is that enormous task for which no one has ever been entirely and perfectly prepared —yet for which students in seminaries regularly prepare.

Ministry has been described, studied, and defined by various individuals and groups within the church. Until now, however, there has been no description of ministry that represents the perceptions of the majority of Lutherans in the United States. This book is an attempt to make that larger image of Lutheran ministry concrete, visible, and available for study and discussion.

Audiences

For whom was *Ten Faces of Ministry* written? Broadly speaking, it was written for pastors, for those who relate to or work with pastors, and for all, members of the laity or clergy, who participate in any way in ministry.

We anticipate that parts or all of this book will be particularly useful to members of congregational, district, and synodical call committees. People preparing for ministry, those who help them prepare, and those who are thinking about preparing for ministry will probably also find it a useful reference. Pastors will no doubt find it helpful, especially if they are evaluating their own needs for continuing education or personal growth.

This book will also be of special interest to bishops, synodical presidents, and other denominational officials responsible for placing pastors and aiding them in carrying out their assignments.

Uses of this book

This book has two basic uses. First, the responses of 5000 Lutherans as reported and analyzed here provide a comprehensive portrait of how Lutherans in the United States view ministry. This portrait should provide a good starting point for discussions of ministry on many levels.

A second, and equally important, use of this book will be in helping individuals and groups reflect on *their own* values and expressions of ministry. Chapter 1 provides a model checklist for use in exploring a particular area of ministry: "Personal Faith, Spiritual Depth." Suggestions on how pastors, church councils, call committees, and personnel committees can use this checklist are included there. Some possible uses would be:

- as a personal checklist
- as a means toward goal-setting
- as a way of offering information to others
- as a way of asking for evaluation of yourself from others
- as part of a group discussion of the ministry of your congregation

By referring to the suggestions and data in Appendix C at the back of this book, readers can develop similar checklists for any of the areas of ministry discussed in *Ten Faces of Ministry*.

Origin

Why was *Ten Faces of Ministry* written? Initially, a number of seminary presidents and others involved in the education of pastors wanted a more accurate way of discovering the needs and potential of incoming seminary students as related to pastoral work. Seminary faculty and staff members have long known that each group of incoming students differs in some ways from previous years' classes. Differences are also apparent between individual incoming students in background, ability, and commitment. What are the new students like? How do they differ significantly from last year's class? How do they differ from each other? Answers to these questions do emerge gradually throughout the year, of course, but it was recognized that it would be an advantage for a faculty to have more information at the outset.

It soon became evident that in order to develop a means of measuring these needs and potentials it would be necessary to know what was required for the pastorate—and to know it in a more precise and systematized way than by simply relying on the memory and experience of a few wise persons. It was necessary to know what Lutherans as a whole believe ministry to be, and the best way to find out seemed to be to collect information from a great number of persons who view it from various vantage points.

Method

Who provided this picture of ministry? Five thousand Lutherans speak from these pages. To be sure, there are some individual names on the cover, and the words on the pages are ours. But the realities conveyed are those of 5000 Lutherans who cared enough about ministry and those who prepare for it so that they were willing to commit a number of hours to pondering what ministry is and what they hope it to be and do.

At various times during the fall of 1974—in parish basements and classrooms, in dormitory rooms, in offices, on planes, and sometimes by the flickering of midnight oil—5000 Lutherans throughout the United States pored over a questionnaire. Its cover read, "What Contributes to, What Detracts from Effective Christian Ministries." In it were 461 statements that marched through more streets, alleyways, fields, and byways of ministry than many had realized existed.[1] They were statements like these:

1. These questionnaire statements had been produced through months of study, research, and meetings. About a third of the items were the same as those used in the Association of Theological Schools' Readiness for Ministry questionnaire. [See David S. Schuller, Milo L. Brekke, Merton P. Strommen, *Readiness for Ministry*, vol. 1: "Criteria" (Vandalia, Ohio: Association of Theological Schools in the United States and Canada, 1975).] Another third of the items were similar to those in the Readiness questionnaire, but modified to fit the Lutheran frame of reference. A third of the items were new. The modifications and new items were gleaned from interviews with Lutherans of all sorts—seminary theologians (who often concentrated on the Scriptures and Lutheran Confessions for what they shared), pastors, seminary interns, members of organized women's groups in the church, church business managers, campus pastors, church secretaries, parochial school teachers, members of ministerial examining boards—people in good positions to see ministers in action. These and more were asked to say what characteristics, qualities, skills, or actions would make a pastor most effective (or least effective) in carrying out ministry as they saw it. The series of interviews was continued until new ideas were no longer being generated in them. A sorting and editing of the information from these interviews, plus the already developed statements, made up the questionnaire.

"Helps people experience the Lord's Supper as a joyous celebration."
"Declares a willingness to run for public office in the community."
"Helps people use the resources of faith in coping with personal problems."
"Shows the mission of Christ to be first in own life."
"In embarrassing situations can laugh easily, even at self."
"Takes time to know parishioners well."

The task for each person was to mark each statement as to the degree of its contribution to, or hindrance of, effective ministry. The readers of the statements came from five groups.[2] There were, in all, 4033 lay persons, 364 parish pastors, 151 seminary professors, 352 senior seminary students, and 99 district or synodical presidents and executives.

The number of participants, by church body, was as follows:

The American Lutheran Church	1896
Lutheran Church in America	1576
The Lutheran Church–Missouri Synod	1527
Total	4999

The responses from each church body were weighted equally; regardless of the number of participants, each body had a 1/3 influence on the final result. There are some differences in what members of the three groups value in ministry, and we will report these differences in the succeeding chapters. However, our general observation is that the differences are relatively few, and the similarities far outweigh them.

It was considered important to give the perceptions of the clergy as much weight as those of the laity. Therefore the responses of clergy and lay persons were weighted 50–50 in analyzing the results of the questionnaire. Though there were not as many differences between the clergy and

2. All district/synodical presidents, all faculty members, and all seniors in United States seminaries of the three Lutheran bodies included in this study were invited to complete the questionnaire. Choosing parish pastors and lay people for participation was more complex. A random sample of 2% of congregations was invited to participate. The congregations were chosen in such a way that they appropriately represented each church body according to its membership, its strength in various regions of the country, and the range of size of its congregations. Members were randomly chosen within the congregations. (The questionnaire was completed before the founding of Christ Seminary–Seminex, so that while present members of the Association of Evangelical Lutheran Churches completed the questionnaire, their responses are included with the Lutheran Church–Missouri Synod information. Since the movement of individuals and congregations between LCMS and AELC continues, the task of separating AELC from LCMS information would be prohibitively expensive, if not impossible). Three hundred seventy congregations were invited to participate in the project by asking their pastoral staff and a representative fraction of their total membership to complete the questionnaire, and 268 of the 370 agreed, making a participation rate of 72%—a phenomenally high percentage of cooperation, as national studies go.

laity as many might be prepared to believe, there were quite a number, and we will report them also.

Content

The total of 461 statements about ministry conveys a sense of covering a vast territory. (Some lay persons, commenting on the questionnaire, speculated that an entering seminarian who caught sight of the sheer size of the territory might turn and flee in fear.) Such a large group of statements is more complex and unwieldy than can be easily kept in mind. Therefore the statements have here been grouped into larger categories and organized for sensible presentation.

The questionnaire participants, by rating each *item* (statement), gave the means needed to group, categorize, and organize the raw materials presented in the statements. When placing values on individual questions or situations, people usually express themselves with a consistency that allows for groupings of items having common elements. Each of these groups of statements—which we call a *characteristic* of ministry—presents a single recognizable facet of ministry. Mathematical treatment of the set of responses from each of the 5000 Lutherans produced 77 of these characteristics.

But even 77 facets of ministry are a rather large set to comprehend or hold in mind. When analyzed by the same statistical methods, the 77 ministry characteristics fell into 10 larger groups. Apparently the corporate Lutheran view of ministry is composed of 10 major aspects or *areas* of ministry. Each area consists of a number of *characteristics* of ministry, and each characteristic is composed of a number of *items*.

461 items (statements about ministry),
each describing some ministry behavior,

formed

77 characteristics of ministry,
each consisting of a group of related items,

formed

10 areas of ministry,
each consisting of a group
of related characteristics.

One kind of information this book offers, therefore, is an organized presentation of Lutheran ministry, together with its parts and pieces, as assembled by Lutherans. These can be studied and discussed at three levels of specificity: in terms of either item, characteristic, or general area of ministry.

The second kind of information resulting from analysis of the questionnaire is the value or importance that Lutherans, on the average, placed on each of the items, characteristics, and areas of ministry. Throughout this book these averages are presented as ratings, since each questionnaire participant rated every item on a scale from "absolutely essential" (+4.00) to "absolutely disqualifying" (−4.00).

The ratings given to each of the items, characteristics, and areas of ministry are also presented in three groups: all Lutherans, laity only, and clergy only. (The clergy only or "professional" rating consists of the combined ratings of seminary professors, seminary seniors, parish clergy, and district or synodical executives.) The corporate ratings assigned by each of these three groups to each *area* of ministry and each *characteristic* are listed in Appendix A. Ratings given on each *item* by each of the three groups appear in Appendix C.

Note: the fact that 5000 Lutherans, on the average, ranked one aspect of ministry higher than another does not mean it should be that way in your congregation. You may determine another order of priorities based on what your congregation and community need most. Though the research reported here may aid your powers of observation, *it is not meant to cancel out or be a substitute for your own efforts to evaluate what your congregation needs* (see the section, "Uses of this Book" above). Yet we hope that the framework of areas of ministry and ministry characteristics presented here will make your task of evaluation easier.

Organization

Each of the 10 major areas of ministry is treated in a separate chapter. Chapters 1–5 deal with five areas of ministerial perspective. They have to do with how pastors view their faith, people, church, purpose, and themselves. Readers should be prepared for a marked shift between Lutheran enthusiasm for the first three of these areas of ministry and their view of the next two. These chapters include first the three highest-ranked and then the two lowest-ranked areas of ministry.

Chapters 6–10 treat five areas of skill and performance. They have to do with how pastors preach and teach, administer, counsel, reach out into the community, and lead worship. They are introduced in sequence according to their rank, from IV through VIII.

Each chapter is presented in three sections. The first part is descriptive. It explores in detail the nature of that feature or area of ministry. In presenting these descriptions, we offer neither our own definitions of the named characteristics nor a standard Lutheran position on ministry.

Instead, we are describing the content of questionnaire statements which fell into a certain group as a result of Lutheran responses. If, therefore, sometimes a description sounds unbalanced or incomplete, it is because we are adhering closely to the meaning of the set of statements we are describing. In this first descriptive section of each chapter we attempt to clarify and illustrate what makes up that facet of ministry—but to restrain as much as possible our desire to editorialize, to neatly balance the presentation, or to speculate why the responses turned out in a given way.

The second section of each chapter, "Emphases and Contrasts," also presents a report of what we found in our research. Where we know of other research that corroborates, contradicts, or illuminates what we found, we have presented that information, but here also we have tried to resist the impulse to offer our own individual interpretations of what we found. This second section outlines particular emphases that certain groups—women, the highly educated, and others—placed on all or part of an area of ministry. It also points out unusual contrasts between the ratings given by identifiable groups. This information is significant because what a person says he or she values in ministry probably describes the kind of ministry that is most likely to reach and affect him or her. Different ministries reach different people, either because of different dispositions or because of particular needs at particular times in life.

This is not to suggest that the primary concern of any pastor ought to be giving people what they say they want. But if ministry that reaches home is significantly different in content, style, or emphasis not only between individuals, but from one group to another, pastors will find it helpful to know about differing preferences or expectations. This knowledge will be valuable neither as a means of staying out of trouble nor as a way of achieving the popularity that may come with presenting only what people want to see and hear; it will be worthwhile, rather, in the spirit of Paul's statement to the Corinthians:

> For though I am free from all men, I have made myself a slave to all, that I might win the more. To the Jews I became as a Jew, in order to win Jews; to those under the law I became as one under the law . . . that I might win those under the law. To those outside the law I became as one outside the law . . . that I might win those outside the law. To the weak I became weak, that I might win the weak. I have become all things to all men, that I might by all means save some. I do it all for the sake of the gospel, that I may share in its blessings (1 Cor. 9:19-22).

Let us underline one point about the "Emphases and Contrasts" portion of each chapter: overall, *Lutherans agreed much more frequently than they disagreed* in their perception of what contributes to ministry or hinders it. In discussing a given area of ministry, we may say that younger people differed from older people in their enthusiasm for two characteristics, that the laity and the clergy also differed in their desire for some of the characteristics, and that more-highly-educated people as a whole rated one characteristic lower than other Lutherans did. Those are differences, and we point them out. But what we ask you to keep remembering (even when we do not say it) is that Lutherans *did not differ on the rest* of the characteristics according to age, evaluator group (such as seminary professors, pastors, or lay persons), sex, education, region of the country, church body, frequency of attendance at worship, degree of satisfaction with participation in church activities, type of ministry, ministry setting, level of income, or size of congregation. If differences between these groups are not mentioned, it is because in each case they have been looked for *and not found.*

In the third section of each chapter, "Reflections," we offer our own personal comments on the implications of the chapter, either for all Lutherans or for specific individuals or groups. Since our writing team includes two clergy and one lay person, we are speaking from within the frame of reference of both lay persons and clergy, men and women.

In a general sense, each chapter presents a kind of dialog, with the first two sections presenting what we understand Lutherans to be saying and the third section offering some of our own comments or reflections on that message.

Some possible misconceptions

We have discovered in the course of this research that, on initial introduction to our work, people tend to draw some natural but erroneous conclusions about the nature of the information presented and its proper use.

We offer a picture of things as they are—characteristics of ministry as Lutherans viewed and preferred them. We suspect that there are some who, seeing that picture, will be ready to stride out to change the church. Others will be pleased to find the perceptions and desires for ministry as we present them. Our first priority is to make clear what *is,* so that those intent either on preservation or on change will get an accurate sense of where they can begin.

We do not present the faces of ministry as a full-blown prescription for the way a pastor ought to be. We do not seek the impossible perfect. No human being can hope to fit equally well every desirable characteristic presented. Those who completed the questionnaire did not deal with the question of how much one person can do. They were not limited to a fixed number of items that could be rated highly. They simply declared which things are effective in ministry and which are not. That information is useful, but we hope it will not be rigidly interpreted as having the force of a set of rules, or become fashioned into a standard to be applied to everyone in the same way.

We have no overall desire to shape ministry to "what people want." We had no intention of spending more than three years conducting a pastoral popularity contest. Members of the clergy and laity bear equal responsibility for what is presented, since their declarations of their hopes and expectations for ministry were given equal weight. If their expressions sound either idealistic or demanding—though we do not think they do—the clergy and the laity are equally culpable.

We have not been able to capture in the names of the characteristics all the nuances of meaning presented in the items that comprise the characteristics. The characteristics have been carefully named. The research team, an advisory council, a design panel, and various other seminary persons have worked with naming and revising the names of the characteristics. Yet it is next to impossible to capture the full meaning of five to ten statements in a five-word title. Frequently when people disagreed about the importance of a particular characteristic, they found much of their disagreement resolved when they looked at *the statements the name represents.* Names of characteristics are as clear and accurate as several minds could make them, and serve as useful tags in discussion. However, if you find yourself in doubt or disagreement over a characteristic, read the whole characteristic—description, statements, and all—from Appendix C.

Lay people are more perceptive than clergy sometimes give them credit for. We think clergy sometimes unfairly downgrade the perceptions of lay persons (and perhaps vice versa). We were often pleased at the rigor and depth of insight in the expressions of the laity on what is important in ministry. It is clear that lay people generally do not harbor a vision of an unfailingly warm, nurturing ministry that offers pie in the sky by and by, and nonstop personal ministerial hand-holding while we wait. A number of characteristics of ministry came to life because lay persons perceived them more clearly than did clergy. The relatively sophisticated and highly valued characteristic, "Communication of Life-Related Theology," arose not from the perceptions of the clergy, but of the laity.

Rank, organization, and centrality

At the start of each chapter we present two listings of the characteristics that make up that area of ministry—one in order of *rank*, and one in order of *centrality*. The two lists say different but equally important things.

Rank is the easier of the two to explain. The number attached to a characteristic of ministry defines its rank order among all Lutherans, presenting the order in which Lutherans prefer it—or the order in which they think it contributes to effective ministry.

But rank isn't all there is to say, because characteristics of ministry were not grouped into particular areas because of their rank. The listing of the rank orders at the beginning of Chapter 1 shows that nine characteristics ranging from a rank of 1 down to a rank of 34 have membership in that area of ministry. If they were grouped simply by rank, we would presumably have listed Characteristics 1 through 9 in that grouping. Something else pulled them together—giving them their *organization*. That something was the fact that large numbers of people, whether or not they were conscious of it, responded to some common element or likeness among the parts of these characteristics.

To give a simple example, suppose we listed 40 foods and asked a large number of people to say whether they "like them very much," "like them a little," and so on down to "dislike them very much." Analyzing those declarations of preferences, suppose we found a set of four to which people often responded similarly: carrot salad, bran muffins, mince pie, and oatmeal cookies. For some reason, people who liked one of those tended to like them all, and people who disliked one tended to dislike them all.

All of those foods (as we know them, at least) have raisins in them, and it wouldn't take much of a leap to assume that it was the presence of raisins in the foods that caused people to respond similarly to them. "Raisin-ness" caused this grouping, and it is not important whether people knew when they listed their likes and dislikes that it was raisin content that influenced their preferences.

People's responses, then, *organized* the characteristics and areas of ministry. The next task was for the research team, together with help from a number of people from Lutheran seminaries, to identify the element that caused the characteristic or area to form. The names and descriptions of the characteristics and areas of ministry are a result of that process of identification.

Now, back to *centrality*. The same mathematical process that grouped the items into characteristics, and characteristics into areas of ministry, also presented them in order of highest concentration of their common, organizing element. First on the list is whatever has the most pronounced degree of whatever is being identified, and last on the list has the least of it. That is the order of *centrality*, and it differs in meaning from *rank*.

To return to our food analogy, the rank order of those four foods might be as follows:

In order of rank
(1) oatmeal cookies
(2) bran muffins
(3) mince pie
(4) carrot salad

This is the order in which, in our hypothetical situation, we discovered that people preferred them. However, in order of centrality, the list would be:

From central to peripheral
(3) mince pie
(4) carrot salad
(1) oatmeal cookies
(2) bran muffins

At least in the recipes we use, mince pie has the most raisins and bran muffins have the least. The matters we are dealing with in the ministry characteristics are more complex and subtle than raisin content, but we think this is a good illustration of the basic principles involved.

To leave the analogy and return to our subject, at the beginning of Chapter 9, where the 14 characteristics of that feature of ministry are listed, "Assertive Civic Leadership" comes next-to-last in rank order. It is not one of the characteristics large numbers of people preferred, or thought contributes greatly to effective ministry. But in order of its centrality to the organizing principle (the thing all these characteristics have in common that causes people to respond similarly to them) "Assertive Civic Leadership" heads the list. People may not be enthusiastic about it, but they tell us that this characteristic presents the clearest expression, the strongest essence, of whatever it is that draws all these characteristics together. It is central to the meaning of that whole area of ministry.

Who ministers?

One informed lay person put it this way: "Ministry is too important and demanding a task to leave entirely to ministers." Certainly, given the enormous responsibility and scope of ministry, it is obvious that the ordained clergy cannot fulfill the task alone. Ministry is the shared opportunity and responsibility of the whole church, including both lay persons and ordained clergy. Each has distinct roles to fill, but ministry is the work of both.

Ministry cannot be fully realized in isolation. Much of ministry is, or should be, interactive. To use a simple illustration, my pastor cannot minister to me as I deal with my present anxieties unless we are together and talk with each other. As my pastor speaks, I am ministered to. But I also minister to my pastor through the trust and confidence I display as I tell about my anxieties and my faith, and by means of the expressions that cross my face as I talk and listen. We minister to one another as we hear each other and make new discoveries that grow from our conversation—discoveries that neither of us would make alone.

The whole ministry of the church is a process of interaction between pastor and people, between individual members and all the people whose lives they touch, between pastors, between church members, or between a particular congregation and a governmental institution—the patterns of interaction in ministry are endless. In short, we in the church are *all* involved in ministry, and in enabling one another to engage in ministry.

The education, development, and sustenance of ministers is a shared responsibility. Seminary professors perhaps most visibly participate with students in education for ministry. But so do lay persons and pastors of teaching parishes where beginning seminarians and interns are placed. District or synodical presidents, together with ministry support committees, provide counsel, match interests and gifts of pastors to specific parish characteristics and needs, and otherwise provide special guidance to pastors. Parish pastors provide models with their own lives, and in this and countless other ways train lay persons for ministry, as well as receive ministry from them. Therefore lay persons also influence and shape the development of their pastors in the partnership of ministry.

The research which provided the basis for this book focused on ordained ministers and their vocation and roles in congregational leadership. However, if we accept the concept of the priesthood of all believers, then we should see most pastoral tasks and roles as carried out in partnership with the entire congregation, and particularly with its lay leaders. Pastors, in their call and vocation centered in Word and sacraments, are servants among servants, providing congregations with the leadership they need to carry out their mission and ministry effectively.

Therefore this book is not just about pastors, but about congregational leaders: church council and committee members, church officials—in fact, all congregational members. If we are to take seriously the word of Lutherans about what is effective and ineffective in ministry, most of these characteristics will affect the ministry of any Christian, whatever the calling or role.

Glossary

area of ministry   one of 10 groups of *characteristics* which describe a
    larger aspect of *ministry*

central-peripheral   an arrangement of *characteristics* or of individual
    items that places them in descending order of their closeness to
    the essential meaning of the *area of ministry* to which they
    belong

characteristic (also *criterion*)   one of 77 facets or features of *ministry*,
    formed by the way in which Lutherans value them, and com-
    posed of from three to a dozen or more individual *items* or state-
    ments about *ministry*

church   either a denomination or church body (such as the ALC) or
    the universal church (all Christians), but not a local *congrega-
    tion* (see below)

clergy   sometimes used as a synonym for *professionals*, sometimes re-
    ferring specifically to parish clergy (context should clarify which
    use is intended)

congregation (also *parish*)   a local group of believers, in the broad
    sense of either a conventional parish or something like the con-
    stituency of a hospital chaplain, including patients, patients'
    families, hospital visitors, and hospital personnel

district/synod   the first subunit of administration in a church body
    (what members of the LCA call a *synod*, both the ALC and
    LCMS refer to as a *district*)—a geographical division like the
    Minnesota Synod of the LCA or the Southwestern Minnesota
    District of the ALC

item   a statement about some aspect of *ministry*—one of 461 which 5000 Lutherans evaluated as the basis for this study

judicatory   a *district/synod*

minister   anyone who does *ministry*

ministry   that witnessing to his grace to which God has called all Christians, consisting of a single act, or of a lengthy, sustained, and complex series of events (as in "the ministry of a lifetime"); especially that done by *pastors*

pastor   a minister serving a *congregation* in the broad sense defined above, not limited to the role of shepherd of a conventional parish

professionals   seminary faculty, parish clergy, denominational officials, and seminary seniors—four of the five groups (all except lay persons) who completed the original questionnaire

rank   the ordered sequence in which Lutherans, according to the degree to which they valued them, arranged *characteristics* of ministry

rating   the expression in numbers of how highly Lutherans valued a particular *item, characteristic,* or *area of ministry,* ranging from + 4.0 ("absolutely essential") to − 4.0 ("absolutely disqualifying")

Part I

Five
Pastoral
Perspectives

1. Personal Faith, Spiritual Depth
   Composite rating 3.02
   "contributes very much"

2. A Person for Others
   Composite rating 2.91
   "contributes very much"

3. Critical Awareness of
   Lutheran Heritage and Theology
   Composite rating 2.74
   "contributes very much"

4. Not Wanted: Dominating Influence
   Composite rating – 0.19
   "contributes/hinders little or nothing"

5. Not Wanted: Ministry-Defeating Behaviors
   Composite rating – 2.59
   "hinders very much"

Component characteristics: Chapter 1

From central to peripheral
1   Personal Devotional Life
22 Ministry as a Calling
9   Christian Example
2   Confidence in Christ's Lordship
14 Scripture-Based, Resurrection Faith
7   Pastoral Guidance
29 Evangelism and Mission Concern
34 Pastorally-Oriented Biblical Scholarship
13 Accepting Mutual Ministry

In order of Lutheran ranking
1   Personal Devotional Life
2   Confidence in Christ's Lordship
7   Pastoral Guidance
9   Christian Example
13 Accepting Mutual Ministry
14 Scripture-Based, Resurrection Faith
22 Ministry as a Calling
29 Evangelism and Mission Concern
34 Pastorally-Oriented Biblical Scholarship

Personal Faith, Spiritual Depth

The woman was understandably provoked. "I know I shouldn't be making comparisons," she was saying, "but it's hard not to. Our new pastor is a nice enough young man. He preaches interesting sermons, and people like him. But there's something missing. He tries to be so fair and open-minded that it's hard to know where he stands. The other night the young people were talking about shoplifting at their study group, and he said it depended on 'what your values are.' Hasn't he heard of the seventh commandment? He talks a lot about doubts, too. My husband's had enough trouble getting his own mind straight, and then one Sunday morning the pastor gets up and says it's important to doubt—that he's sometimes doubted that Jesus rose from the grave. I know he has a right to his doubts, like everybody else, but as our pastor I don't think he ought to raise them without helping us find a way to handle our own!

"It's enough to make me long to have Pastor Peterson back. He may have had his faults, but I'll tell you one thing—he knew what the church stood for. And he knew what he believed—and told us. Actually, he wouldn't have had to tell us. It was written all over him. You could see it in the way he did things. I think that's pretty important in a pastor."

Pretty important, indeed. Though not all Lutherans would state it in her terms, most would agree with the sense of this woman's statement.

In our study Lutherans placed highest importance [1] on a pastor's having a firm personal faith and living it out in ways that constitute visible affirmations of that faith.

The quality of a life founded on a deep relationship with God is difficult to describe in concrete terms because it involves a faith so internalized that it is inseparable from a person. It infuses everything one says or does with a special quality. It blends and becomes part of a person in the way C. S. Lewis described the invisibility of genuine humility. He observed that if you ever met a perfectly humble person, you probably wouldn't notice anything other than that he or she would be a nice person who would seem very much interested in what you had to say.

Lived-out, unselfconscious awareness of God as the center of life is an essential part of being the people of faith Lutherans most want their pastors to be. When you meet one so centered on God, you may not be aware of anything special at the time. The effects come as a kind of afterglow, as if you had been in touch with a source of light, warmth, inspiration, and edification. People used to say of one associate pastor, "After he's been with you, you feel as if you're walking four inches off the ground." They were saying that, for a time thereafter, life held a new quality of clarity and hope. In persons of faith, everything seems attached to the source of life—not because they have made a decision to see it that way, but because it has become clear to them that all of life grows from God as leaves grow from stems. Being with such a person helps one come to a new perspective.

Another fact about this quality that Lutherans want most in their pastors is that persons generally possess it quite unconsciously. A pastor who is active in politics, or one whose special strength is in working with the ill or in community life, is usually aware of the part such interest plays in personal identity. When that strength is pointed out, a pastor will probably nod in agreement, saying, "I know that about myself. I wouldn't know how to carry out my ministry without including such interests and skills as a major ingredient."

But persons so centered on God as to be living examples of a faith deeply held and consistently lived out will probably react with surprise if someone points to those spiritual foundations as part of their identity. It would be almost as if you had announced that they had skin on their

---

1. The reading habits of many people cause them to begin books with Chapter 1. If you are one of those, we recommend a return to "Partners in Ministry: An Introduction" to begin your reading. Without the information contained there, much that appears in the next 10 chapters may be hard to comprehend. The statement above and many like it will be fully understandable only if you have read pp. 9-20, which present the 10 faces, describe the reason for the sequence in which they appear, and outline the research which the 10 chapters report.

arms, or a fourth lumbar vertebra. Such a person often seems to forget there is any other possibility.

Among Christian youth, as among adults, this quality is very highly valued. Many a high school student has been started on the road to a seminary education and the pastorate because of the magnetic presence of a pastor who so thoroughly embodied the Christian faith that it was powerfully communicated to young people. One such young person said of his pastor, "I like the way he is, the way he sees God working in everything, the questions he asks that make you see connections between things, the way he doesn't have to be running the show all the time because he knows God's running it. That's the kind of person I'd like to be some day."

The nine characteristics that form this area of ministry intercorrelate strongly with one another, showing that Lutherans view them similarly. The nine divide themselves logically into two primary categories. One category includes attributes a pastor *has*—a set of personal qualities—including knowledge, attitudes, beliefs, and values. The second includes things a pastor *does*—a set of pastoral practices, skills, or activities. Although the two components are not entirely discrete (they overlap somewhat), they do represent two distinguishable facets of pastoral identity. They divide personal expressions of faith into *disposition of faith* and *faith lived out* in pastoral witness.

Disposition of faith: "It was written all over him."

Four of the nine characteristics comprise this facet of ministry: "Personal Devotional Life" (1);[2] "Confidence in Christ's Lordship" (2); "Scripture-Based, Resurrection Faith" (14); and "Ministry as a Calling" (22). These are all essentially attitudes, beliefs, and values. Together they amount to a firm and balanced Christian faith, a world view, a set of lenses through which everything in life is perceived, interpreted, understood, and responded to. Little wonder that a person with this perspective will not necessarily be aware of it. To have this disposition of faith is an entire way of *being*, and what we *are* is what we are least able to perceive about ourselves. Outlined in these four characteristics is an approach to life based on the assumption that a gracious God, our heavenly Father, is the source and center of life. All else flows from that assumption.

Being ordained does not guarantee this perspective. The clergy are as human as the laity, fighting the same battles with sin and Satan. More than one pastor has fought a losing battle with the calendar and the

---

2. Numbers in parentheses refer to the ranking the 5000 Lutherans gave to the characteristics in order of their desirability or contribution to effective ministry (1-77). "Personal Devotional Life" was the highest-ranked of the 77.

clock, and discovered that time for prayer and meditation are often casualties of the battle—losing out to the demands of an emergency call, the needs of family, or to extra time needed for sermon preparation.

Other pastors report that though they preach the truth that with God all things are possible, they are not always able to live with that confidence. So often disappointed in people, so often working hard with results that remain stubbornly invisible to the naked eye, they suffer discouragement, doubting their abilities and even their fitness and call to the ministry.

Knowing more theology (or less) does not make it easier to repent and believe in Christ. Knowing theology does not make it easier, when one is under pressure or in crisis, to place one's ultimate confidence in the power of God. Knowing theology *does* make it easier to understand what one is experiencing in matters of faith, but it *does not* make belief more accessible or experiences of faith easier to come by. This is all the more reason why these qualities, when present in a pastor, are so highly valued.

Personal Devotional Life (1). This is the highest-ranked of all 77 ministry characteristics. It is like a capsule statement of the Christian life. Lutherans want a pastor who follows the practices commended to those who would live in God's presence: confession of sin to God, use of Scripture for personal nourishment, seeking out the guidance of the Holy Spirit, living with a sense of daily forgiveness, receiving Holy Communion regularly, and showing that the mission of Christ has first priority. This list strikingly recalls Luther's daily baptismal cycle of dying to sin and rising again to new life in Christ. When Lutherans hear the Word of God proclaimed, they want to hear it from one who from daily contact knows the one proclaimed.

Confidence in Christ's Lordship (2). "*Christos ho Kyrios!*"—"Christ, the Lord!" was the cry of the early church. It rocked the Roman Empire. Jesus is not only Savior, but Lord, Ruler, King, Emperor, and omnipotent God. Therefore as his faithful subject I need not fear.

Lutherans want to sense in their pastor such a confidence in the ultimate outcome of Christ's kingdom. They want to sense a profound and underlying hope, an assurance that God is at work in the midst of everything, and a belief that ultimately the forces of good are greater than the forces of evil. They want a pastor who communicates this understanding of life to others, and who lives with the sense of freedom that comes when one relies fully on the presence and power of God.

Scripture-Based, Resurrection Faith (14). Lutherans also want their pastor's beliefs to be firmly grounded in Scripture, and to be held with such conviction that they are not easily altered, swayed, or otherwise threatened when they meet opposition. Lutherans want pastors to know, affirm, and communicate a faith that is biblically based. One specific desire expressed is that pastors affirm Christ's resurrection from the dead.

Ministry as a Calling (22). The idea of working under a sense of a call from God is still very much alive among both the laity and clergy. The ministerial call, as viewed by Lutherans, encompasses both the subjective conviction of being called by God and the more objective matter of being asked by a congregation or the church at large to accept a specific position as pastor. A call is not seen as a one-time-only or occasional experience, but as a continued sense of vocation that is a source of sustaining power when difficulties arise.

In summary, what the clergy and laity have underscored as most vital in ordained ministry—"Disposition of Faith"—reflects a traditional stance of Lutherans, once outlined by Thurneysen:

> The decisive sign of a real call is the pastor's own faith. It is the root of that inner compulsion that is operative in all genuine cure of souls. From it grow the zeal and patience, the willingness to make haste and to wait, the search for one's neighbor, the sympathy for him, and above all the certainty with which we administer the Word to him and which wins him to the Word. It may be a weak faith, a tempted and struggling faith (and where is there ever real faith without doubt and struggle?), but it must be faith, one's own personal knowledge of grace and sin, of repentance and rebirth, one's own existence in prayer and supplication.

> Then, a second sign; back of pastoral care is a call. But this call is not only being called *through* the Word; it means also being called *to* the Word. That is, the pastor of souls who is to lead others to the Word must himself be one who is led by the Word, grounded and practiced in the Word. Therefore, mediation of the Word of God is the most important requirement of the pastor. He must be steeped in the Word. . . .[3]

Faith lived out: "You could see it in the way he did things."

The five remaining characteristics or qualities of ministry that comprise the area of "Personal Faith, Spiritual Depth" have to do with actions that a pastor takes, or, sometimes, the effects on others that occur because of something a pastor does. They are: "Pastoral Guidance" (7), "Christian Example" (9), "Accepting Mutual Ministry" (13), "Evangelism and Mission Concern" (29), and "Pastorally-Oriented Biblical Scholarship" (34). All of these overlap to greater or lesser degree with the firm grounding in faith discussed in the previous section, but the primary component of each is *action.*

---

3. John W. Doberstein, ed., *Minister's Prayer Book* (Philadelphia: Muhlenberg Press, n.d.), pp. 204-205.

Pastoral Guidance (7). [The data show that when Lutherans go to a pastor for counseling, they usually expect more than psychological counseling. They look for the kind of skilled guidance that links their wounded memories with accounts of what God has done and will do.] In helping people deal with problems, a pastor may speak of God's forgiveness or help them recognize the ways God is working in their lives. In other situations, a pastor may confront counselees with the need for a heightened personal commitment, or assist them in relying on the resources of faith. This characteristic points to a desire that ministers retain their pastoral role and identity as they work with persons who are under stress or facing problems.

Christian Example (9). Wanted: [an exemplary personal life manifested in generosity, a joyous attitude, and a life of high moral quality.] When one looks at the items that make up this characteristic, one finds that the bulk of them are specific actions performed by a pastor: for example, providing personal witness to the gospel by one's own generosity, demonstrating the joyous character of the Christian life, and behaving morally in a way that is above reproach. But the central element essentially talks about effect—setting a Christian example that people in the community respect. Like the final item on the criterion list, which speaks of a spouse who is a companion in the faith, this is not something that comes off well if consciously done. Lutherans want a pastor and spouse to be respected examples of Christian life in the community—but unselfconsciously. Otherwise the potential for tacit and subtle impressions of legalism, aloof propriety, too much caution, and too little freedom in the gospel will be forever present—and perhaps realized. A Christian example, like the habit of faith, is best worn without the knowledge of the wearer.

Accepting Mutual Ministry (13).   Another characteristic Lutherans associate with this area of ministry is the willingness of a pastor not only to minister, but to be ministered to. This is an attitude that personal experience and observation of others suggests is not universally possessed. It means, first of all, being open and receptive to the ministrations of another pastor or lay person, and giving evidence of being willing to forsake complete independence for mutual interdependence. This characteristic also includes a reciprocal willingness to offer a ministry that reaches out to others through intercessory prayer. Associated with both is a freedom of spirit that comes from living in the gospel—not being bound to a set of rules.

Evangelism and Mission Concern (29). This is [commitment to an evangelism and service outreach that involves a congregation in local and worldwide efforts to reach all with the gospel.] Based on a desire for everyone to know God's love in Jesus Christ, it includes stimulating interest and support for world missions and organizing evangelism programs that involve congregational members in witnessing to Jesus Christ in their communities. The major thrust is clearly toward what is traditionally known as reaching out with the Word, the good news of the gospel. Yet it is not just bringing the words of the gospel, but rather ministering to the whole person, that is implied in the item: "Urges members to respond to critical needs in the world through sacrificial giving."

Pastorally-Oriented Biblical Scholarship (34). The motivation for this aspect of ministry comes from a knowledge of the Scriptures and sound theological foundations. In a sentence, pastorally-oriented biblical scholarship involves thorough and continually-renewed knowledge of the Scriptures and theology, *applied to current pastoral issues.* Lutherans want their pastors to know the Scriptures thoroughly, continuing to study them in the original languages for further clarification and understanding. They expect them to be aware of the scriptural and theological background of current religious movements and to be able to present a solid theological basis for the entire mission of the church. There is no anti-intellectualism in this expectation expressed by Lutherans; rather, sound and diligent scholarship are required and applauded.

Emphases and Contrasts

Among the various groups studied, who cared most about a pastor's personal faith? Which characteristics did certain groups accent? The questions below deal with some of the different expectations of various Lutheran groups. As you read, however, remember that most people placed great importance on all of these characteristics, rating each as contributing very much to effective ministry. Some groups simply pronounced the *very* more loudly than others.

Who felt most keenly the need for a pastor with a vital faith?

Those who were most concerned about a pastor's personal faith were (a) seminary professors, parish pastors, and denominational officials, especially those who (b) are older, (c) attend worship once a week or more, and (d) consider their own participation in congregational activities a major source of satisfaction in life.

Among the laity, those who placed highest priority on this area were those who (a) attend worship frequently and (b) find deep satisfaction in congregational life, particularly (c) older Lutherans—those over 45. Persons' estimates of eight of the nine characteristics in this chapter increased steadily with age up to the age of 65. The one characteristic older Lutherans did not accent is "Pastorally-Oriented Biblical Scholarship" (34).

Those who (a) worship less frequently than once a week and (b) reported less than major satisfaction with congregational life showed a marked drop in their rating of these characteristics. People whose worship attendance was lagging and whose dissatisfaction with the church was considerable usually showed less concern and appreciation for a spiritually oriented ministry. Those who were least concerned about pastors exhibiting a deep faith were (a) youth under age 21, particularly those who (b) attend worship less than once a week and (c) do not find much satisfaction in congregational activities.

Figure 1 gives, in descending order, the makeup of seven groups and their evaluations of the importance of the characteristics in this chapter.

Did men and women differ in the value they placed on a spiritually-oriented ministry? The opinions of women resembled three other groups: older Lutherans, those who attend church every week, and those who are the most satisfied participants. Women consistently placed greater importance than men on these characteristics. The one exception is that women emphasized no more strongly than men the importance of "Evangelism and Mission Concern" (29).

What effect did education have on the importance people placed on this area of ministry? Our findings here may come as a surprise to anyone who thinks those with the least education exhibit the most piety. More-highly-educated Lutherans usually placed greater importance on a pastor's personal devotional life and commitment to evangelism and missions. This may be evidence that Lutheran church colleges foster in their graduates an appreciation for the life of faith, since a large proportion of the more-highly-educated members of Lutheran congregations were educated at Lutheran colleges.

Did members of different Lutheran church bodies differ in their emphases on expressions of faith? Church body differences in preference for a spiritually-oriented ministry were relatively slight, though statistically significant. The primary pattern of difference was between the Lutheran Church–Missouri Synod (LCMS) and the other two bodies—sometimes contrasting with one, then with the other.

Both the LCMS and the American Lutheran Church (ALC) were slightly more appreciative of a pastor who has a strong "Personal Devotional Life" (1) and who emphasizes "Evangelism and Mission Concern" (29). The LCMS alone placed greater importance on "Pastoral Guidance" (7). Members of the Lutheran Church in America (LCA) placed somewhat less emphasis on all three of these characteristics.

The ALC, in contrast with the LCMS, slightly accented a "Scripture-

Fig. 1. Lutheran groups that place significantly different degrees of importance on ministry Area I, "Personal Faith, Spiritual Depth."

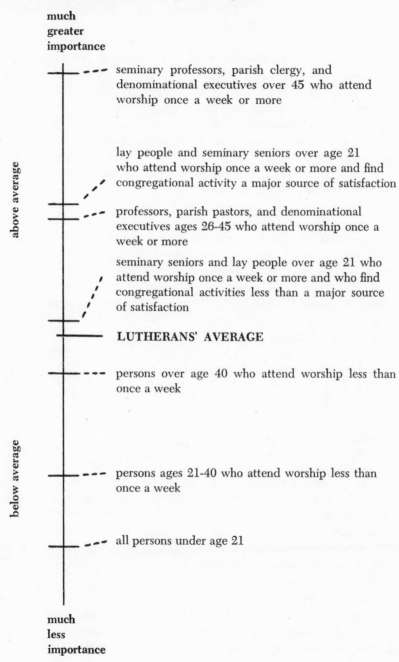

**much
greater
importance**

- - - seminary professors, parish clergy, and denominational executives over 45 who attend worship once a week or more

lay people and seminary seniors over age 21 who attend worship once a week or more and find congregational activity a major source of satisfaction

- - - professors, parish pastors, and denominational executives ages 26-45 who attend worship once a week or more

seminary seniors and lay people over age 21 who attend worship once a week or more and who find congregational activities less than a major source of satisfaction

LUTHERANS' AVERAGE

- - - persons over age 40 who attend worship less than once a week

- - - persons ages 21-40 who attend worship less than once a week

- - - all persons under age 21

above average

below average

**much
less
importance**

Based, Resurrection Faith" (14) and "Pastorally-Oriented Biblical Scholarship" (34). But the members of the ALC, by contrast with both the LCMS and LCA, slightly de-emphasized the relevance to effective ministry of "Ministry as a Calling" (22).

Did pastors differ in the value they placed on these expressions of faith? Younger pastors are less likely than older pastors to value the characteristics of this area of ministry; seminary seniors, about to graduate and be placed in congregations, gave a significantly-lower-than-average priority to six of the nine characteristics described in this chapter. They rated "Evangelism and Mission Concern" (29) *much* lower; rated "Ministry as a Calling" (22), "Christian Example" (9), and "Pastorally-Oriented Biblical Scholarship" (34) *lower;* and rated "Pastoral Guidance" (7) and "Scripture-Based, Resurrection Faith" (14) *slightly* lower than Lutherans as a whole.

In conclusion, one can expect older, more-well-educated clergy and women who go to church every Sunday and find major satisfaction in their participation in congregational life to appreciate this area of ministry more than others. Generally speaking one can expect younger, less-well-educated men who attend church less frequently than once a week and who find their participation in congregational life less than a major source of satisfaction to de-emphasize the importance of this area more than others. This fits together with what we found in *A Study of Generations* (a 1972 study of Lutherans, ages 15-65), that blue-collar males have a greater tendency to feel alienated—not to feel that they really belong and are well accepted in a typical Lutheran congregation. (It seems to us that those who give the lowest ratings to these kinds of pastoral ministry may be most in need of them.)

Reflections

What Lutherans look for first and foremost in their ministers is that they be persons of faith, unquestionably Christians for whom Jesus Christ is both Savior and Lord. This is not to say they look askance at honest questions or doubts. But Lutherans value a clear expression of *faith* more highly than a constant emphasis on open-mindedness and searching. This has implications for the entire church, and especially for lay leaders of congregations, seminary educators, and pastors.

Thoughts for lay persons

Granted the importance of these qualities of ministry throughout the church, how important are they for the leadership of your congregation? The average opinion of members in your congregation would most likely not be dramatically different from what we found among the 5000 Lutherans who participated in this project. One way to identify your own sense of your congregation's needs would be to use the checklist at the end of this chapter, prefacing each of the items with "How important is it for our congregation or our pastor to . . . ?" or "How important is it to me to . . . ?" For each item check one of the categories on the left side of the checklist.

A checklist could be used twice by a church council—first with the pastor in mind, and second with themselves in mind. A useful comparison could be made between members' expectations of pastors and members' expectations of themselves.

A church council could profitably spend the first half-hour of a meeting discussing results from using a checklist, concentrating on the full content and meaning of one of the characteristics, or considering what they are doing and could additionally be doing to promote the development of themselves, their pastor, or their fellow members in a particular area such as incarnating the Christian faith.

This also suggests the importance of congregational lay leaders examining their own values and actions. For this first area, the question might be raised: Am I taking God and my own faith seriously in decision making? Related questions are: What do the Scriptures or my faith say to this decision? If I look at this situation with the eyes of faith, what do I see, both as the issue and as the potential? When I confront a decision within the congregation, do I bring to bear primarily my business experience, my application of the principles of psychology, or what? How long does it take me, in decision making, to come to the question, What is likely to be God's will in this matter?

Committee evaluation

One congregation in five is involved each year in selecting a new pastor or staff worker. *Call committees* take the responsibility for selecting candidates with the strengths especially needed at a particular time. What use can be made of this chapter—or this book, and the checklists included? The items of the checklist given at the end of this chapter, together with the items of checklists that could be developed for other chapters from the material in Appendix C, would be useful to a call committee as it tries to discover its own priorities. We do not envision that the checklists would become the total agenda for an interview with a candidate, but their use by a call committee prior to an interview would pinpoint matters of particular interest to members of the committee that should be dealt with during the interview.

An important and beneficial contribution of a *personnel committee* might be to recommend, based on dialog concerning the chapters of this book, mutually chosen continuing education experiences for clergy and lay church staff workers.

Seminary educators

Luther made a distinction between historical faith and faith that saves. Historical faith is knowledge of Christian teaching and belief, and especially acknowledgment of the events of the life, death, and resurrection of Jesus Christ. But it is possible to keep all of that knowledge at a safe distance of 2000 years and regard it largely as a matter of information. Faith that saves, however, is acknowledgment that God's saving activity in history is personal: *"It is for me!"* A church college student illustrated the difference when she reported, "In my New Testament courses I learned a lot about the Christian faith and theology, but it wasn't until I got into Professor Abel's class that I felt real concern on anyone's part for what I believe personally."

Seminary educators typically recognize the need for students to be confronted by the living God, as well as the need to receive instruction in church history, dogmatics, liturgics, homiletics, and the like; they see the need for students not only to learn about prayer, but to have opportunity to develop a prayer life. Members of a seminary community might very profitably identify and discuss the seminary's particular traditions of piety, or the range of pieties represented there. By that identification and discussion students might be helped to explicitly evaluate and reflect on the varieties of piety available for observation in the seminary community, and to consider them in relation to development of their own expressions of the faith, rather than simply allowing that development to happen through a less conscious process.

Lutherans expect their ministers to have a definite sense of calling that can serve as a source of strength when the going gets tough, a kind of gyroscope when others lose their sense of direction. A seminary curriculum might therefore include definite times when each student is helped to confront the questions: Am I called? What does it mean to be called? To what, specifically, am I called?

Two of the nine characteristics discussed in this chapter emphasize the importance of the Bible to this area of ministry: "Scripture-Based, Resurrection Faith" (14) and "Pastorally-Oriented Biblical Scholarship" (34). Clearly, Lutherans are less than pleased with biblical illiterates, like the recently-graduated seminarian who tells members of his first parish, "I feel that I've learned a lot of theology—just ask me about Tillich or Barth or Pannenberg—but I'm not all that familiar with the Bible itself." What is valued, of course, is not *either/or,* but *both/and.*

"Pastoral Guidance" was ranked 7th out of 77 in importance for effective ministry. Lutherans perceived pastors counseling in two different ways: as pastors who help people relate their personal problems and crises to their Christian faith, or as would-be psychologists who minister to people under stress without reference to their faith. Lutherans clearly preferred the former. That Lutherans perceived these differences in emphasis, however, does not mean that ministers must necessarily counsel from a frame of reference that is either exclusively religious or exclusively psychological. However, while field-testing our research instruments on incoming seminarians we did discover that seminarians gravitate toward one or the other—not both. Perhaps seminarians should be alerted to this potential dichotomy and helped to interrelate, if not integrate, the two.

We have reported that seminary seniors tended to de-emphasize six of these nine characteristics. Some readers might view this as cause for considerable alarm, as if it means there is less faith or less interest in spiritual matters among younger pastors. But with this research we cannot tell whether or not that is really the case. We can only report that the seminary seniors involved in this project showed less concern than Lutherans as a whole for evangelism and doctrinal agreement, and somewhat more concern about quality of congregational sharing and communion and about the need for persons' lives to be consistent with what they believe. Whether this is a trend toward a new breed of pastor, we do not know; but seminary professors and students might discuss how they would feel if it were to become a trend.

Implications for pastors

What Lutherans as a whole would say is, "What makes about as much difference to us as anything is the degree to which our pastor incarnates the Christian life of faith." As one pastor put it as he reflected on a preliminary version of this chapter, "The first issue it raises for the pastor is the question of spiritual formation. The question is, How do I incarnate (or let God incarnate) my faith in my thinking, acting, and living?"

"Personal Devotional Life" is at the top of the list of characteristics Lutherans believe contribute to effective ministry. Therefore the second question raised by this chapter is: What about a pastor's devotional life? The question is not so much, Does a minister have one? (surely, that question too!), but, What kind of breadth and depth does it have? *Breadth* means including enough different kinds of reading, thinking, praying, meditating, and reflecting to be recognized by a wide variety of people as incarnating the faith. *Depth* in devotional life is a question of taking all of oneself into one's devotional life—relationships, struggles, and inner thoughts and feelings. Does one's devotional life get into dialog with one's life-style and priorities? These questions are inherent in the issue of how well one incarnates the faith, for some types of devotional life can feed a compartmentalized faith and become only a matter of words and thoughts that do not affect one's attitudes, decisions, investments, and commitments.

At the very heart of the Christian faith is letting go of our own attempts to justify ourselves and letting God be God and save us. One way we can do this is by "Accepting Mutual Ministry" (13). The very core of this characteristic is willingness to forsake complete independence for mutual interdependence. Lutherans associate "Accepting Mutual Ministry" with other characteristics of faith that is lived out, offering a firm reminder that ministry is not only individual but corporate. It is the interactive activity of the living body of Christ. We pray not "My Father . . ." but "Our Father. . . ." The fact that we are "believers incorporated" [4] applies also to the doing of ministry. This implies that ordained ministers need also to be open to receiving the counsel, guidance, and prayer support of their fellow Christian ministers—whether lay or ordained. It is important to recognize ministry in its various forms. Sometimes evaluative comments, suggestions, criticisms, and contrary opinions, so often perceived as unnecessary irritations or burdens, are instead another form of Spirit-led mutual ministry.

Because Lutherans as a whole look first for faith and faith lived out in their ministries, it might be profitable to pay some detailed attention to the various facets of this disposition. One way of doing that would be for pastors to use the checklist that follows as a means of clarifying the importance they accord a personal faith, and the degree to which 27 expressions of faith characterize them. Evaluations of oneself are often surprisingly accurate. If pastors compare their estimates of the *importance* of each expression of faith with estimates of the degree to which they *possess* each one, they will have some raw material from which to develop goals for personal growth.

Checklist Instructions

The 27 items on the checklist are the best descriptors of the nine characteristics of the spiritual foundations Lutherans associate with effective ministry. The heart of each of the nine is described by three items. These 27 form a checklist that provides a brief inventory of the attitudes and behaviors commonly associated with this area of ministry.

---

4. "Believers incorporated" is an expression perhaps not coined, but admirably articulated and emphasized, by Dr. Walter R. Wietzke in his book *Believers Incorporated: The Message of Ephesians for Evangelical Outreach* (Minneapolis: Augsburg, 1977).

As you fill in the left side of the checklist, begin with the phrase "For a minister to . . . ?" and check one of the possibilities for each item from "somewhat desirable" to "very desirable."

On the right, begin your reflection about each item with the phrase, "Do I . . . ?" and again check one of the possibilities from "usually" to "seldom or never."

The results may be more accurate if you complete the left side for all items before turning to the right side, rather than going from left to right, item by item.

When the inventory has been completed, add the scores on each side separately and divide by 27. These average scores will provide a basis for comparing your view of the "should be" and "is" of living out one's personal faith.

Your average scores from the right side summarize how you perceive your faith is expressed. You might use the checklist a second time to discover whether you place higher importance on these matters for someone else than for yourself. After completing the list with yourself in mind, try completing it with your church council or some other congregational leadership group in mind.

If you find your use of the checklist prompts you to want further detail regarding the whole area or some part, turn to Appendix C and use the full set of items for this area. There you will find not just three, but all the items for each characteristic, together with suggestions for developing a variety of checklists from those and other items.

Checklist 1: Reflecting on "Personal Faith, Spiritual Depth"

extent needed						extent true		
3 very desirable	2 quite desirable	1 somewhat desirable	◄ For a minister to . . . Do I . . . ►			3 usually	2 sometimes	1 seldom or never
			Personal Devotional Life (1)					
			acknowledge own sin and confess this to God?					
			use Scripture as a source of spiritual nourishment?					
			spend time daily in prayer and meditation?					

extent needed					extent true		
3 very desirable	2 quite desirable	1 somewhat desirable			3 usually	2 sometimes	1 seldom or never

◄ **For a minister to . . .**   **Do I . . .** ►

Confidence in Christ's Lordship (2)

express profound hope because of a belief in the kingdom of God?

acknowledge a personal need for continued growth in faith?

approach life as one who believes the forces of good are greater than the forces of evil?

Pastoral Guidance (7)

lead people to recognize ways God may be working in their lives?

lead people to deepened spiritual growth and commitment?

help people use the resources of faith in coping with personal problems?

Christian Example (9)

set a Christian example that people in the community respect?

provide a personal witness to the gospel by own generosity?

demonstrate the joyous character of the Christian life?

Accepting Mutual Ministry (13)

accept the ministries of another?

go about work in a way that reflects the liberating power of the gospel?

actively engage in intercessory prayer on behalf of others?

extent needed				For a minister to . . . Do I . . . ▶	extent true		
3 very desirable	2 quite desirable	1 somewhat desirable			3 usually	2 sometimes	1 seldom or never

◀ For a minister to . . .   Do I . . . ▶

Scripture-Based, Resurrection Faith (14)

treat the Bible as the norm in matters of faith?

affirm with conviction the historical resurrection of Jesus Christ from the dead?

express beliefs regardless of opposing views?

Ministry as a Calling (22)

interpret ministry as a personal calling from God?

view appointments to a parish or office as a calling of God?

appear to be sustained by a sense of God's call when the going gets rough?

Evangelism and Mission Concern (29)

seek to bring everyone to know God's love in Jesus Christ?

speak and act as one concerned about reaching others with the gospel?

stimulate the congregation to interest and support for world missions?

Pastorally-Oriented Biblical Scholarship (34)

demonstrate knowledge of Scripture?

give evidence of continued and thorough study of the Scriptures?

present a theological basis for the mission of the church?

Component characteristics: Chapter 2

2

A Person for Others

Everything ought to have been going right at Faith Lutheran. Located in a middle-class suburb among a population of well-educated, active, highly motivated people, the congregation, until recent months, had increased steadily in size over a period of almost 10 years. Its senior pastor was both an able administrator and an astute theologian. Through the efforts of a dynamic youth pastor, the church enjoyed a booming youth program.

But the adult program of the church was another story. To attend any task group or decision-making body was a painful exercise. One had the feeling that all the real decision making was being done elsewhere. People spoke in tight, careful sentences. Most proposals were either rubber-stamped without discussion or were opposed on what frequently seemed to be irrelevant grounds. Business meetings were rehashed over the phone or over late-night coffee sessions, with speculations over "why they're pushing so hard for this new project" and guesses about why a given decision had gone a particular way. In speaking of those responsible for the general program of the church, members usually said "they."

People threatened to leave the church over a puzzling variety of issues. Some of them went so far as to carry out the threat. Those lay persons

most responsible for church programs spent agonized hours trying to divine the source of the trouble—without successfully identifying it.

Then came a change in pastor. Three years later, the tone of the church
was perceptibly different. People no longer threatened to leave. Sunday
morning visitors spoke of an atmosphere of warmth and friendliness
among members that reached out and drew them in.

Business meetings were still work sessions, but people expressed themselves openly; one sensed that the real decisions were being made at the
meeting, not elsewhere. A curious new phenomenon arose. When a business meeting was over, people no longer cleared out quickly to head for
home or for a coffee shop postmortem on the meeting. Instead, they stood
around in the meeting room, chatting with one another, exchanging
greetings and family news. "Takes me an hour after adjournment to get
this group on its way," one chairman grumbled cheerfully.

When asked to describe the new pastor, people spoke variously about
him. "I get the feeling that he likes himself, and that he likes me." "I
know he has strong convictions, but I can disagree with him and know
he will listen to me and still like me." "He asked me to do this thing I'd
never tried before, and he really believed I could do it—so I did." "I
think he respects himself, and he respects us as a congregation." "What
we're all doing is living up to what he really believes we're capable of."

This pastor's first action, on moving into the parish, was to visit once
in every home in the congregation: four nights a week, three calls a
night. It took more than a year to complete the round of calls, but he
completed it.

His dedication to people was clear to see. He developed an astonishing facility at learning and remembering the names of congregation
members, and was endlessly interested in what people did at work or
through their hobbies. His conversation was studded with references to
this member's skill or that member's achievements. There may be other
factors at work as well, but it is perhaps not too much to say that this
pastor loved and affirmed a troubled congregation back to health.

The area of ministry presented in this chapter was ranked second in
importance only to the expressed-in-life faith treated in Chapter 1. The
foundation of this area of ministry has to do with being mature, personally
secure, and of such integrity as to be unthreatened and unflappable.
Operating from the rock-like solidity and security of this base, such a
pastor then appreciates people and participates with freedom in the
give and take of life. A pastor oriented to people is not only so invulner-
able but also so concerned about, so invested in, and so committed to
the welfare of others as to be always affirming them. The effect on a
congregation is likely to be evident in a spirit of freedom to exercise

creative potential within the family of God. In the words of Goethe: "Treat people as if they were what they ought to be, and you help them become what they are capable of being."

The characteristics of this area of ministry fall into two logical groupings. The first describes a solid ground of personal confidence and a habit of reflecting theologically on life and experience. The second grouping describes a pastor's active participation in the give and take of life—enjoying people, seeking them out, and treating them as valued and desirable parts of life's experience.

On solid ground: "A rock-like security"

Five of the eight characteristics belong to this grouping. They are "Nondefensive Integrity" (4), "Positive Approach" (19), "Theologically Integrative Reflection" (26), "Imperviousness to Threat" (28), and "Adaptive Self-Confidence" (30). A pastor who possesses these qualities will express the type of self-confidence that research shows most powerfully affects one's relationship with others.

Nondefensive Integrity (4) How does a pastor respond when mistakes or weaknesses become apparent in public or before people who are of particular significance or in authority over him or her? Does that pastor find it necessary to make excuses or cover up the blunder? Does he or she find it difficult to apologize, or to admit being wrong? This is the major issue involved in "Nondefensive Integrity." Just how much can ride on this issue was illustrated, in public life, in the Watergate debacle. By the high value they placed on it, Lutherans seemed to be saying that this characteristic is as important for ministers as for presidents. It includes recognizing one's emotional and physical limitations, showing willingness to admit that certain situations are beyond one's own experience or competence, and being able to enjoy an occasional laugh at one's own expense.

Such nondefensiveness about one's abilities is a quality that inspires the trust of others. Another trust-inspiring facet of this characteristic is integrity that cannot be compromised; a person possessing it will not be swayed from a principle by outside pressures. The characteristic includes yet another quality—trustworthiness. Such a person's promise to complete a given act or task can be relied on.

Lutherans also associated "Nondefensive Integrity" with having a spouse equally committed to ministry. Having a spouse who is not sympathetic to a pastor's vocation was apparently associated with a lack of integrity, or seen as a potential source of defensiveness.

Positive Approach (19). A second characteristic of a pastor who is "On Solid Ground" is a positive approach to relationships or situations that are potentially difficult: handling distasteful tasks, relating to superiors, and dealing with difficult or critical members. All these pose at least potential discomfort, yet a pastor who maintains a positive approach deals with them head-on and pleasantly. Whether an unpleasant task is keeping parish records, answering correspondence, preparing sermons, or making hospital calls depends on the preferences of an individual pastor, but a "Positive Approach" pastor resists the temptation to postpone such work and gets it done on schedule.

Relating to superiors in a church structure poses difficulties for some pastors who see these persons as threats; a "Positive Approach" pastor works cooperatively with them. Difficult members can sometimes be *very* difficult, indeed, but such a pastor is able to remain positive and constructive in relationships with such people.

Though this characteristic bears some similarity to the one that follows, the difference is perhaps in the depth at which it operates. The "Positive Approach" characteristic deals mainly with observable behavior. By itself, in isolation from other characteristics in this area, it signals a kind of gentle, accepting, optimistic position. The one to follow has a sturdier, more resilient, perhaps more assertive note. Linked as they are, however, by the item about cantankerous members (which is the most peripheral item in "Positive Approach" and the most central in "Imperviousness to Threat"), the two characteristics clearly have a strong similarity.

Imperviousness to Threat (28).   This characteristic came into existence because of the way lay persons ranked the items (a testimony to the perceptiveness of the laity), who evidently saw this as an observable entity more clearly than did clergy.

Two strong elements in this characteristic are sturdiness and resilience, and of the two, sturdiness is dominant. A pastor who possesses this trait can deal with angry or troublesome people, open opposition, and negative experiences without being squelched or overcome. In such situations he or she is able to express personal opinions without showing anger or undue anxiety. Such a pastor is also emotionally equipped to bounce back after negative experiences and plunge into the fray or the routine once again. This characteristic includes the further step of helping others see the best in people, even when there may be much to be seen that is anything but good. The final item in the characteristic underlines its Gibraltar-like nature. It speaks of an ability to accept comfortably the discrepancy between pastors' status and income and that available to people in other professions.

The emotional resilience that makes this kind of behavior possible bespeaks a considerable degree of ego strength and emotional maturity. The crux of this characteristic exists not so much in being positive when threatened as, rather, in *not being threatened* by what most people would find very threatening.

Adaptive Self-Confidence (30). It is not uncommon to hear people say, "New situations throw me." When "thrown," some become afraid and withdraw. Others become overly impressed, saccharine, or ingratiating. Still others, consciously or not, try to get everyone around them to appreciate what a difficult time they are having. "Adaptive Self-Confidence" is a vital quality for ministers, who never know what the next ring of the phone or knock at the door may bring. It is a quality of dealing calmly and consistently with potentially intimidating people and unfamiliar situations. Pastors with this quality are *not* easily "thrown."

Theologically Integrative Reflection (26). The appearance of this characteristic makes the portrait of a pastor "On Solid Ground" something more than a purely psychological one—he or she is something other than a warm, open, loving humanist. This characteristic indicates that what Lutherans want is a pastor whose approach to people is grounded in theology. They value a person who combines thought and action—who constantly seeks to understand what is happening within the framework of Christian theology.

The emphasis here on a consciously theological base for interpersonal relationships does not suggest that Lutherans want a pastor to be weighed down by a legalistic albatross of rational, conscious decision making before every word or action. But it does suggest that Lutherans want pastors to take time for systematic reflection on their experiences with people, testing their habits and patterns of interaction against the theology they preach and teach, and the values and faith they espouse. Lutherans believe it is appropriate, if not imperative, for pastors to ask, "Where is God in the midst of all of this? What is he attempting to reveal or say to me, to this congregation, and to the individuals with whom I interact?"

The appearance of "Theologically Integrative Reflection" in this area of ministry really signals that Lutherans perceive another Person in the mix of interpersonal relationships: God. All of the discipline, sensitivity, and devotion to persons that appears throughout this area of ministry applies to relationships with him as well. And vice versa: being a person of integrity who enjoys and affirms people (as Lutherans want their ministers to do) consists of applying to one's relationships with others all the sensitivity, concern, devotion, discipline, freedom, and adventure experienced in relationships with God through Jesus Christ.

Affirming others: "Participating freely in the give and take of life"

The second logical grouping of characteristics in this area of ministry describes a person who wades into the mainstream of human interaction —intentionally, with zest, and in a way that affirms people. The three characteristics belonging to this grouping are "Commitment to Family" (3), "Loving Devotion to People" (6), and "Exuberance for Life" (43).

Commitment to Family (3). Both the clergy and laity placed high value on pastors' disciplined commitment to their own families. "Commitment to Family" ranks third of all the long list of characteristics desired in a pastor. Both clergy and lay persons sense that what does or doesn't go on in a pastor's own home is crucial to an effective ministry. The commitment to family that Lutherans generally believe to be so highly important boils down to pastors treating their spouses with the same care given to other parishioners. It means keeping commitments to one's children as carefully and faithfully as one keeps professional appointments, and seeing that time is intentionally set aside to spend with one's family. However much parishioners may need the presence of a pastor at a particular time, they know that pastors who regularly neglect their families in order to clear more time for parish work are being shortsighted. On the other hand, pastors who devote time and energy to keeping family relationships in tune are developing an unassailable asset to their emotional health and general happiness, as well as helping to keep life in balance.

It is at least implicitly clear, however, that Lutherans retain the idea that it is appropriate for them to place expectations on a pastor's spouse as well as on a pastor. Confidentiality is one of those expectations. A pastor's spouse may sometimes become aware of situations and information that should be kept confidential. Just as lay persons expect that their pastor will respect confidential communications and observations as his or her professional responsibility, disclosing them to no one, they also appear to expect a pastor's spouse to protect any confidential information he or she may become aware of.

Loving Devotion to People (6). This characteristic forms the core of the area of ministry discussed in this chapter. It is the dominant characteristic—the one that comes closest to containing the central meaning of the set of eight characteristics. It bears the stamp not so much of the happy, gregarious mixer, but of a disciplined person who is sensitively and wholeheartedly engaged with people and their concerns, who is open and accepting of them, and who is concerned for their welfare.

Discipline is shown in not avoiding distasteful tasks of ministry, finishing what one starts, and working cooperatively with superiors. (If there is a familiar sound to that quality, it is because two of the three descriptive items in "Positive Approach" also appear in this characteristic.) For some clergy, taking time to listen carefully and well to their own children may require some of this same sort of discipline. The *sensitivity* that is also a part of that act of listening would be evident in accurately sensing the concerns and needs of people, relating well to persons of various cultures, even such specifics as making eye contact in conversation. A decided *openness* is required in order to learn from other people through accepting their criticisms and suggestions. This includes the ability to demonstrate honest affection and to converse easily with just about anyone, regardless of sex, culture, or background. It includes manifestation of a pastoral heart through accepting and affirming people, and maintaining a good, candid, relaxed balance between seriousness and humor.

There is simply no room here for an attitude that "loves humanity but can't stand people." This characteristic requires discipline, great sensitivity, and the expression of warmth, acceptance, honest affection, and benevolent candor.

Exuberance for Life (43). Though its number in rank (43) makes it evident that this is not one of the absolute imperatives for ministry in the eyes of most Lutherans, it is a distinctly desirable characteristic. Lutherans prefer pastors who plunge with gusto into the adventure of living. They admire a pastor who shows eagerness for new possibilities, and enthusiasm for exploring new friendships, ideas, and cultures. According to this characteristic, Lutherans generally approve when a pastor forms and enjoys friendships within a congregation, and spends some time —precious though that time often is—simply having fun. They appreciate being drawn into their pastor's interests in diversity of culture, experience, and thought.

The final item of this criterion gives further insight into the thinking of the laity. They are not attracted to clergy who deny or attempt to hide their sexuality behind a pose of holiness or dedication. Rather, a majority (three out of five) consider it highly important that pastors show positive acceptance of sexuality and reflect an appreciation for this aspect of God's creation.

Emphases and Contrasts

The highly educated

The group that placed highest value on a ministry marked by a firm integrity and an affirming approach to people was the highly educated, particularly women. Though a warm, affirming approach was appreciated by everyone, the more education Lutherans had, the more con-

Table 1. Groups that place higher value on specific characteristics of Area II, "A Person for Others."

	more educated	older	younger	female	clergy
4 Nondefensive Integrity	HH	HH			H
19 Positive Approach	HH			H	
28 Imperviousness to Threat		H			
30 Adaptive Self-Confidence				H	
26 Theologically Integrative Reflection	HH				
3 Commitment to Family	HHH	HH		HH	
6 Loving Devotion to People				H	
43 Exuberance for Life			H		H

As compared with Lutherans' average: HHH = much higher
HH = higher
H = slightly higher

vinced they were of the importance of sensitivity to others. They perceived such sensitivity as a visible evidence of the gospel—the Word becoming flesh and being manifested in the way people are treated. It follows that when these qualities are lacking, the first to notice and react will probably be the well-educated.

The very high value placed by the educated on "Commitment to Family" (3) came as something of a surprise. That educated women valued it was merely verification of a commonplace, but we were not prepared to discover that well-educated men also placed especially high value on it. There are a number of possible reasons why the well-educated would feel "Commitment to Family" is especially important. One possibility is that the highly educated often have jobs that spill over into personal time. Many of them may have come to recognize, through personal experience, that setting aside ample time for family life is both essential and difficult.

The preference of the better educated for "Theologically Integrative Reflection" (26) was less surprising. So also was the value they placed on "Nondefensive Integrity" (4) and on "Positive Approach" (19), since both of these represent values implicit in the American educational system—taking an optimistic, positive approach, and being less pugnacious and more nondefensive in the face of opposition.

Young people

Young people who participated in this study did not show a particularly high degree of preference for this area of ministry. This lack of enthusiasm was surprising in light of the emphasis on human relationships during the late 1960s. Their single point of emphasis, and it was a slight emphasis, was on "Exuberance for Life" (43).

Clergy

Although clergy gave slightly higher value to "Nondefensive Integrity" (4) and to "Exuberance for Life" (43), the emphases were not great. The most notable event here was that, in their pattern of preferences, the clergy were much like the laity.

Older people

Older people in particular valued a pastor who honors personal commitments to spouse and children. They also wanted a pastor to be sufficiently secure and stable so as not to be threatened and "thrown" by opposition or negative experiences. A Study of Generations showed a somewhat greater desire among older Lutherans for a dependable world. The special preference shown here for evidences of self-confidence and of dependable family relationships may have a logical link to that earlier finding.

Reflections

The characteristics of an affirming person, though intensely desired in a pastor, have larger implications. They are essential in any helping ministry on the part of either the clergy or laity. Unless a loving, accepting relationship is established, little ministry can occur. In *Five Cries of Youth,* Strommen [1] has shown that two elements found in homes where children share their parents' faith are (a) religiously committed parents and (b) a congenial, loving home atmosphere. It is difficult to over-emphasize the equal value, in an effective ministry, of these two qualities: personal faith and the ability to relate well to people.

There are two sides to being able to relate well to others. One of them is seeing persons as lovable, trustworthy, and important. People quickly sense, appreciate, and are drawn to a person with this view of them. This represents more than a technique or a psychological device—it is a broad perspective or belief that sees possibilities and worth in people and in life. Given this perspective, a response of love and patience is the mark of a personally secure, caring person. It is a Christ-likeness that people find persuasively attractive.

The musical *Man of La Mancha,* which retells one of the most-loved stories of all time, had a phenomenally successful run on Broadway some years ago. The central figure is Don Quixote, who mistakes inns for castles and windmills for giants. Further, he imagines the tavern prostitute Eldonza to be a lady of beauty and character. He demonstrates his genuine esteem and love for her by naming her Dulcinea—"sweetness and light"—a name which he exalts in a hauntingly beautiful song. At first she listens to him with contempt, angrily ridiculing him as a dreamer. Later she listens again, but now with a note of wistfulness.

In the final scene, as Don Quixote is dying, Dulcinea enters, no longer a self-despairing tavern prostitute, but the woman of beauty and character Don Quixote believed her to be. Audiences which regularly accorded this final scene a standing ovation may have been cheering something more than the play. They may have been applauding, as well, the message of the releasing and transforming power of affirming, visionary love.

The second side of relating well to people is an intensification of a positive, affirming view of people: the predisposition not to react negatively to persons who act in unloving, deceitful, and cruel ways. The natural reaction to cruelty is more cruelty, and the natural reaction to attack

---

1. Merton P. Strommen, *Five Cries of Youth* (New York: Harper and Row, 1974).

is defense. Lutherans value a pastor who responds to destructive criticism or a scolding attack with a nondefensive, accepting spirit. Overcoming evil with good is not one of the easier aspects of the Christian life to live out, but a pastor or lay person who can do it has laid hold of a pearl of great price—and Lutherans know it.

Among the surprises in our study was the discovery that the majority of Lutherans see the enjoyment of life as an enhancement of one's ministry. People in parishes live with an appreciation of God's creation as well as redemption. They want their pastors to enjoy their families, to engage with exuberance in new life experiences, and to enjoy life with them. Presumably those who want this of their pastors also want the same for themselves.

Congregational leaders

The material in this chapter is relevant to the laity of a congregation in two ways. First, the insights it offers into the nature of an affirming person can be profitably applied to anyone. With a few deletions or modifications of items, any lay person could profit from a self-rating using the items on which this chapter is based (see Appendix C, Area II, p. 212). Second, it is important for congregational leaders to know how significant a part they can play in creating an atmosphere where both pastor and congregation as a whole can offer a person-affirming ministry.

A support group within a congregation is one of the most powerful resources one could offer to help a pastor grow in the area of affirmational ministry. If a pastor is to continue to be affirming, he or she must be affirmed. A pastoral support committee, whatever its official title or make-up, can offer ministry to a pastor that can have far-reaching effects in the lives of group members as well as in the congregation as a whole.

Such a group could offer a listening ear; be available; give positive feedback; take seriously a pastor's needs (financial, family, and educational); bear emotional burdens; speak the truth in love; offer intercessory prayer; be involved in mutual study of the promises of God; and simply care. It would be imperative that such a group take seriously the responsibility of maintaining strict confidentiality on all matters discussed, so that members can express themselves honestly and fully, trusting other members to deal responsibly with whatever is conveyed in the group.

Such a group need not focus exclusively on the pastor. A group might well begin with members completing a checklist twice: once for themselves and once for the pastor, and discussing, over a period of time, the insights that develop from that experience.

Sometimes the person-affirming support offered by a congregation is not of the formal, structured sort at all, but is instead a kind of environ-

ment provided, tone established, and set of expectations communicated
that affirms the pastor as a valued, loved, and respected person.

A pastor we know served successively two churches with very different
atmospheres. In church A the expectation was that the pastor was ultimately responsible for everything. The members expected him to be
available 24 hours a day, present at all meetings, and available for questions and personal consultation at any time. If the pastor heard nothing
from the congregation, he was to assume that things were going well;
he would hear from them only if things were going wrong. Church
leaders were impatient with any discussion that centered on long-term
goals—the needs of the moment were all that counted with them, and
therefore all that should count with the pastor.

In church B the expectation, both expressed and unexpressed, was that
the congregation as a whole had a ministry to perform, and that the pastor's role was that of facilitator and enabler. Members often approached
the pastor with an opening like, "We expect to carry out the work of
this particular program, but we'd like your counsel on it before we begin."
After receiving the counsel, they carried through. They assumed that the
pastor needed days off, and set up office structures and congregational
policy that prevented all but the most extreme emergencies from inter-
rupting those days off. They assumed that the pastor needed time with
his family, just as they themselves did, and saw that he got it.

The set of assumptions of church B were not so much formally stated
as they were informally carried out, appearing in little nudges here and
there, verbal reminders, raised eyebrows when the pastor showed up on
his day off, and invitations to the pastor and sometimes his family to join
members and their families in nonchurch recreation and relaxed enjoyment of one another. Such an atmosphere is person-affirming in quite a
different way from that of the support group, but it had a profound
influence on the ability of the pastor to offer his own affirmative ministry
to others.

Seminary educators

The high rank accorded this area of concern for ministry should make
it clear that a seminarian's growth in self-confidence and in ability to
affirm and to be affirmed is an important ingredient in preparing people
for ministry. Seminaries where it is not already part of the structure
might well give serious consideration to developing opportunities within
the life of the seminary for something that might be called "person-
formation." One of the more common vehicles for this is the small support group, where the focus is on understanding oneself more thoroughly
—discovering one's strengths and abilities, and having them highlighted

and affirmed—and on becoming more confident of one's own abilities to relate positively and affirmatively to others.

It may be important for seminaries to offer such opportunities not only to students but to the spouses of students, since Lutherans see spouses as an integral part of pastoral ministry. Granted, a spouse should not be considered an auxiliary staff member. Even so, the presence or absence in a spouse of an attitude of self-respect, self-confidence, and of value, respect, and affirmation of others will have an effect both on congregational members and on a pastor, and will accordingly help or hinder that pastor's ministry.

Such person-formation groups should not center narrowly on the psychological. The presence of "Theologically Integrative Reflection" (26) in this area of ministry suggests that small groups of Christians may be able to help one another develop abilities to learn from and reflect on life's experiences. In the academic arena, seminarians learn to move with facility from the general to the specific—from biblical or systematic foundations to application in human life. Small support groups may help learning to move in the opposite direction, from current life experiences to a generalized discovery of some of the principles of God's activity in creation or the work of the Holy Spirit within the group.

Example is a powerful teacher. A child's way of walking, speaking, and using body gestures is often a clear, though usually unconscious, copy of his or her parents. The personal style of a teacher—dress, phraseology, tone of voice—often turns up in a pupil, particularly when the pupil is discussing that teacher's subject. It is probably safe to assume that much of a pastor's style, tone, and manner develops from seminary experience. Given the high value of a style that affirms people, it may be worthwhile to look at the thrust or tone of seminary educational methods and, indeed, the whole tone of seminaries. Are the educational methods person-affirming? Are they person-respecting, or do they emphasize negative criticism and competition? Are there ways in which professors offer (or could offer more) models of a secure, stable, person-affirming style in the process of making and correcting assignments, leading discussion, responding to students' questions, and dealing with disappointing or failing students? Consideration of this question by seminary faculties, with the aim being to affirm one another and help one another find new ways of further developing this kind of atmosphere, might have salutary and far-reaching effects.

Pastors

The central issue raised here for pastors is the question of self-love: the degree to which a pastor senses his or her own self-worth. This chapter highlights the very considerable contribution to ministry that a pastor's self-esteem can make. Without a sense of self-esteem, of personal worth, a pastor can probably affirm and support others in a congregation, with some positive effect. But such a person will probably not have the impact of one who has a sense of self-esteem, and who therefore finds it easy and natural to like others and to be an affirming person for them.

One way to look at this area of ministry is to consider which way one's decisions habitually tip—toward meeting the needs of others and ignoring or postponing one's own needs, or toward an appropriate respect for one's own needs as well as the needs of others. A pastor may go to a church subcommittee meeting, even though it was called at the last minute, or go ahead with a previous promise to his or her family. When there is a choice, do pastors habitually decide *against* themselves? Perhaps taking a count of one or two recent decisions is not so useful as noticing over time how often they sacrificed their own needs or schedules for others, and how often they were firm about their own needs and schedules. To make the latter choice some of the time is to say, "I'm worth something." Too little self-affirmation of this sort may be a danger signal.

Those who consistently and regularly sacrifice their own needs often extend that expectation to their families, sacrificing their needs as well. This kind of shortsighted unselfishness can have bitter long-term results.

Pastor "Severson" was always a person of gracious availability. He was always willing to pick up the slack for others, stay late into the night for an after-meeting meeting, interrupt dinner, or postpone a family shopping excursion in order that his congregation be ministered to. It was not until his children were into their teens that he noticed that his wife and children had developed a family style that operated entirely without him. They carried on without him because they so often had to.

For pastors who, like Pastor Severson, have gradually become outsiders and strangers to their own families, the long-term effects of day-by-day decisions can be disastrous. To have estranged oneself from one's family —one's most close and lasting support group—is to have wandered unawares into a very lonely place.

A pastor who wants to offer a ministry that affirms others should realize his or her own need of support in order to offer that ministry. One of the best potential support groups is one's own family. A spouse can be not only one's own best critic, but best affirmer. Certain types of marriage enrichment now available through churches are especially good at training couples to establish patterns that help them appreciate, encourage, and affirm one another, and at teaching them to include their children in that person-affirming process. A pastor whose primary support group is a lively, joyously, and affirmatively interacting family has a great asset in ministry.

When we speak of a pastor's need for a "family," we recognize that single pastors have the same need as married pastors for some person or small group to provide a focus in life other than a congregation. All need someone to tease them, bore them, lose their temper with them, be companionably silent with them, and generally make them feel like ordinary mortals. Whether single or married, pastors need persons who address them and think of them primarily as someone other than "Pastor."

Naturally we are not recommending that pastors suddenly adopt a "me-first" policy. We take it for granted that pastors will be available in case of crisis or real need in a parish (note the relatively high priority Lutherans placed on "Gracious Availability" [21] discussed in Chapter 8). But it is also a good thing for pastors to have people who encourage them, now and then, to put their own plans first—to miss a particular meeting, and instead go off to read a book, play tennis, or fish for trout.

Pastors, in order to see more clearly the degree to which you exhibit the characteristics of this area of ministry, you might complete a checklist based on the material in Appendix C that relates to Area II, "A Person for Others" (page 212). As you read each item, say to yourself, "Concerning myself, this item is (very true, somewhat true, not true)." Check the appropriate column for each of the items. You might then review your choices and circle those items on which you would most like to change.

You might also consider asking one or more trusted persons from your congregation to complete the checklist as they see you. But it is best not to begin that process unless you intend also to discuss the checklists with them, either as a group or individually. In order for the checklist to make a difference, it should be used as the starting point for continuing discussion, prayer, and mutual help.

Churchwide and district/synodical leaders

Given the importance among Lutherans of this area of ministry, churchwide and district/synodical leaders might do well to see that a pastor's ability to offer this kind of ministry is enhanced in every way possible. The concerns we have expressed for seminary education have their parallel implications for parish pastors and those offering ministry in nursing homes, prisons, hospitals, in the military, and in other noncongregational settings.

Where a congregation, whatever its nature, is not able to offer support, a pastoral conference, study group, or local ministerium could well serve a similar function. In taking seriously its supportive function, members of such a group should make a practice of affirming one another, speaking the truth in love, giving positive feedback, and lending their minds out to one another when a member of the group is wrestling with a particularly knotty problem. Members of such groups need, of course, to be scrupulously careful to preserve confidentiality in order that group trust may be protected.

One potential obstacle in a group of pastors is the usual tendency to enlarge on one's successes and hide one's failures. However, in order for a group to serve the purpose intended here, members must be willing to become increasingly vulnerable—by being open about their own areas of weakness, confessing their own imperfections, and asking for help and support. Such an atmosphere of openness is usually possible only when some of the more secure, more firmly established, or "successful" members lead the way by being willing to discuss their own problems, uncertainties, or failures and asking for help. Support and affirmation are far more meaningful when they are offered by those who know both one's successes and failures, strengths and weaknesses. They come then as affirmations of the person one really is.

Component characteristics: Chapter 3

From central to peripheral

In order of Lutheran ranking

3

Critical Awareness of Lutheran Heritage and Theology

"Why do we baptize infants? They don't know what's happening and haven't made a decision to live for Christ."

"Why do our kids have to take two years of instruction before being confirmed? In churches I know, they're confirmed after eight weeks of instruction."

"Why do we use the same liturgy every Sunday at our church? All I really need is some music and a good sermon."

"I can't understand why our pastor won't support the seminar 'Basic Youth Conflicts.' She calls it legalistic because it stresses what a person is supposed to do. But as far as I can tell everything presented in the seminar is based on Scripture. Bible verses are given for everything we are to do."

"Why doesn't our congregation join the all-city evangelistic campaign? Our pastor is interested in evangelism, but he says he doesn't like the techniques being used. What difference do techniques make if people are being converted?"

These are some typical and persistent questions that pressure pastors to stop stressing distinctive Lutheran emphases. Pastors are usually more conscious of these subtle but real distinctions, and often puzzle devout lay people by stands they take.

It is often hard to define those things that are most firmly a part of one's identity. When asked to describe the uniqueness of their home atmosphere—the special quality of family life that distinguishes their family from all others—many people respond with a puzzled silence, or flounder helplessly in search of an answer. For similar reasons many Lutherans are unclear about what makes them distinguishable from other Christians. But by asking a person what home life *should be* like, one can often discover what that person's family life *is* like. When one asks Lutherans what ministries they want, as we did, the hallmarks of Lutheran-ness become visible in their replies. Lutherans take theological stances, interpret Scripture, and adhere to doctrine in identifiably Lutheran ways.

Three distinctive Lutheran emphases emerged from people's statements about ministry:

- the centrality of justification by faith
- a view of Christians as both sinners and saints
- a particular kind of emphasis on doctrine

These emphases, though not unique to Lutherans, are nevertheless distinctive, highly valued, and well-nigh essential to the continuing identity of Lutherans. The strong accent on these three explains in part why some Lutherans drag their feet on some ecumenical ventures. More importantly, they identify theological perspectives most Lutherans want to find in their pastors. If a pastor does not exhibit these distinctively Lutheran emphases, members of that congregation, even though unable to put their fingers on exactly what is missing, will be uncomfortable. This is because the features discussed in this chapter are ones Lutherans associate with their spiritual home. Clergy consider them especially important. But the laity also give them high rank. Of the 10 areas of ministry identified in this book, how pastors view this distinctively Lutheran perspective ranks third in importance.

The centrality of justification by faith

Some people experience the church as concerned primarily about right living, concentrating its teaching and preaching on what people should do. They feel the focus is on what God considers right words, right thoughts, and right behaviors. Over time, such emphasis on "oughts" leaves the impression that being a Christian is determined by whether one has attained a sufficiently high moral standard or adequately pleased God. Lutherans have traditionally maintained that such experience amounts to legalism, or life under the law.

Other people experience the church as emphasizing the scriptural account of what God has done and is doing. They feel the focus is on becoming acquainted with a living, active, holy, yet *justifying* God. Their attention is drawn to the good news found in Jesus Christ that salvation is not a reward for our good works, but a gift of a gracious God which is received through faith. Over time, this emphasis encourages belief in a personal, gracious, saving God. Confidence that one is a Christian centers in what Christ has done, rather than in what one can do. Such a gospel-oriented approach is a distinctive, though not unique, Lutheran accent.

Luther's fundamental question was, How do I find a gracious God? Upon what can I rest my confidence that I am righteous before him? The Scriptures and the Lutheran Confessions answer with one accord: Nothing human whatever, but only God's grace in Christ Jesus, is the true ground of our salvation. They see this doctrine as the article by which the church stands or falls: "Nothing in this article can be given up or compromised. . . . On this article rests all that we teach and practice. . . ." [1]

Lutheran Confessional Stance (38). A confessional stance centering in the authority of the Scriptures and in the doctrine of justification by grace alone through faith alone is the dominant characteristic of this distinctively Lutheran area of ministry. Its uniting theme is a personal theological stance reflecting a Lutheran confessional position, but one held neither rigidly nor in a way that ignores insights from biblical scholarship. (The fourth and first items of this characteristic read: "Interprets Scripture using tools of biblical scholarship," and "Makes the Lutheran Confessions own personal confession without feeling obligated to every nondoctrinal detail.")

The Lutheran Confessions referred to here are the documents found in the Book of Concord: the three ecumenical creeds, the Augsburg Confession, the Apology of the Augsburg Confession, the Smalcald Articles, the Treatise on the Power and Primacy of the Pope, Luther's Small and Large Catechisms, and the Formula of Concord. These confessional statements guide the interpretations of Scripture made when teaching and preaching in Lutheran congregations. (The third item of the characteristic reads, "On controversial issues, shows sensitivity to the relationship between Scripture and traditions of the church.")

These Confessions present the point of view that pastors should find their authority in the gospel message—in what Scripture says God has done, is doing, and will do for a lost humanity. Because the gospel is dependable, authoritative, and trustworthy, so are the Scriptures. That

---

1. Theodore G. Tappert, trans. and ed., *The Book of Concord,* Smalcald Articles, part II, article I (Philadelphia: Fortress, 1959), p. 292.

is to say, the authority of Scripture resides in its gospel message. (The second of the four items of this characteristic reads, "Interprets the authority of Scripture as being in the gospel message.") [2]

The Lutheran Confessions embody this gospel tradition of interpreting Scripture. They are an expression of the Christian faith that Lutherans hold as normative. Those most conscious of the gospel-orientation in the Confessions are clergy—parish pastors, seminary professors, seminary seniors, and denominational officials. They rate such an orientation as contributing "very much" to an effective ministry. The laity scale it down one level to say it contributes only "quite a bit."

A view of Christians as both sinners and saints

In Luther's Latin, a Christian is *simul justus et peccator*—at the same time righteous and sinful. In using this phrase Luther (and countless Lutherans after him) acknowledged that those who live within the promises of Christ and trust their lives to him have dual natures. On the one hand they have been born again into the kingdom of God and are new people in whom the Holy Spirit dwells. Simultaneously, on the other hand, their old sinful natures still persist and lead them to sin daily; original sinfulness is not done away with in Baptism, but its guilt is forgiven. Christians are righteous, clothed with the imputed righteousness of Christ. But in this life they remain sinners still, though their sin is covered through forgiveness in Christ.

Simul Justus et Peccator (12). This second distinctive accent of Lutheranism showed up in a set of items that drew an exceptionally high rank— 12th of 77—and for whose title we have retained Luther's Latin phrase. Though it ranked 12th in importance when the responses of all Lutherans were taken into account, clergy as a group put it second from the top. Its three items find their uniting idea in the truth that persons in Christ are at the same time sinners and saints.

There is a close relationship between being gospel-oriented and being aware of one's own two states as a Christian. *A Study of Generations* found that people who overemphasize Christ's divinity and deny his humanity tend more toward law orientation. Among gospel-oriented persons one finds more acceptance and ready acknowledgment both of Christ's humanity and one's own humanity. Lutherans clearly want

---

2. There were other items in the questionnaire that placed emphasis on historical accuracy and verbal inspiration of the Scriptures. Lutherans did not rate those items with comparable enough consistency for them to become part of the set that comprises this distinctively Lutheran characteristic. Rather, they became part of Characteristic 61, "Extreme Adherence to Scriptural Authority," described in Chapter 4.

pastors who acknowledge their humanity, sinfulness, and inadequacies, and who at the same time recognize their sainthood in Jesus Christ.

There is also an element in this characteristic that speaks of balance— the ability to hold two ideas, positions, or sets of needs in tension, and to live within that tension without being pulled either to one extreme or the other. To see oneself as both sinner and saint implies that one escapes the fate, on the one hand, of being overimpressed with one's own membership in the community of saints, and on the other, of being weighed down under the burden of one's sinfulness. One can live life somewhere in between. This characteristic speaks of the similar ability to achieve a balance in the way one spends time, neither being constantly overextended to serve the needs of a congregation, nor neglecting congregational responsibilities for one's own personal agendas. It also includes a balance between the confidence that one can fulfill a calling that demands both sophistication and expertise, and the recognition, at the same time, of one's own deficiencies and the need sometimes to ask for help.

A particular kind of emphasis on doctrine

To emphasize doctrine is not distinctively Lutheran. To emphasize it with the particular pattern of accents that emerged from our study *is* distinctive. We discovered that Lutherans value pastors who (a) are competent theologians, (b) are not dryly academic theologians, but have integrated their theology into their lives and beings, and (c) take a position of critical acceptance of their Lutheran heritage—with about equal emphasis on "critical" and "acceptance."

Communication of Life-Related Theology (8). This characteristic's rank —8th among 77—indicates the high regard in which Lutherans hold the ability (point "a") to think theologically, and to express that thought competently. Point "b" is explicitly conveyed in the items of this characteristic. Lutherans want a minister who is a seeking, thinking, and learning scholar of Scripture and doctrine. But they want very much a minister who makes both doctrine and Scripture relevant to their own current needs and circumstances. If we are to believe their declared priorities, they want life-relatedness even slightly more than doctrinal clarity or biblical scholarship. Lutherans are saying to their pastors through this characteristic, "We want you to be clear on theology; but we want you to be able to make it clear to us in language familiar to us, and we want that theology to be related to our experiences and to meet our present needs."

Scholarly Openness and Objectivity (50). The third accent of the distinctively Lutheran emphasis on doctrine (point "c" above) is that a pastor be committed to the Lutheran heritage, but also free to test it against subsequent learning—thus submitting it to critical thought. Most

Lutherans do not want to be bound uncritically to the past. They hope for pastors who maintain an openness to truth that does not bind them to every nondoctrinal detail in the Lutheran Confessions. They want pastors who exhibit scholarship. When the Scriptures are interpreted, the laity want an informed interpretation, bearing the marks of a pastor's own biblical scholarship. On the other hand, they don't want Scripture subjected to a kind of freewheeling, highly individualistic interpretation. They want an interpretation that is not one person's opinion, but a communication of the heritage and wisdom of the church.

The laity and clergy differed in their willingness to endorse a pastor's freedom to criticize the Lutheran heritage. Though 70% of the seminary professors deemed such an attitude highly important, and 65% of parish pastors agreed with them, only 37% of the laity shared this opinion. In fact 15% viewed it as a hindrance to effectiveness.

A young pastor serving his first parish in a rural district reported, "I thought learning was what seminary was for, but I'm still learning, and a lot of it is from the people in my church. I've been visiting a not-so-pretty, white-haired old lady in a nursing home. She's 87, and most of the time in pain from a broken hip that isn't healing well. The other day I visited her, and as I drove away I was thinking how cheerful she always is, and so serene, really beautiful, and it came to me what 'the peace that passes understanding' looks like when it is communicated in the face of a person who will probably never walk again."

Lutherans believe a pastor should be willing to learn theology from lay persons. Seventy-two percent of seminary professors and 71% of parish clergy said it is highly important to do so. It is the high value that clergy place on this ability that makes it central to the meaning of this characteristic. Lay persons are generally less committed to the idea. Only 43% said it "contributes very much" or is "absolutely essential" to an effective ministry. This may not mean that the laity truly reject the idea. More likely, although this is a strong theme in the teaching of certain professors, it is an unfamiliar idea to most lay persons. Since many of them may not have thought through its implications, it did not immediately rise to the top of their priority lists. In addition, some pastors may (intentionally or unintentionally) discourage the idea that pastors can learn from lay persons. Pastors may discourage the idea when they preach sermons devoted mostly to the drawing of fine theological and doctrinal distinctions. Lay people, having their attention constantly drawn to a field in which they have no professional preparation, may then believe that the connections they make between the gospel and their own experiences of life are of little value either to the pastor or to other Christians.

Table 2. Major areas of ministry as perceived and rank-ordered in importance for readiness or effectiveness in ministry by all Christians vs. Lutherans.

rank of Lutheran equivalent	rank	pan-Christian areas of ministry, 47 denominations combined	rank of pan-Christian equivalent	rank	Lutheran areas of ministry
(2)	1	Open, Affirming Style	(7)	1	Personal Faith, Spiritual Depth
(6)	2	Caring for Persons Under Stress	(1)	2	A Person for Others
(5)	3	Congregational Leadership	(6?)	3	Critical Awareness of Lutheran Heritage and Theology
none	4	Theologian in Life and Thought	none	4	Community Through Word and Sacraments
(8)	5	Development of Fellowship and Worship	(3)	5	Making Ministry of Administration
(3?)	6	Denominational Awareness and Collegiality	(2)	6	Ministry of Counseling
(1)	7	Ministry from Personal Commitment of Faith	(8)	7	Reaching Out with Compassion to Community and World
(7)	8	Ministry to Community and World	(5)	8	Informed Leadership of Liturgical Worship
none	9	Priestly-Sacramental Ministry	(10)	9	Not Wanted: Dominating Influence
(9)	10	Privatistic, Legalistic Style	(11)	10	Not Wanted: Ministry-Defeating Behaviors
(10)	11	Disqualifying Personal and Behavioral Characteristics			

Another study of ministry

Another perspective on ministry that bears some similarity to the one presented here is available from the Readiness for Ministry Project involving the 47 denominations which are represented in the Association of Theological Schools of the United States and Canada (ATS).

In that study, a questionnaire of about the same length, and containing some of the same items, was presented to representative samples of the 47 denominations. The information was treated in much the same way, and a ranking of areas of ministry developed. The pan-Christian ranking of areas of ministry is presented in Table 2, along with the Lutheran ranking of areas of ministry.

There are differences between the two projects, and between the two lists. The pan-Christian data at the left of the page were ranked in terms of importance to readiness to begin the professional practice of ministry. The Lutheran data were ranked in relation to effective ministry performed by ordained ministers—whether beginning or experienced. The terminologies used in the rating scales were slightly different, and the items in the two questionnaires were about one-third the same, one-third slightly different, and one-third completely different. The categories of ministry that developed from the data of the two projects are not entirely parallel. However, it is possible to examine the two lists and draw some conclusions from that comparison which may throw further light on the question of what is distinctive about Lutherans.

One discovery that becomes apparent in looking down the pan-Christian list, along with its Lutheran approximate equivalents, is that the Lutherans did not develop, through their responses, a separate category to parallel the pan-Christian "Theologian in Life and Thought," which is ranked fourth. Lutherans do not see theologizing as a separate area of ministry, but as integrated with other areas, whereas apparently most other Christians consider the task of being a theologian and scholar as more of a separate and distinct activity. Lutherans see it differently. Among Lutherans, we find characteristics having to do with theology turning up in a variety of areas of ministry. One appears in the area of pastoral counseling (Characteristic 46, treated in Chapter 8). Two of them turn up in the discussion of ministry to the community and world (Characteristics 37 and 45, treated in Chapter 9). As Lutherans see ministry, theological thought is interwoven in the whole fabric of ministry, fitting in here and there where it belongs. Lutheran theology is less a separate ingredient and more of a leaven for the whole.

In looking at the Lutheran list at the right, the first and perhaps most significant difference that appears is that the area of ministry to which Lutherans accord top rank is most closely approximated by the lower ranked pan-Christian ministry area called "Ministry from Personal Commitment of Faith." Though none of the features of ministry are exactly parallel in the two studies, these two are good approximations, since six of the nine Lutheran characteristics of this area have parallel characteristics in the Readiness grouping. For Lutherans to rank first that which appears as seventh in the pan-Christian ranking speaks powerfully of the importance Lutherans place on having a pastor who presents an example of a faith firmly believed and visibly lived out in their midst. This does not imply that the rest of the Christian community devalues a lived-out faith. Many of the individual characteristics that make up "Ministry from Personal Commitment of Faith" (one called "Christian Example" and another called "Commitment Reflecting Religious Piety") received very high rank across denominations. However, the area, taken as a whole, stands considerably down the list in the pan-Christian ranking from the place given to it by Lutherans.

Another difference is the high importance Lutherans give to a pastor's emphasis on the Lutheran heritage. This has no pan-Christian counterpart. It looks as though the pan-Christian "Denominational Awareness and Collegiality" might be much the same, but it is not. This consists of knowledge of, and comfort with, the polity and general characteristics of one's own denomination. It lacks the sense of the internalization of the theological heritage and faith that Lutherans placed third in importance for effective ministry. The final difference of note is the relatively low rank Lutherans gave a counseling ministry—sixth, as compared with the second rank given it by the pan-Christian group. The two, again, are not entirely parallel. The pan-Christian version concentrates more on techniques of counseling, and ministering to personal need. The Lutheran version includes an expectation of pastoral skill, but is based on a considerable foundation of theological reflection, intentionality, and scholarship. Nevertheless, the two have much in common, and the difference in rank bears a significant message.

When taken as a whole, this is what the two lists appear to imply: *the distinctively Lutheran answer* to what makes for effective ministry is that (1) it centers in personal Christian faith, an affirmational approach to people, and adherence to a solid theological core such as is expressed in the Lutheran Confessions; (2) it then broadens to providing for individual, community, and world needs; and (3) theology is a leaven that moves through many areas of ministry, rather than a separate task.

The general *Christian answer* is that effective Christian ministry includes (1) open and affirming personal qualities; (2) responsive sensitivity and provision of help for the gamut of individual and corporate needs and hurts; and (3) ultimately includes the development of Christian community and mutual, spiritual ministry based on personal faith and commitment.

Emphases and Contrasts

What we failed to find

Though Lutherans differed somewhat from one another in the degree of emphasis they gave to this area of ministry, our findings fail to support certain widely-held assumptions within the church. For example, we were not able to find that Lutherans in any one region of the country put markedly greater emphasis than others on Lutheran distinctiveness. We also found that members of the Lutheran Church in America, the American Lutheran Church, and the Lutheran Church–Missouri Synod do not differ significantly from one another in the value they place on Lutheran distinctiveness.

In the light of the present controversies within the LCMS, some might have expected that a significant number of LCMS members would place higher importance on a ministry that emphasizes the authority of Scripture and the Lutheran Confessions. However, consider the interpretation that is placed on that authority by the items of "Lutheran Confessional Stance" (38). The emphasis is upon use of tools of biblical scholarship—and not on verbal inspiration or historicity, but rather on the authority of the gospel as the source of biblical authority. These emphases drew no significant variations by church body. (But significant differences by church body were found in average ratings of "Extreme Adherence to Scriptural Authority" [61], which has quite different content and is discussed in Chapter 4.)

Further, in the value they gave to this area of ministry, we found no significant difference between:

- members of urban, rural, or suburban congregations
- people in various types of ministry settings (such as hospital chaplaincy, visitation ministry, evangelistic ministry, or youth work)
- higher and lower socioeconomic levels
- members of large and small congregations

To find variations in the desire for ministry with a distinctive Lutheran accent we must look elsewhere.

Where variations appear

The group most convinced of the importance of Lutheran distinctiveness is the clergy. Lutheran laity not only placed much less importance on taking a Lutheran confessional stance (38), but also on ministers seeing themselves as at the same time sinners and saints (12). The laity were also not as impressed as the clergy with the contribution that scholarly objectivity (50) and communication of life-related theology (8) make to good ministry. Part of this is a matter of terminology or knowledge, since many lay people are not aware of most of the Lutheran Confessions as historical documents. Tools of biblical scholarship are also not familiar to large numbers of lay people. Therefore they may be hesitant to place high value on what is unfamiliar to them, though they may generally agree with the principle of a pastor being a good scholar of the Scriptures and of the heritage of the church. On the other hand, lay people are simply not as impressed with the fine nuances or the present-day significance of doctrinal positions articulated centuries ago as they are with a realistic living-out of personal faith today.

Among the laity those most likely to appreciate a distinctively Lutheran minister are the highly educated and older. Generally speaking, the older the person, the more importance one can expect will be placed on pastors both taking a Lutheran confessional stance and being aware of their simultaneous sainthood in Christ and their sinfulness. Well-educated Lutheran lay persons, however, are inclined to show slightly more than typical appreciation for scholarship, and much more appreciation for well-conceived and theologically sound commentary about human problems (8).

There is a slight but perceptible difference between lay women and lay men in the importance they attributed to Lutheran distinctiveness; women, together with most-frequent worshipers, placed a little more importance on a personal awareness that resembles Luther's "Simul Justus et Peccator" (12).

Reflections

Perhaps a key word for this entire area of ministry is one that we mentioned in connection with "Simul Justus et Peccator": *balance*. What comes through almost every characteristic is an ability to hold two opposing forces or ideas in tension, make use of the best of both, and resist the temptation to go all the way toward one extreme or the other.

Lutherans want a minister to maintain the Lutheran heritage, but not uncritically. A minister should be open to additional insights of biblical scholarship, and to the possibility that the Confessions can be freshly stated in a way that will speak more clearly to the people of this generation. But a minister must still be committed to the Confessions, not holding them lightly.

Another point of balance is a minister's identity as both a sinner and saint. The ability to live in this dual identity was placed second in importance among *all* characteristics by the professionals, perhaps because they realized its difficulty, but more likely because they recognized the problems attached when one slips too far toward either one identity or the other.

The expectation is that a minister will be theologically sophisticated, but this sophistication is valued less for its own sake than for the way it illuminates life and interprets the "this-world" concerns of people. Rather than a theology of glory, full of speculation about "realms beyond the sky," such a theology deals with the mundane, the painful, and the difficult—the places where God meets human beings.

Lutherans value scholarship, but scholarship which is objective and open to change, that feels free to test the wisdom of the past against recent discovery or critical thought, neither afraid that the past will crumble under this scrutiny, nor hopeful that it will.

Seminary educators

One thing comes clearly through from study of this area of ministry: this is a place where Lutheran seminaries have done their work well. The clear difference between the patterns of preference of the clergy and laity in this area speaks for itself. Professionals (people who have experienced a Lutheran seminary education) generally see this area clearly, identify it with apparent ease, and rate it high. Lutheran ministers know who they are, why they are Lutheran, and what value that has. Seminaries are apparently doing a good job of keeping the Lutheran tradition clear and alive in generations of students.

Lay persons

Compared to their clergy, the laity are usually less sensitive to distinctions between what may be law-oriented rather than gospel-oriented. Hence, they are likely to be less critical of certain evangelistic programs that emphasize specific rules for living backed up by quotations from Scripture. Therefore they may be puzzled when their pastor is unenthusiastic about such programs. Also they are less likely to detect the dangers in the programs that stress human efforts toward salvation. Though seeing the distinctions once they are explained, lay people are less likely to see that the negative features outweigh the positive ones. Does this mean the laity are less Lutheran than the clergy? Not necessarily. The truth of justification by faith is often lived, prayed, and proclaimed by those who do not know the formulated doctrine (at times better than by those who *do* know). But this does mean that the laity's lesser ability to differentiate between a law or gospel emphasis can lead to a loss of Christian substance. This fact, which poses a serious issue, underscores why pastors who can make these distinctions are vital to the church. To illustrate, *A Study of Generations* found that two-fifths of Lutheran lay people are best classified as law-oriented in their concept of the faith. The study also showed that what a pastor accents—law or gospel, precept or promise, correction or possibilities—makes a great difference to Lutherans.

Lay members of call committees

Suppose you are a member of a newly-elected call committee. Your pastor has resigned and your committee faces the responsibility of seeking a new pastor. Perhaps after considerable study and discussion you find that you have settled on a fairly extensive and thorough list of priorities. Even without a book such as this before you, it is probable that you would have developed a list that includes many of the desirable characteristics of ministry outlined here—the qualities of a deep personal faith, an ability to counsel and truly support people in troubled times, an interest and sincere respect for people, a sense of responsibility and appropriate skills for improving the life of the community outside the congregation, and a gift for preaching and leading worship in ways that consistently capture the interest and enthusiastic participation of the congregation and enlighten the hearts and actions of most members.

But even though you have been as thorough as this—or even more thorough—in identifying significant pastoral qualities needed in your parish, another important element may remain to be considered: the pastor's approach to the interpretation of Scripture.

How important is it to you that his or her ministry maintain the Lutheran distinctiveness described earlier? Those interviewing candidates for public office want to know a candidate's political stance. School boards inquire into the educational philosophies of a candidate for superintendent of schools. People know that one's basic philosophy or stance toward one's work influences everything that is said or done. It seems sensible, therefore, that Lutheran call committees should want to know the specific Lutheran stance of a pastoral candidate. The material in this chapter could be used as a call committee prepares to talk with such a candidate.

Each member of a call committee might rank the items included in the characteristics of Lutheran distinctiveness in Appendix C (see p. 217). A composite of those rankings will represent the committee's priorities and suggest those areas most important to pursue when talking with candidates.

Congregational leaders

Besides its practical value for call committees, the material in this chapter may provide a fruitful subject for adult study. Since this is an area where there is a marked difference between the typical perceptions and understandings of the clergy and laity, some lay persons may be interested in broadening their understanding of Lutheran heritage and theology. A study that would go a step beyond mere understanding would also take seriously the question of how well the programs currently operating in the congregation work toward distinctively Lutheran goals.

Pastors

Given the evident finding that seminaries do a good job of imparting an understanding of the distinctiveness of Lutheranism to their graduates, pastors might be pardoned for taking comfort in the thought that here is one topic on which self-examination is not imperative. However, there is occasionally a difference between one's ability to perceive the value of something and one's tendency to practice it. Some pastors may want to know whether there has been some slippage over the years since they finished seminary. A pastor might wish to ask, How far have I moved away from my original intentions in this area? Or (taking a somewhat different approach), Can I take the four characteristics of this area of ministry and develop for myself a statement of the faith on which my ministry is now based? Pursuing such questions will not be merely an academic exercise, for one's statement of faith has ramifications in every area of ministry. One's awareness of being both sinner and saint affects preaching and counseling; one's certainty of justification by faith affects teaching confirmation, administration, and every other aspect of ministry. One's scholarship and application of theology to life comes through even in holding casual conversations with people. Just what is distinctively Lutheran about your present ministry?

Why, after all, is it important to be a Lutheran? Is it a matter mostly of ecclesiastical pride? Is it parallel to if not synonymous with an effort at preservation of an ethnic tradition? Is it in order to keep from drowning in a sea of ecumenism? No, it has more profound roots than that. The content of Lutheran distinctiveness is at the heart of the gospel and the Christian faith. There are awesome ramifications for those who begin to acknowledge their justification by faith that move them worlds away from the self-justified. Lutherans stand as a reminder of the importance of that perception and declaration not only for themselves but for the rest of the Christian world.

Justification by faith, forgiveness, grace—it is the never-ending task of the church to keep holding up the reminder that these are the great realities of life. It is a lesson that is never permanently learned; left to our own devices, we human creatures will inevitably return to self-justification. Pastors therefore must expect to offer the message again and again, sympathetically, patiently, persistently, in faith and in realistic humility.

Component characteristics: Chapter 4

From central to peripheral

In order of Lutheran ranking

Not Wanted:
Dominating Influence

This chapter and Chapter 5 deal with two areas of ministry Lutherans as a whole do not prize. In fact, in order of preference, they are at the bottom of the list, ranking IX and X. They are included here because, along with the three highly valued areas of ministry described in the previous chapters, they represent personal characteristics, or pastoral perspectives, rather than the skills discussed in Part II of this book.

The pastoral perspective of this chapter is illustrated in the following quotations from lay persons:

"I hate to say this because he's such a kind person. But we can't get anything passed or changed in the church council if our pastor disapproves of it. If persons oppose him in a meeting, they're soon off that committee. I think our pastor is actually more political than he realizes."

"I'm puzzled. Why does our congregation have the reputation of being aloof from community life? Is it our pastor? It's true that she seldom pushes any community or cooperative activity, and we're seldom informed of activities that take place outside of our congregation."

"I know our congregation should be Lutheran in its teachings and preaching and music. But does that mean excluding everything that is a little different? I'm really less worried about people being 'led astray' by an occasional speaker or visiting group than I am about our members going to sleep. If nothing new is ever introduced, people quit thinking about their faith."

Comments such as these reveal a kind of pastoral leadership familiar, through experience or by hearsay, to many Lutherans. Some lay persons like it, some get used to it, and some find it discouraging. The central issue is one of pastoral purpose. Is the purpose of ministry to bring people to believe and behave in specific, preconceived ways, or is it to help people grow toward becoming valued, responsible partners in Christian ministry?

The importance of a leader's perception of purpose is now becoming evident in the serving professions. Studies have shown that what professionals hope to accomplish with people—their purpose—has a shaping effect on how they approach them. The way teachers treat students, for instance, is shaped by what they believe is the purpose of schools, of classes, and appearing before students. It has been found that those teachers judged to be most effective try to *free* students. Their concerns are usually to help them become excited about learning, grow in their knowledge of a subject, and learn how to learn. On the other hand, teachers judged to be least effective try to *control* students. The concerns of such teachers are to make students behave, keep them from getting out of hand, and get them to learn anything at all. The accent with the first group is on providing the conditions and stimuli for growth. With the second, the accent is on getting students to engage in—or not engage in—certain quite specific behaviors.

Ministry presents similar contrasts in style. At one pole is the pastor who, conscientiously living out a particular view of pastoral ministry, brings a tightly disciplined, controlled, focused, and carefully delimited approach to ministry. At the other is the pastor who—equally conscientiously living out another view of pastoral ministry—shares ministry with the laity, is open to variety in interpretation of Scripture, and is cooperative with other churches and institutions in carrying out a shared vision of ministry.

These opposite purposes, together with various positions in between, profoundly affect how lay persons and pastors approach their ministries. Lutherans in our study were sufficiently aware of some pastors' desire to exert a dominant influence to have caused six sets of items to form the undesirable area of ministry described in this chapter. These six characteristics describe pastors whose style of ministry is to use the weight of authority and role to carry out the agenda they alone have established for the congregation.

Some pastors are probably unaware of the extent to which they engage in this type of leadership. Its effect is like the blue tint in a glass dome, which outsiders see easily, but insiders cannot detect. Other pastors may be entirely and comfortably aware of exerting a personal, firm, and direct influence at all levels of congregational behavior. They are usually confident of their abilities, do many things well, and are very willing to take charge. Though currently-popular leadership styles flow counter to this, most Christians know at least one strong pastor who has made a success of a dominant style of ministry. "Homer Johnson" was one. It was a proud moment when Homer's son "Dan" decided to follow in his father's footsteps and study for the pastoral ministry. Homer announced proudly to his congregation and friends that he expected Dan to "carry on the family tradition" and "pick up where I leave off."

Dan privately, and perhaps a bit cynically, speculated on his father's pleasure. "I think Dad's happy because he has a small dynasty founded, and he can see it being perpetuated for generations to come. I wouldn't be surprised if he is secretly entertaining the notion that I should take over First Lutheran when he retires. Frankly, I don't think I'd want to work in the kind of atmosphere he's developed. It's not my style at all."

The disparity between Dan's pastoral style and his father's, though evident to almost any casual observer, did not really come clear to Homer until he visited Dan in his first pastorate. After observing his son's leadership of an evening Bible study class, Homer could scarcely wait for the last participant to leave before taking his son to task.

"What kind of teaching do you call it when you ask a few questions and then sit and listen while everyone else talks? You're the one who knows, the one who has the education. What was all that seminary training for if not to prepare you to guide people to a proper understanding of Scripture? You're not providing the kind of instruction and leadership they have a right to expect from their pastor.

"You made no effort at all to set that young woman straight with her ideas about 'meaningful social involvement' as a way of preaching the gospel—or to correct some of the other strange ideas people were putting forth.

"And another thing, I see from reading your church bulletin that your church council has decided to open the church to an Alcoholics Anonymous group to meet here. Did they decide that without your knowledge? A pastor who isn't truly in charge in his congregation is simply shirking his responsibility."

One's attitude toward this area of ministry depends on whether one thinks it legitimate and right that there be clearly delineated roles in the church for leaders and followers, and that the leaders, insofar as possible, be clergy. There is certainly an efficiency and clarity about such a division of roles that makes it attractive to a good many people.

This chapter attempts to describe a dominating style of ministry that Lutherans view somewhat negatively. Those involved in ministry should be aware of this style of ministry and the attitude of most Lutherans to it, or else risk unknowingly undermining the effectiveness of their ministry.

It must be made clear that the view of most Lutherans that we present here does not deny that there is such a thing as authority in the church. The authority of Scripture, of the gospel, is seen as being present in the message that the whole church and its ordained clergy carry to the world. The Word gives pastors authority to proclaim both law and gospel, and in so proclaiming they judge and heal both themselves and others. But a "Dominating Influence" pastor goes beyond conveying this authority to using the influence that attaches to it to get particular things done in a particular way.

The six characteristics of this area of ministry divide themselves into two groups of three. One group is composed of characteristics that are principally psychological in nature, and a second set is composed of those that are principally theological. Their rank orders (all but one are in the upper 60s among 77) convey the generally—though by no means universally—low esteem in which they are held among Lutherans. Lutherans disagree considerably, but on the average view the psychological characteristics as "somewhat hindering" to an effective ministry, and the theological characteristics as "somewhat helpful."

Psychological characteristics: The "shepherd-in-charge"

Three closely intercorrelated characteristics—"Law unto Self" (67), "Spiritual Superiority" (68), and "Unbusinesslike Leadership" (69) describe a distinct style of leadership—a strong, dominating, controlling, take-charge approach. This style is premised on the belief that a pastor has more knowledge and ability than others in a congregation. It assumes that a pastor is uniquely equipped to preach, teach, interpret Scripture, and make decisions. Personally assured of this, such pastors tend to lead more by intuition than by careful planning and logically worked-out decisions. Feeling called to shepherd a flock, they work hard at it, completely caught up in the demands of the task.

Because of taking personal charge of so much, the "Shepherd-in-Charge" pastor is often overworked. As a result he or she frequently evades or postpones decisions, or makes hurried or ill-considered ones. Such a pastor becomes the taker of final responsibility—by whom everything must be approved. Nevertheless, the data show that some of the laity prefer a congregation where the pastor is clearly the leader and the members are amiable followers.

Law unto Self (67). "Law-unto-Self" pastors give the impression not so much of serving a congregation as of owning and operating it. This characteristic describes a lordly style in which a pastor assumes total responsibility for all congregational activities and their outcomes. The pastor functions in the manner of the missionary stereotype of former years, who supervised the local personnel at a mission station like a benevolent father, around whom all activities revolved, and who made all decisions, large and small.

Such pastors dominate group discussions, want to be viewed as the ultimate decision makers, and create the general impression that if any job is to be done right, they must do it. They prefer to rely on personal charisma and intuition to make things work, rather than to take the time for careful planning or for consulting members of the congregation for their opinions. This independent, take-charge approach prevents them from being able to delegate responsibility. The idea of shared leadership or shared ministry is entirely foreign to this characteristic.

Spiritual Superiority (68). The assumption that pastors know best carries with it the overtone of spiritual superiority. Though pastors who demonstrate this characteristic may give lip service to the concept of the priesthood of all believers, they are likely to treat nonordained Christians as second-class citizens in the kingdom, particularly when theological issues are under discussion. They would be unlikely to ask a lay person to preach a sermon or lead an adult Bible class. The dynamic underlying this attitude is not so much a matter of feeling threatened by the capabilities of lay people—a characteristic treated in Chapter 5—but rather believing that a pastor's training and ordination have conferred special insight in spiritual matters. This air of being a spiritual superior in the parish is expressed in the now often uncomplimentary term *Herr Pastor.*

Unbusinesslike Leadership (69). The third psychological characteristic of the "Shepherd-in-Charge" is highly correlated with the previous two. In other words, Lutherans perceive that when you find one or two of those characteristics in a pastor, you will also often find this third one. This characteristic reflects a certain regal disregard for the details of leadership or for the needs or desires of the people with whom one works. Such a pastor frequently makes plans without paying sufficient attention to their concomitant financial implications, tends to ignore deadlines (or shift them to suit personal convenience), and cannot be depended on to arrive on time, to complete promised work on time, or to keep any but the sketchiest records. Occasionally, when the congregation wants and seeks direction he or she fails to provide it.

There is some evidence that the behaviors summarized in this third characteristic are related to a sense of inferiority or threat. The strategem of belittling a person in front of others is included with the characteristic, as is the habit of measuring one's success by the size of the church budget, buildings, or membership. Such pastors betray defensiveness and the need to be bolstered by external evidences of success.

If one puts together all three of these characteristics the picture emerges of an "I'm-in-charge" person who pilots the members of a congregation without their advice or mature involvement. Such pastors waste the potential ministries lay people could offer, and in time often lose some of the most competent and creative people in their congregations. Such people, if they have the option, will often gravitate to churches where they are encouraged to exercise their gifts of competence and creativity. Among those who remain, the "Shepherd-in-Charge" leadership style produces a mind-set in the congregation that successors find difficult to reverse. One minister confessed ruefully, "I inherited a rubber-stamp church council that wants me to tell them what to do. I find myself having to repeat constantly, 'This is not my congregation, but yours. I'm not here to act as if I'm the president of a corporation; I've joined you to carry out a partnership in concern.' Although they seem to hear what I say, I frankly think they're more concerned about the success of their bowling team."

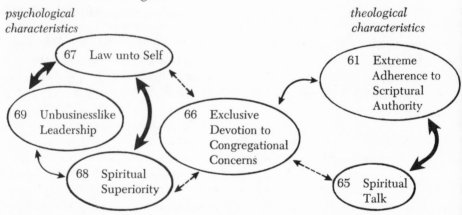

In the diagram above, heaviness of line indicates the strength with which Lutherans view the characteristics as being connected.

Theological characteristics: "Minister to the faithful"

What has been described so far in this chapter is not the exclusive preserve of pastors. There are school superintendents, M.D.s, public officials, and other people-servers who also fill their leadership roles in this style. For many pastors, however, the style of leadership described in this area of ministry includes a theological as well as psychological stance. This, too, is shaped by a pastor's perception of purpose, role, or mission—by what he or she believes ministry should be and do. As the characteristics describe them, such pastors believe it is their role to be God's exclusive "Minister to the Faithful."

These characteristics also relate to a pastor's view of the Christian faith. One Lutheran seminary dean, describing this area of concern, suggested that it has to do with whether one sees one's Christian identity as a matter of *stasis* or *process*—something static, given, and once and for all the same; or something interactive, developmental, and changing.

However they are summarized, these three characteristics—presenting a combination of extreme orthodoxy, verbal piety, and disciplined attention only to those matters readily identifiable as spiritual or congregational—represent a face of ministry about which Lutherans disagree. About equal numbers of Lutherans oppose and favor them. These theological characteristics, which intercorrelate tightly (see the diagram on p. 82), find their primary linkage with the psychological characteristics through one characteristic, "Exclusive Devotion to Congregational Concerns" (66).

Exclusive Devotion to Congregational Concerns (6). This characteristic involves avoidance of involvement in civic, social, economic, and political activities. Pastors who fit this description devote themselves more fully to those matters to which they believe they are distinctively called—the more strictly religious and spiritual concerns associated with the salvation of persons. This exclusive devotion to congregational concerns includes (1) insisting that clergy should stick to religion and not concern themselves with social, economic, and political questions, (2) remaining uninvolved in civic activities, and (3) showing little concern for persons outside the congregation.

Spiritual Talk (65). This is a conversational style that includes a specific vocabulary, often called "God-talk" (or at least one form of it). Such pietistic talk is highly subjective, and concentrates on personal experience and one's relationship with God. Those who favor it will usually view it as a mark of holiness to use a specialized vocabulary that emphasizes one's closeness to God. They may talk of having been "born again," of being aware of what the Lord has recently done, and of having received certain gifts from God such as the ability to speak in tongues. Those who do not appreciate such talk usually find it stilted, pompous, or too threateningly intimate. There is a great deal of difference of opinion about the contribution this does or does not make to effective ministry. The range of ratings is very wide.

Extreme Adherence to Scriptural Authority (61). The very heart of this stance is a belief in verbal inspiration of the Scriptures: that God directly supplied not only the inspiration and motivation to write, but

84 FIVE PASTORAL PERSPECTIVES

the words used in writing the Bible, including those referring to scientific matters. Pastors who show this characteristic will give answers based on specific Bible verses not only to ethical but to many other kinds of questions. They will insist, for instance, that Adam, Eve, and Jonah were historical figures. They believe that Satan is a personal devil present and active today.

The belief that this is the proper understanding and use of Scripture is widely held by lay people, but is generally opposed as being too rigid or legalistic by the majority of professional Lutheran church leaders. Concerning the item, "Teaches that God directly supplied the words used in writing the Bible, including those referring to historical, geographical, and scientific matters," 55% of the laity believed that such a belief either contributes very much or is absolutely essential to an effective ministry. Only 21% of the professional ministers thought so. In fact, 55% of the clergy believed that such a position hinders ministry either "somewhat" or "very much."

This characteristic also represents an orthodoxy that views Luther and the Confessions through the eyes of the "age of orthodoxy" (16th and 17th centuries). It views that theology as being the final and complete Lutheran position. Such pastors will take the kind of stands on doctrinal issues that accept no other positions as tenable.

There is disagreement on this matter between the laity and clergy, as on the matter of the use of Scripture just mentioned. Concerning the item, "Tends to give authoritative answers based on specific Bible verses," 50% of the laity believed that such an approach either "contributes very much" or is "absolutely essential," whereas only 15% of the clergy thought so. On the contrary, 37% of clergy viewed such a tendency as hindering ministry either "somewhat" or "very much."

Significantly, this group of items concerning the Bible correlates almost as strongly with the characteristics of the first area of ministry (Chapter 1). Almost as many Lutherans associate this theological stance with deep spiritual foundations as with the characteristics of this chapter. It may be fair to say that though a literal interpretation of Scripture often characterizes pastors whose approach is dominating and controlling, it often does not. For some pastors it is an underlying stance within a distinctly gospel-oriented approach.

In this chapter, the set of items including verbal inspiration tips in the direction of a legalistic stance. This is indicated not only by the characteristics with which this one correlates but also by the items which joined the set. For instance, concerning the item, "Preaches sermons which accent people's need to work at gaining faith in God," 66% of the laity (vs. 29% of the clergy) said it is highly important that sermons stress people's need to work at gaining faith. Forty-eight percent of the seminary professors saw such an emphasis as harmful. This evidence suggests that the doctrine of justification by grace through faith in Jesus Christ is de-emphasized by the approach to Scripture some pastors employ.

Emphases and Contrasts

Lutherans range across the spectrum in their opinions of this type of leadership. Some believe it is "absolutely essential" that a pastor assume an authoritative position in all matters, because they believe that the Bible presents the truth in all matters. Others believe that such a position is detrimental, that it "very much hinders" the ministry God intends.

At opposite poles

In general, lay persons with less education, who are older and living in either rural or inner city locations, see this type of ministry as contributing something to ministry. Members of the clergy, especially those who are younger and living in urban and suburban ministry settings, rate it lowest. These two groups represent the extremes of opinion on the strongly dominant style of pastoral leadership.

Education

People usually disagree about all six characteristics in direct proportion to the amount of education they have had. Those with less education place much-greater-than-average value on all six, with a heightened emphasis on the first four listed on the chart.

Laity vs. clergy

Lay persons differ from clergy on whether this set of characteristics is a slight asset or a liability in the practice of ministry. The laity view it somewhat more kindly than the clergy. The four groups of clergy—parish pastors, seminary professors, denominational officials, and seminary seniors—are in essential agreement (on the average) that this style of leadership is a hindrance to ministry.

Church body

Members of the three Lutheran church bodies do not differ in how they view the three psychological criteria. They all see them as hindering ministry. They differ markedly, however, on the theological criteria. Members of the Lutheran Church–Missouri Synod accord a higher value to these characteristics than do members of the American Lutheran Church and the Lutheran Church in America. Much of the stance described in

Table 3. Groups that show greater appreciation for the characteristics of Area IX, "Not Wanted: Dominating Influence."

	laity (vs. professionals)	less educated	older	LCMS (vs. ALC & LCA)	rural & inner city	men
67 Law unto Self * (hinder somewhat)	HHH	HHHH	HH (plus very youngest)		HH	
68 Spiritual Superiority (hinder somewhat)	HHH	HHHH			HH (not rural)	
69 Unbusinesslike Leadership (hinder somewhat)	HH	HHHH				H
66 Exclusive Devotion to Congregational Concerns (contribute/hinder little or nothing)	HHH	HHHH	HHH	HH	H (not inner city)	H
65 Spiritual Talk (contribute somewhat)	HHH	HHH		HH		
61 Extreme Adherence to Scriptural Authority (contribute somewhat)	HHH	HHH	HHH	HH	HH	

* average Lutheran evaluation of this characteristic's contribution to effective ministry

As compared with Lutherans' average (or with the groups specifically listed):
HHHH = very much higher
HHH = much higher
HH = higher
H = slightly higher

"Extreme Adherence to Scriptural Authority" (61) and "Exclusive Devotion to Congregational Concerns" (66) generally fits the position of Francis Pieper as stated in his three-volume work, *Christian Dogmatics*.[1] Dr. Pieper was president of the LCMS from 1899 to 1911, and president of Concordia Seminary in St. Louis from 1887 to 1933. It is not surprising to find that the teachings of a man whose dogmatics shaped the theological education of a church body for 45 years are given high priority by members of that church body.

Ministry setting

Firm leadership on the part of pastors is appreciated more in rural and inner city parishes than in any other situations. Rural parishioners are more tolerant of pastors who are quite highly independent and slightly more tolerant of those who devote themselves rather exclusively to congregational concerns. Pastors who are often dominating, spiritually superior, dogmatic, and independent can expect to encounter the greatest trouble in specialized ministry settings such as those overseas, on college campuses, in the military chaplaincy, or in service institutions such as hospitals, prisons, retirement homes, welfare agencies, and the like. All of these settings place a pastor on a highly structured team where independent action will be more disturbing than when performed by a lone pastor or member of a small ministry team in the usual sort of congregational setting. Nevertheless, such a pastor can expect to run into just about as much trouble in urban and suburban settings. Pastors who view themselves as being somewhat spiritually superior, with little confidence in the competence of lay people, will find some inner city parishes more tolerant of this attitude.

Older members

The very oldest (over 65) and the very youngest (under 18) persons are usually the most tolerant of pastoral leadership that assumes responsibility for all activities and their outcomes. Since the very youngest and the very oldest will, for different reasons, often consider themselves somewhat less competent than others, this is not altogether surprising. Nor is it surprising that older Lutherans should be more appreciative or tolerant of "Exclusive Devotion to Congregational Concerns" (66). With rare exceptions, that was the common practice among Lutheran pastors until the last few decades. Older Lutherans' preference for "Extreme Adherence to Scriptural Authority" (61) is consistent with the pattern we note in other chapters among older Lutherans; they appreciate a conservative

---

1. Francis Pieper, *Christian Dogmatics* (St. Louis: Concordia, 1953), vols. 1-3.

doctrinal stance, expression of a strong personal faith, concern with the spiritual, and formality in worship.

Men

Men are slightly more tolerant of "Unbusinesslike Leadership" (69) and "Exclusive Devotion to Congregational Concerns" (66). That they should be more tolerant of the former may be related to the fact that fewer men than women are involved in congregational life. Those who have been involved in church projects are most aware of the problem that can be presented by those who try to run things principally according to their own intuitions, guesses, and hunches.

Reflections

Though Lutherans see the six characteristics in this area of ministry as being related to one another, there is nothing that arises from our study that would tell us whether Lutherans believe all six are usually embodied in the same person, or whether the characteristics appear in a group simply because people feel similarly about them wherever they appear.

Our own experience suggests that these characteristics *do* come in groups more often than singly. We can remember persons who amply illustrated three, four, or more of these behaviors or attitudes. It is highly probable that the theological characteristics, where they are present, reinforce the psychological characteristics, and that the psychological often reinforce the theological.

This area may reflect a gradually vanishing tendency in ministry. Just as "Dominating Influence" ministers are less prevalent now than fifty years ago, so their number may continue to diminish even further in the future. Since these characteristics are most acceptable to the less well-educated and most strongly rejected by the highly educated, and since the general level of education among Lutherans is rising rapidly, the acceptance level for a strongly dominant ministry will probably drop steadily in the future. But it is alive and well in some quarters today, and well worth reflecting on.

Pastors

Some readers will discover in the theological characteristics of this area of ministry a description of their own thoughtfully-chosen approach to the spiritual guidance of their congregation. As we reported earlier, the theological characteristic "Extreme Adherence to Scriptural Authority" (61) correlates almost as closely with the spiritual foundations of Chapter 1 as it does with this set of characteristics. It is entirely possible for people who possess the theological characteristics to minister completely free of the related psychological tendencies. However, given the close relationship of these two, pastors may find it worthwhile to take a good look at whether they are, indeed, engaging in some of the "Dominating Influence" leadership styles as well. Because they are so closely related, an unintentional drift into the psychological leadership styles might be relatively easy to make.

We do not believe that most pastors deliberately set out to offer the "Shepherd-in-Charge" style of ministry described in this chapter. The clergy in general agree that the characteristics of this area of ministry are a hindrance. Why, then, do they exist? We think ministers often develop this style unawares—mostly inadvertently. This may be in part a result of unrecognized psychological tendencies, in part the particular circumstances of the pastorate, and in part a response to encouragement from congregations.

There is much in pastoral experience that encourages the impression that pastors are knowledgeable, worthy, wise, and should at all times and in all places be deferentially regarded. It is seductively easy to confuse the respect people accord the office, and the Word taught and preached, with their response to one's own personal qualities and merits. Over the years, without ever consciously intending it, a pastor can become a "Law-unto-Self" leader, a "Shepherd-in-Charge," dominating discussions and behaving as the only one who knows how things should be done—a kind of ultimate authority in all things.

Many lay persons, perhaps equally unintentionally, encourage pastors in this estimate of themselves. There may, in truth, be some intellectual laziness mixed in with this encouragement. If a pastor tells people what ought to be done, they don't have to struggle to find the answer themselves, or take responsibility for the consequences. There may also be an exaggerated humility at work among some lay persons, who assume that a pastor, from sources not altogether clear to them, knows more than they do or always has better judgment.

Where a pastor and congregation combine in this kind of unintentional but mutually-reinforcing activity, the penalty for the church is the loss of many functioning, creative talents. Lay persons learn to bring inside the church only their well-meaning, loving, obedient hearts, and to park other gifts of the Spirit and their critical faculties at the church door. Attractive as that prospect may sometimes seem, especially to an overworked and beleaguered pastor, its effect is that members come into the church as less-than-whole persons who provide less than the edification they could.

How might you discover whether or to what extent you are exerting a too dominant influence? One informal way is to be sensitive to your own feelings of restlessness and impatience when you are away from your congregation. Do you have the sense that people are not paying attention to you? Are you unaccountably unable to turn the direction of a meeting or attract attention simply by clearing your throat at a significant point in the discussion? Are even your best-presented proposals surprisingly defeated, or, worse yet, ignored? If you experience a sharp drop in the deference scale whenever you are out of your congregational setting, that may present a clue not so much to the nature of the world outside as to the tenor of what is happening on your own turf.

A further exercise might be for you to complete a checklist—based on the items of Appendix C related to Area IX (p. 248) as they apply to you. A still more searching examination of the extent to which this style is present might be to undertake, with your church council, an assessment not only of your own style, but also of the style of the congregation. Since much of this area relates to leadership, it would make sense to enter on such a joint study using both the checklist of Area V, administration, (treated in Chapter 7) and the items related to this area. In considering these items one by one, what picture develops of the way the council works? The way you work? What strengths and weaknesses are discovered? Are there ways in which you and the council can help produce change for the better?

The task of keeping clear and separate their office and person is a never-ending one for pastors. It is a fine line to walk, requiring the help of others to avoid slipping too far either in the direction of overvaluation or undervaluation of their knowledge, judgment, and authority. A free and open discussion between a council and pastor concerning what is happening in the whole decision-making and leadership area of church function can open the way for members to point out unconscious and unintended slips into authoritarianism.

Lay members

Some lay persons reading this chapter will recognize their pastor in many or all of the characteristics. These lay persons may find that some elements of their pastor's style are reflected in or encouraged by their own behavior. Two kinds of congregations seem to produce "Dominating Influence" pastors. One kind believes that leaders should lead: make decisions, give directions, take responsibility, chart new ways, and give answers. A congregation firmly convinced that this is the way things ought to be can usually produce a matching dominance in its pastor with remarkable efficiency. "Just tell us, Pastor, and we'll get right at it." Such congregations need not be at all lackadaisical. They may be involved in continuous whirlwinds of activity. But they persistently seek direction and approval from their pastor, and work (knowingly or unknowingly) in large part to please him or her.

A second kind of congregation that often produces an authoritative style of leadership is one with a history of broken promises, responsibilities shirked, programs halfheartedly carried out, and opportunities for service refused. Pastors in such congregations may be driven to believe that the only way to get anything done properly is either to do it themselves or to issue precise directions and practice close supervision. Lay persons who see their pastor as having a "Dominating Influence" should be prepared to find some of these characteristics in themselves, and to deal with correctives not only of their pastor's behavior, but of their own.

In a group study it might be helpful to have lay persons work through the Appendix C checklist for this area of ministry twice. The first time they could read each item as preceded by the statement, "I believe it is a good thing if a pastor . . ." and check the appropriate column. The second time they could mark each item according to how true it is of them personally. Discrepancies or similarities might be worth noting and acting on.

District/synodical presidents, call committees, and churchwide leaders

As we have already implied, the "Dominating Influence" style is produced as readily by external forces as by deliberate choice. Congregations are not the only forces influencing their pastors. Denominational structures and processes also have their effect, both as direct forces and also by means of the examples they set. Do pastors feel that decisions from the denomination are being handed down to them, or do they feel involved in the process, and free, at least, to provide input or minority opinions that will be heard? Whatever style they perceive as operating in denominational polity is likely to be reproduced to some degree in the way they deal with their congregations—as authoritarians, or as participants in a democracy.

The call process, a memorable occurrence in the lives of most pastors, can be structured in an authoritarian, hierarchical way, creating in pastors a feeling that they are dependent on the approval of others, making them feel judged and less like pastors than pawns. Or it can be structured to make them feel consulted, regarded, heard, and valued by those who are in positions of authority. The tones of respect, or of authority imposed, that surround this process are likely to have echoes in the kind of leadership pastors offer to congregations they serve.

Seminary educators

The evidence presented in this chapter may suggest course work to be offered in seminary with particular emphasis on leadership. It seems likely to us that some of the undesirable behaviors of "Law unto Self" (67) and "Unbusinesslike Leadership" (69) originally spring as much from ignorance of more appropriate or more democratic methods as from strong tendencies of personality or conviction. Young pastors may go into their first parishes and begin firing decisions from the hip, making plans that are inadequately reasoned out, and relying principally on intuition in planning because they have not been exposed to more sound and sophisticated ways of doing things. If seminary students routinely emerged from seminary with as much built-in scorn for a sloppily-planned church enterprise as they now have for a sloppy theological argument, some pleasant changes might be in store. One part of teaching about leadership styles might well include offering seminarians advance warning of the power of congregations and denominational structures to bend and shape even the most determinedly-open and egalitarian style.

The issue this chapter raises for seminaries is the possibility of additional integration—of recognizing that pastors' personal formation and theological formation have close links with the specifics of how those identities and positions will be spelled out in action as pastors relate to people in decision-making and in the whole area of congregational program-emphasis and leadership.

Component characteristics: Chapter 5

From central to peripheral
74 Self-Isolating Behavior
75 Insecure Authoritarianism
73 Instability
71 Self-Centered Isolation
77 Impersonalness Without Trust
70 Secular Life-Style
72 Evidences of Insecurity
76 Undisciplined Living

In order of Lutheran ranking
70 Secular Life-Style
71 Self-Centered Isolation
72 Evidences of Insecurity
73 Instability
74 Self-Isolating Behavior
75 Insecure Authoritarianism
76 Undisciplined Living
77 Impersonalness Without Trust

Not Wanted:
Ministry-Defeating
Behaviors

"I've given up suggesting improvements for our congregation. No matter what we mention, our pastor immediately starts defending. She can't seem to hear that we would like to think out loud about whether the youth program, or the stewardship emphasis, or the worship service might be changed or improved. She apparently thinks that any mention of weakness in our church program is a criticism of her."

"It seems as though our pastor never stops running. Even when he visited me in the hospital last fall, he kept looking at his watch all the time. And he's always leaving meetings early, or coming to them late. It seems as though he's trying to impress us with how much he does and how important it all is."

"I know that on camping trips things get pretty relaxed around the campfire. Just the same, I don't like the tone of some of the jokes the pastor told on the high school camping trip. I think you can be funny and 'real' without telling shady stories."

The total effect of any pastor's ministry is largely dependent on the pattern of strengths and weaknesses in that ministry. Trouble that arises in the practice of ministry is, in many situations, the result of the *absence* of one of the characteristics—or weakness in a whole area of ministry— described in this book. But with this chapter the reverse is true. With these characteristics, trouble arises because of their *presence*. Lutherans essentially have a single unanimous opinion of these characteristics: *they hinder*. Any ministry that exhibits them is to some extent crippled. The combined presence of several of the characteristics will damage or even negate the positive influence of any ministry a pastor can offer. People differ on how negative they think these characteristics are, but there is agreement that all of them are an impediment to effective ministry.

Though the behaviors described seem quite different from one another, they appear to arise from a common source—a pastor's sense of being inadequate. He or she feels like one lost in the jungle, with a thousand unseen threats lurking in the shadows, or like one adrift in the ocean, facing the simple, stark possibility of death by drowning or exposure. The major preoccupation of such pastors is their own survival. Ministry may occur, but it is hampered by their ever-present need to survive—to produce evidence that they are worthy, capable, and of value.

The effort to survive appears in several guises. It may come in the activity of chipping away at the self-esteem of others, cutting them down in size in order not to feel so small beside them. Some pastors attempt to survive by presenting the image of being in total control, manipulating the lives of other persons, or taking up a pose of certainty and security in all situations. Still others try to avoid disaster by attacking first, and attacking so aggressively that others are repelled and keep their distance. One, two, or all three of these guises may exist in the same person.

All of the eight ministry-hindering characteristics were ranked in the 70s, with 70 being least and 77 most negative. The first four, numbered 70 through 73, are judged on the average by Lutherans to "hinder quite a bit." Those numbered 74 through 77 are judged to "hinder very much."

The eight represent three distinct routes taken when a pastor is preoccupied with self and survival. The first is *isolation* from contact with others. The second is an approach to others that has to do with control, but manifests itself in *vacillation* between dominating others and being subservient to them. The third route is involvement in *deviant behavior* styles that alienate people and diminish the effectiveness of ministry because they undermine people's respect for their pastor. Both a mild and a severe form of each method of survival appear among the eight characteristics.

To those pastors who will be described on some of the pages to follow, who will offer ministry? Because pastors can be the loneliest people in congregations, Martin Luther stressed their own need for pastoral care. "No man is to be alone against Satan. God instituted the church and the ministry of the Word in order that we might join hands and help one another. If the prayer of one does not help, then that of the other will." [1]

Though the ministry of the laity is addressed throughout this book, both implicitly and explicitly, this is the area where the laity may be called on to offer their most taxing, delicate, yet most needed ministry. This chapter addresses a need for "mutual conversation and consolation of brethren" that is vital to the health of both clergy and laity. Beneath the self-defeating behaviors commonly seen in pastors, what such pastors are really crying out for is acceptance, encouragement, support, and correction. What is described here is reversible if that kind of help is offered in a way the sufferer can trust and accept. Change is possible, perhaps through the ministry of a pastoral support team, perhaps through more radical means: change of assignment, counseling therapy, or hospitalization. Whatever the means eventually taken toward health, the laity may well be called on to take the first steps and to assume leadership in initiating ministry on behalf of the one who bears the title *minister*.

Isolation

Three strongly correlated characteristics describe a minister who treats the pastor's study as if it were a private island or the castle keep, emerging to deal with the populace only when necessary. These characteristics describe the plight and behavior of pastors who survive by keeping personal contacts to a minimum because they need to hide.

Self-Centered Isolation (71). Of the forms of voluntary withdrawal from human contact, this is the least objectionable to Lutherans (which, of course, scarcely constitutes a ringing endorsement of it). In the struggle for psychological survival, persons who exhibit this characteristic become preoccupied with themselves and with performance. They worry excessively about what others think of them, take criticism of parish programs personally, and are jealous of other staff members' popularity with parishioners. Because of this strong focus on themselves, meaningful relationships with others get crowded into the background. Such people seldom spontaneously convey news about their own family to others. Tasks are so much more important to them than relationships that they keep others at arm's length by giving the impression of being terribly busy and terribly hurried. By these and other similar strategies, self-centered isolationists keep themselves protected from meaningful human contacts. If their needs for isolation go no further than this, such pastors will probably never hurt anyone in a congregation very deeply, but neither are they likely to be able to offer deep and personal help.

---

1. John W. Doberstein, ed., *Minister's Prayer Book* (Philadelphia: Muhlenberg Press, n.d.), p. 322.

Self-Isolating Behavior (74). This characteristic describes a deeper form of isolation, because it is no longer primarily passive. Instead, it consists of behaviors that push people away, that warn them to keep their distance. The heart of this characteristic centers in an inability to forgive oneself and, along with it, a tendency not to be accepting or forgiving of others. Such persons are abrupt when talking with people, and impatient with those who resist their proposals or ways of doing things. Self-isolating behaviors like these prevent people from coming to know what such pastors are really like and what they are experiencing. Whether the behaviors are unconsciously or deliberately motivated, they isolate pastors from others, and sometimes cause people to feel disregarded or ignored.

Impersonalness Without Trust (77). This characteristic bears the dubious distinction of being tied for last place (with 76—"Undisciplined Living") among the characteristics. Among clergy it comes in dead last by a considerable margin—the least-to-be-desired of all characteristics of Lutheran ministry. Persons suffering from the presence of this characteristic are out of touch. They show an inability to commit their lives and work to God's care. They are cold, impersonal, and insensitive to the feelings of those nearest to them. They show additional insensitivity in a careless sharing of confidences, discussing publicly what has been said privately. Conscious of this indiscretion, people are afraid to come to such pastors for counseling, even during times of crisis.

These three isolating characteristics cut a pastor off from the essential ingredients of health: supportive, in-depth, caring relationships with other people and with God. Those who surround such hurting clergy must break through the invisible walls before they can provide the loving, caring, supportive affirmation so desperately needed.

Vacillation: Struggle for control

Persons showing the second set of behaviors attempt to put up a front of security. The facade rests on a foundation of deeply-felt insecurity—basically the same underlying dynamic that causes others to retreat into isolation. A person who struggles for control deals with insecurity not by withdrawing from human contact, but by heeding Hamlet's advice to "assume the virtue, since you have it not." What results is someone who is either pompous, dominating, and authoritarian, or is submissive, eager for approval, and compliant—or one who vacillates unpredictably between the two.

Evidences of Insecurity (72). This characteristic combines a claim of authority with a need for constant reassurance. Such a person sets up meetings so as to be in control, questions the motives of anyone who opposes, and uses the pulpit to express personal irritations. Though seeming strongly in control of others, this person also seeks public acclaim and reassurance, suffers deep humiliation over mistakes made in public, and sometimes compromises personal principles in the interest of winning approval. Such a person, alternately dominating and plaintive, in effect simultaneously declares and asks, "Dammit, I'm right! . . . Isn't that right?"

Insecure Authoritarianism (75). Those who exhibit Characteristic 75 dominate. They survive their insecurity by being tough, playing "king-of-the-hill," and winning. They act as bosses (second only to God), assuming that the only right way to do things is their way, and that their roles as ministers qualify them to make unquestioned pronouncements on all subjects. Pulpits are their private preserve, from which they may attack persons or ideas with impunity. They are more impressed by who says things than by what is said; they are not impressed by the opinions of women, but the opinion of a single influential person can cause them to make a complete about-face. The most evident sign of underlying weakness in this characteristic appears when things are going badly; such pastors' first approach to real problems is to look for another call or appointment.

Deviant behavior

Persons who take the route of deviant behavior in their effort to survive are somewhat different from those who are inclined more toward either of the other two routes. Their insecurity shows more in their style of living than in the quality of their relationships. In all three of the characteristics described here one can hear pastors simultaneously asking a question and making a declaration. The question is, Am I really in the right profession, serving the right role in life? The declaration is, I'm afraid I'm *not* in the right profession; I wish someone would discover it and either pull me in closer or push me out altogether.

All three of the characteristics in this group hinder ministry, not only because of the attitudes that underlie them, but because the behaviors are shocking and offensive to many people and "turn them off" to the possibility of ministry from pastors who engage in them.

Secular Life-Style (70). This characteristic was judged by Lutherans to be least negative of the eight negative characteristics. With the exception of one item, it is made up of behaviors that are not so much harmful to others as they are offensive because they violate the norms of behavior expected of clergy. Telling dirty jokes, displaying mannerisms associated with members of the opposite sex, obviously enjoying visiting cocktail lounges, dressing in an overly casual way, not getting along well with one's spouse—all these, it could be argued, are a pastor's own business.

The sole exception—becoming known as a fast and careless driver—is not. Whether the behaviors truly are a pastor's own business or not, the attitude they present is a truculent declaration: I'm important enough to do as I please, whether it pleases you or not. As far as Lutherans are concerned, both this attitude and its related behaviors hinder ministry.

Instability (73). This characteristic is exemplified in a person whose actions are not deviant, but who raises in conversation the questions which are assumed to underlie all three of these characteristics: Should I be in the ministry? Perhaps I shouldn't. The pay isn't adequate. I deserve better. Maybe then it is all right for me to live beyond my means. This attitude is one that also appears in the conversations and behavior of people in other areas of work who frequently move from one job to another. They are restless and dissatisfied with their lot in life—unstable.

Undisciplined Living (76). This characteristic, tied for last place in the 77, and rated as most negative of all by Lutheran lay people, presents behavior that violates social norms not only for clergy, but for society in general. Occasional drunkenness, gambling, and illicit sexual relationships, even when tolerated in the general population, are scarcely approved. They shock and offend.

Such behavior may spring from prideful, sinful insistence on "doing my own thing" or "living my own life." It may represent a repeated pattern of weakly succumbing to temptation. It may also be a cry for help. These behaviors constitute professional suicide. If they represent anything more than a once-and-never-again capitulation to temptation, they may convey the cry, "I respect myself so little, and am in so much pain! Either help me make a new beginning, or reject me altogether."

These negative behaviors—whether in their major or minor versions—are both self-defeating and ministry-defeating. They are diametrically opposed to what Lutherans expect of their pastors and consider necessary for an effective ministry. They present a special challenge to the church: How does one minister to clergy who behave in these ways that hinder ministry? How can congregations help pastors back onto their feet to become effective again?

Emphases and Contrasts

Those who are more highly educated, those who are older, and women tend to view these behaviors, with a few exceptions, as more detrimental than other Lutherans do. Less-well-educated, younger men are less inclined to be disturbed by them. Whether one group or the other is in a better position to help is hard to say. The former may be in a more opportune position because they are more likely to recognize the symp-

Table 4. Groups significantly less tolerant of the characteristics of Area X, "Not Wanted: Ministry-Defeating Behaviors."

isolation *characteristics*	laity	more educated	older	women
71 Self-Centered Isolation ° (hinders quite a bit)				L
74 Self-Isolating Behavior (hinders very much)		LL		LL
77 Impersonalness Without Trust (hinders very much)		LLL		LL
vacillation *characteristics*				
72 Evidences of Insecurity (hinders quite a bit)		LLL		LL
75 Insecure Authoritarianism (hinders very much)		LL		L
deviant behavior *characteristics*				
70 Secular Life-Style (hinders quite a bit)			LLL	
73 Instability (hinders quite a bit)	LL (vs. all professionals)			
76 Undisciplined Living (hinders very much)	LL (vs. sem. seniors)		LLL	

° average Lutheran evaluation of this characteristic's contribution to effective ministry

As compared with Lutherans' average rating (or the contrasting groups specifically listed):

L = slightly lower
LL = lower
LLL = much lower

102

toms. But the latter may be better able to help because they are less likely to be irritated by what they observe.

Education

People differ most about negative behaviors on the basis of the amount of education they have. More-highly-educated Lutherans were *much more* sensitive than others to the hindrance to ministry represented in "Evidences of Insecurity" (72) and "Impersonalness Without Trust" (77). For better-educated Lutherans, total lack of trust in people and the resulting complete isolation from them is about the worst thing that can happen to pastors and their ministry. This group was also *more* sensitive than is typical to "Self-Isolating Behavior" (74) and "Insecure Authoritarianism" (75) as hindering ministry.

Less-well-educated Lutherans were more sensitive to the negative impact of "Instability" (73) in their pastor. As we have observed before, the less-well-educated are usually more disturbed by a lack of dependability. As was discovered in *A Study of Generations,* those with less education are more interested than average in security, and more concerned about being able to count on their world not to present surprises or dramatic changes. Their expectations of pastors reflect a similar attitude.

Older vs. younger

Older Lutherans come down hardest on all forms of deviant, rebellious, questionable, and immoral behavior on the part of clergy. They were much more sensitive than other Lutherans to the negative aspects of "Secular Life-Style" (70), and counted "Undisciplined Living" (76) as most negative of all. This bears out once again the tendency of older Lutherans to want greater spirituality, formality, and propriety from their ministers. Younger Lutherans were most sensitive to the negative potential in "Impersonalness Without Trust" (77). They consider a lack of sensitivity and approachability to be an extreme hindrance to ministry.

Women

Women seem to be additionally sensitive to five out of the eight characteristics in this area. They are more critical of attempts to survive by vacillation and isolation in the face of life's pressures. The deviant behavior which runs contrary to social norms for clergy is viewed no more negatively by women than by men.

Other groups

The laity joined the less-well-educated in being more conscious of the negative potential of pastoral "Instability" (73), when compared with its rating by clergy. Seminary seniors were more tolerant of the behaviors in "Undisciplined Living" (76) than were lay people. They were, in fact, more tolerant of it than any of the other four groups. It is somewhat thought-provoking to discover that seminary seniors are apparently more tolerant of clergy behavior that, according to biblical standards, is sinful.

By contrast, regular-churchgoing Lutherans (those who attend worship at least once a week) viewed "Secular Life-Style" (70) slightly more negatively than other Lutherans did. They found it more difficult to accept actions that fly in the face of what is usually considered appropriate behavior for clergy.

Reflections

It is necessary to approach comment on this group of characteristics with humility and care. It is our experience that we cannot read through the items of these negative characteristics without an occasional flicker of self-recognition. We doubt if many ministers can. In the assessment program for seminarians that grew from this study, we discovered that these characteristics (as is true of nearly all of the other characteristics of ministry) are not something that people either have or do not have. Instead, nearly all are possessed to a greater or lesser degree by most people.

Bacteriologists tell us that we all carry within our bodies an arsenal of viruses, bacteria, and other malevolent organisms sufficient to bring us down with any one of a host of common diseases at any time. Only the vigorous activity of counteracting forces in our bodies keeps us on our feet. So it is with some of the characteristics described in this most-negatively-regarded group. We all carry within us the potential for this kind of behavior. If we now function relatively free of it, it is by the grace of God, not our own merit, that we do so.

There are no easy answers for lay persons or clergy who see themselves reflected in this chapter, those who recognize their pastor in this description, or for denominational officials struggling with decisions concerning someone whom this chapter in part describes.

Behavior that isolates, dominates, vacillates, or repels is a problem for both the clergy and laity. It damages pastors; it damages their ministries both within congregations and in the community; it demoralizes congregations. In the wording of our study, it *hinders* ministry. Where pastors exhibit too much of one or more of these characteristics, ministry often is paralyzed until the underlying ailment is arrested or cured.

Though the ailment is a hindrance, annoyance, and embarrassment, we must keep one fact in mind: a minister showing these behaviors is suffering. To feel engaged full-time in a struggle for survival is not jolly good fun. There is a grimness, a desperation underlying these behaviors that calls for compassion. The behaviors themselves may not be painful to a person who engages in them, but the anxiety, the feeling of being threatened, and the sense of panic that may underlie them *are* painful. The behaviors often represent ways a person has chosen, consciously or unconsciously, to escape or alleviate the pain.

Because people exhibit these negative characteristics in varying degrees of seriousness, it is difficult to map a single action or strategy that will help a person move toward change.

Those who are not severely affected by one or more of these characteristics are more likely to wonder how others see them and to muster the courage to find out. A self-inventory, using the checklist for Area X in Appendix C (p. 252), can alert pastors to tendencies which others usually see long before they might be conscious of them themselves. To carry that self-appraisal a step further, a harrowing but useful exercise might be to ask another person or group for their frank responses to the checklist in terms of one's own ministry. This might be particularly useful if it is a prelude to conversation about the kinds of activity the checklist brings to light.

In a congregation where a pastor is observed to be showing some of these behaviors, lay leaders might well begin with self-examination. Was he or she like this at first? If not, what elements in our congregational life might be causing the behavior? If so, what elements in our congregational life are encouraging and perpetuating it? Are we encouraging our pastor to dominate by an unwillingness to shoulder responsibility ourselves? Are we shortening an already-short temper by demanding long working hours? Do we let our pastor bear too many stresses alone? Are we understaffed? Are we so resisting a prophetic ministry that we increase our pastor's frustration and sense of failure? As a congregation, do we communicate that we care about him or her? A congregation that faces such questions squarely, or asks the head of the particular judicatory to help explore such possibilities as these, may find that the first step toward change and healing is within its own power to take. In addition, whatever the level of presence of these negative characteristics in a pastor, congregational leaders may be sowing the seeds of such characteristics by failing to reinforce that which is positive in the ministry they see—by neglecting to convey appreciation, enthusiasm, support, and approval where it is genuinely felt and where it should, in honesty, be expressed.

Threatened persons especially need the warming encouragement and love of a sustaining group. If pastors can draw on groups within their congregations for this kind of support, they may be able to reduce some of their feelings of threat and turn some of the energies they once used for self-protection to more productive causes, investing more of themselves in ministries to others. Progress in such a healthy direction may be slow, but in any congregation it can be a sure result of the ministry of a group that surrounds the pastor with the human reflection of God's unconditional love.

Given the fact that there are many situations in which ministers who show evidence of instability, insecurity, and isolation can be helped to wholeness by their congregations, there are also many situations in which they cannot. There are situations in which "dis-ease" has taken hold to such a degree that radical measures of some kind are necessary to heal the suffering pastor and the also-suffering congregation. The supportive love of a congregation or friends is always a force on the side of health, but there are cases so severe that such support cannot by itself effect a cure. Intervention by denominational superiors, long-term professional counseling, long-term leaves for retreat, study, and personal redirection, or some other such major action is necessary.

A striking thing occurred as we worked on our research and wrote this book. Repeated experiences that were about the same for each of us occurred with such regularity that we began to expect their occurrence when it became known that our research was connected with entrance to ministry. Whether the person we were speaking with was an old friend, a casual acquaintance, or a stranger in an airport, as soon as he or she took in the nature of the project, the first reaction was a sigh of relief, followed by a statement like, "*Finally* somebody's really going to do something about some of these people that never should have gotten into ministry in the first place. My home church is still recovering from one we had five years ago. The church membership had dwindled down to half its size before we got rid of him."

Eventually, if the conversation went on long enough, it would move on to other topics relevant to ministry, but the subject that usually surfaced first was that of the negative effect ministers can have.

Many of the people we talked to issued what amounted to a plea: that those in authority recognize early the symptoms of those whose ministry is flawed by personal negative characteristics; that ministerial disasters not simply be moved from place to place to visit harm on a series of congregations; and that those in power muster the firmness to deal effectively with ministers whom many recognize as wolves, but whom everyone seems to keep blandly accepting as shepherds or just another one of the sheep.

People want those who keep the gate on entry into ministry and those who supervise ministers throughout the church to make sure they are not playing ostrich. A few emotional cripples *are* getting into ministry. In some cases they are doing considerable harm. In even the best situations their handicaps hinder ministry wherever they serve. In the worst situations congregations struggle for years to recover after such a pastor has left.

The following is quoted from the 1977 Report of the Task Force on Clergy Training and Deployment of the American Lutheran Church:

> At the same time we draw attention to another significant trend in the life of our church: a heightening of the expectations parishes now have as they call and work with pastors. Congregations are less willing than they used to be to tolerate ineffectiveness in pastoral leadership. While that trend must not reach the point where we have a "hiring and firing" mentality, the trend itself is salutary for the mission of the church. It is therefore important that our seminaries discourage those applicants/students who are not really good candidates for effective ministry.

How does one deal with a person who is agreed by a number of competent observers to be consistently exhibiting one or more of these negative characteristics, and to be beyond any of the possibilities suggested thus far? How does one deal with what seems to suggest real "dis-ease" —not just unpleasant behavior, but illness? Whether the setting is a seminary, congregation, or some other place of ministry, it seems to us that the answer is the same: one deals compassionately, but firmly and forthrightly. This is not a time to be "nice." Honesty, thoroughness, and clarity are imperative. The defenses of such persons are probably too well developed for a quiet chat or judicious suggestion to have much effect. Greater drama and greater force may be required to break through their defenses so that they can hear the dual message that their behavior is no longer tolerable, and that people who care about them want to help them change.

Whether the person in question is a seminarian, parish pastor, or minister in some other setting, some—or perhaps all—of the following may be necessary in order to help the process of change begin:

● Several persons should be present who have observed the negative behavior and are generally agreed on the necessity for change.

● The persons present must be able and willing, if necessary, to present specific times and places at which the negative behavior has been displayed, and be able to relate these individual incidents to a pattern of behavior.

● A person with special professional expertise—psychiatrist, psychologist, wise and respected spiritual shepherd, or other person with particular knowledge not only of the problem but of a possible means of cure—should be present.

● The group should be ready and willing to arrange for some kind of help, hoping the person will be willing to accept it or an alternative. Certainly the preceding paragraphs presuppose that possible sources of help have been sought out and identified before the conversation begins. It would be irresponsible to point out problems such as these without offering possible remedies.

● If the seminarian or pastor cannot accept the information communicated, steadfastly refuses help, or continues unchanged to maintain his or her defenses, the intention of the group should be to seek a change in assignment or, in the case of a seminarian, to counsel the person out of ministry and onto some other vocational track.

To prepare thoughtfully and prayerfully for such a significant encounter, to be firm, and to insist on change is in the best interests both of persons who consistently exhibit such behavior and of those whom their ministries affect. In our view we should not, out of a misguided politeness, an overdeveloped respect for the ministry, or our own cowardice, barter away the health and ministry of a whole congregation in order to preserve an appearance of harmony and prevent unpleasantness. Christ overturned tables, rocked the boat, and pointed out the wrongs he saw, and he could scarcely be expected to approve our passivity on an issue of this magnitude—trading the health not only of a person but of a congregation as well for our own temporary comfort. And yet it is far easier to prescribe from a safe distance than to cope with a real situation. Often by the time a pastor's behavior becomes clear enough to motivate some members to take strong action, the congregation is either divided or so demoralized that it cannot come to a decision to take corrective action. All this underscores the importance of detecting these tendencies early enough so that they are correctable without major surgery that leaves both a minister and congregation in a state of shock.

Part II

Five

Ministry

Skills

Component characteristics: Chapter 6

From central to peripheral

11 Creating Sense of God's Family
10 Communicating Grace and Forgiveness
20 Explaining Sacraments and Rites
5 Encouraging Responsibility to Means of Grace
15 Relating Biblical Faith to Everyday Experience
59 Open, Evaluative Stance
36 Personal Approach in Worship
23 Fostering Congregational Gospel Community
18 Relational Preaching and Worship Leading
53 Awareness of Children's Needs
35 Motivating Faith-Consistent Action

In order of Lutheran ranking

5 Encouraging Responsibility to Means of Grace
10 Communicating Grace and Forgiveness
11 Creating Sense of God's Family
15 Relating Biblical Faith to Everyday Experience
18 Relational Preaching and Worship Leading
20 Explaining Sacraments and Rites
23 Fostering Congregational Gospel Community
35 Motivating Faith-Consistent Action
36 Personal Approach in Worship
53 Awareness of Children's Needs
59 Open, Evaluative Stance

Community Through Word and Sacraments

Preceding chapters focused on how ministers view their faith, people, church, purpose, and person. Attention centered on these life perspectives first because Lutherans are more concerned about them than about the skills and abilities of a pastor. This does not mean that competence is viewed as unimportant. It means only that people feel it is *more* important for their pastor to affirm a personal faith, be people-oriented, value Lutheran distinctiveness, and not have low self-esteem or a sense of purpose that is restrictive or repressive to people.

Saying this should not detract from the fact that Lutherans are still concerned about how well their pastors can preach and teach, as well as administer, counsel, provide community leadership, and conduct worship services. These areas of ministry are described in the next five chapters. The first three of these competencies draw an average rating of "contributes very much" to an effective ministry, with the one listed first (the ability to preach and teach) being tied for third in importance among all ten concerns treated in his book. This competency is outranked only by two qualities desired in a pastor—spiritual foundations and a people-orientation. Good preaching and teaching rank high because they are seen as essential to gaining something Lutherans desire deeply, vital congregational community life.

111

Apparently the presence of a spirit of warm community in a church is easy to detect. At any rate, nearly everyone feels free to make informal judgments about it: "We attended a different church last Sunday morning, and we felt at home there right away." Not only do lay people regularly make such judgments, but they often act on them. A pastor's phone will ring and the voice on the line will say, "We've been looking around in this area for a church home, and we think we've found it. We've been attending your congregation for several weeks now, and we'd like to become members."

In spite of the relative ease and certainty with which people make these judgments and act on them, most would find it difficult to trace the sources or to name the elements that make a spirit of community evident in a congregation. But people apparently sense what they are. A clear identification of the shape of this area of ministry emerged from the responses of the 5000 Lutherans. It covers a surprisingly large territory. Eleven characteristics—one-seventh of the total number in the study—combined to describe congregational community developed through pastoral teaching and preaching.

These characteristics, taken together, present a picture not so much of an easy, cozy togetherness, but of life together as the community of faith, the family of God. The picture presented here has to do with the creation, sustenance, and growth of this life together that only the means of grace can create. Lutherans recognize and want to be part of this harmony with God, with oneself, and with other people that can exist nowhere but among Christian believers.

This area of ministry consists of the tasks of building the church as a community of faith, the family of God, a church home. A church home has many things in common with a good family. It is a place where people speak and understand a mutual language, where people care about each other's hurts and problems, and where each supports the other in times of failure, but yet keeps encouraging, enabling, and hoping for each person in the family to move on to greater accomplishments. Members know why they are together; there is an organizing force, a bond that they know and can name that causes them to be and remain together.

In most homes that function well as homes, and in churches that function well as communities, this spirit of community does not stay alive by itself. Communities sometimes will form spontaneously in order to confront an outside threat, but once the threat is gone the spirit of community often evaporates unless someone undertakes activities and arranges structures that sustain it. Viewed from this perspective, a pastor functions as a church homemaker, one who keeps community alive and growing. Or, to speak with greater accuracy, as a pastor becomes a minister of the means of grace in Word and sacraments, God builds the church.

The nature of the church-homemaking task becomes clear in the four categories into which the characteristics of this area of ministry fall. The first has to do with *community building,* and consists of "Creating Sense of God's Family" (11), "Fostering Congregational Gospel Community" (23), and "Open, Evaluative Stance" (59). The second has to do with *building persons,* and consists of "Communicating Grace and Forgiveness" (10), "Personal Approach in Worship" (36), and "Relational Preaching and Worship Leading" (18).

The third category has to do with *providing instruction,* or teaching the significance of practices and activities of the community. It consists of "Explaining Sacraments and Rites" (20), "Relating Biblical Faith to Everyday Experience" (15), and "Awareness of Children's Needs" (53). The fourth has to do with *motivating to action,* and consists of "Encouraging Responsibility to Means of Grace" (5), and "Motivating Faith-Consistent Action" (35).

The first two categories describe functions that help the membership to discover, celebrate, and appreciate their identity as a community under God. The last two describe functions that equip members for better citizenship in the church community, and, to a lesser extent, in the world.

Ministry that builds community

More than any of the other nine areas of ministry, this one is what Lutherans have characteristically identified as distinctive of the ordained ministry—the public ministry of the means of grace, of Word and sacraments. At heart it is the preaching and teaching ministry. It is extremely significant, therefore, that Lutherans clearly view the ordained ministry of preaching, leading worship, baptizing, administering the Lord's supper, teaching, marrying, and burying as *occurring within the community*—rather than as private interactions between an individual, a pastor, and God. Not only do they see these things as properly occurring within the community, but they also see them as serving the purpose of creating, sustaining, and increasing a living, worshiping, serving community which is the people of God.

The ministry of the gospel and the Christian life that Lutherans want is seen as life together as a fellowship of believers. They expect pastors to be the prime builders of that fellowship.

Creating Sense of God's Family (11). The essence of this characteristic is the pastoral skill of helping people experience in worship the confident, joyous sense of being a witnessing family of God, a community of faith in the world. One of the items reads, "Helps people feel confident in sharing their faith with others." Apparently Lutherans generally recognize that people cannot really experience being a community of faith unless they learn to confess and share their faith with one another. According to the rest of the items, members expect to learn to share the faith confidently both through observing pastors in worship and through what they involve them in saying, singing, and doing on Sunday morning and at other times of corporate worship. Approximately four out of five people reached for the words "absolutely essential" or "contributes very much" when describing how important these abilities are in a pastor.

Fostering Congregational Gospel Community (23).   The accent here, though still on community, is not on what happens in corporate worship, but on what happens among pastors and people everywhere else. Members want a pastor to enter into the life, work, and play of a congregation, and by example, to encourage the formation of an atmosphere of mutual friendship, cooperation, and support—especially freedom for use of members' varied talents in ways that provide a sense of belonging, mutual acceptance, and community.

Open, Evaluative Stance (59).   At first glance, it seems strange to find this characteristic as a part of the area of community-building. The characteristic centers on a pastor's efforts to find out about lay people's understandings of doctrine and their reactions to sermons and worship services; its title calls to mind the word *criticism.* Surprising partners—evaluation and community.

At second glance, however, the partnership makes eminently good sense. There are few actions that show respect for other persons as powerfully as asking for their suggestions, criticisms, and evaluations of your work. Mutual respect is the *sine qua non* of lasting relationships and the foundation of community.

This characteristic outlines more than a one-sided kind of evaluation. Although a part of it concerns a pastor's openness to hearing a congregation's reactions to sermons and to the conduct of worship, another part speaks of a pastor's effort to help a congregation be open to ministries from others, even from Christians in other parts of the world. The characteristic also speaks of a pastor's trying to understand or evaluate people's doctrinal understandings in order to minister more effectively to them. In sum, then, the characteristic includes various approaches on the part of a pastor to create an atmosphere in a congregation of openness, both to giving and receiving a ministry of evaluation.

Ministry that builds people

Christian community is unique because it is a union in which each member finds his or her identity—as well as community with all other members—in relationship with God, the head of the household. The community coalesces around the One who brings the household of faith into being through the means of grace. A pastor, as one who leads worship, administers the means of grace, and declares absolution, is in a position to build people up by reminding them of that identity and community, and by helping them to rediscover it for themselves.

Communicating Grace and Forgiveness (10). "I know, intellectually, that God loves me and forgives me when I confess my faults and sins. My problem isn't to *know* that, it's to experience it happening. And that's easier said than done." The lay person speaking here has set the agenda for the pastor who would develop this characteristic of ministry. It is no easy assignment, but it is important—one of every two Lutherans said "absolutely essential." The primary task and joy of the church is to proclaim and *be* the place of forgiveness through grace.

The items of the characteristic give at least some sense of how this can be done. Such pastors believe themselves to be occupying the same plane as their parishioners—under God's judgment and grace. The aim is to help people *sense,* not just understand, the gift of God's forgiveness and the reality of God's grace. The audience is not just the church membership, but all people. One of the symbols of God's grace is the power of Baptism, which one can continually experience through daily repentance. It is clear that, whether it is communicated to a pastor or to church members, no cheap grace is intended. Both the judgment and grace of God are a part of the message, but the accent is on grace, forgiveness, acceptance— the good news.

This set of items includes a peripheral item that reads, "Treats Christian day school teachers as co-ministers in the gospel." Perhaps this is among the most powerful of gospel messages that some lay people, especially commissioned lay staff workers, can hear from pastors: the acknowledgment that they are not in any way less, or second-class, but *co-ministers.* Though they have different offices, those ministries are as important as pastoral ministry.

Personal Approach in Worship (36).   Professional clergy placed higher value than did the laity on a pastor's ability to be warmly personal and empathetic when conducting a service. They deem it important that a pastor preach as one who experiences the problems of living the Christian life. When preaching a funeral sermon, they want a pastor to acknowledge personal grief as being very real, natural, and painful. They believe that a personal approach to worship keeps liturgy from seeming formal or a pastor from appearing unapproachable. When it is led in a spirit of reverent celebration, and when it is personal enough to touch the emotions, a worship experience can powerfully reawaken in worshipers a sense of family and of being part of the community of faith.

Relational Preaching and Worship Leading (18). Whereas the key words in the preceding characteristic were *personal* and *empathetic,* the key words in this one are *come alive.* This characteristic illuminates the value of a pastor's ability to "stab the spirit broad awake." To do that in preaching or teaching, a pastor must have the goal in mind of enlivening and building people up as only the gospel can when clearly and vividly presented. Under such a pastor's preaching and worship leading, people come to a new awareness of their sinfulness and need, feel joy, or experience God as real and close—or perhaps experience all of these things at once. In worship services such as these, people rarely fall asleep. Too much is happening that affects them deeply, and they can't afford to miss any of it.

There is a possible pitfall here, however. A powerful preacher is always in danger of building only the relationship between pastor and parishioner rather than between *pastor, parishioner,* and *God.* This latter relationship is the thrust of this characteristic.

Ministry that instructs

If the Christian community is to remain alert, articulate, and "wise as serpents," it is necessary that information be shared, knowledge communicated, and insight engendered. If there ever was such a day, the time has long passed when the church can get by with only pastors knowing what's going on, or being able to explain what the faith is all about. Only when the general membership of Christ's church is thoroughly grounded in the Scriptures and well informed about the heritage of the Christian community is it in a position to be the living, dynamic, servant organism it is called to be. Therefore there must be wise, well-informed, and effective teachers in the Christian community, and Lutherans expect their pastors to be primary among the teachers in congregations.

Relating Biblical Faith to Everyday Experience (15). There exists in this characteristic the same note of vividness and clarity that was present in the previous one, "Relational Preaching and Worship Leading." But added to it is the important concept of making connections—linking theory and practice. The central item, which describes what lies at the heart of this characteristic, reads, "Presents the Word of God in terms clearly understandable to the modern mind." Lutherans are saying here, "If it doesn't relate in some way to contemporary life as people are living it, what good is it?" To minister, figuratively speaking, with the Scriptures in one hand and the daily newspaper in the other involves three functions: preaching, teaching, and providing counsel and guidance.

The educational specifics appear in being an interesting teacher, explaining changes introduced into worship, and being sensitive to educational needs in the congregation. The specifics of guidance appear in such activities as helping people make choices in daily life that relate the Scriptures to their human condition, and applying biblical insights to current ethical decisions. The specifics of worship appear in preaching with authority and conviction, and in such a way that people remember not so much the preacher, but Jesus Christ who was preached.

Explaining Sacraments and Rites (20). Symbols have power even for those who may not be able to articulate their meaning. Therefore attendance at worship and participation in liturgy are important for children or others who may not fully understand their meaning. Yet understanding enhances the effectiveness of symbols. The perception of this truth by Lutherans emerged in their separating out "Explaining Sacraments and Rites" as an identifiable and desired characteristic of ministry. This characteristic, ranking 20th in importance, underlines the importance of a pastor's efforts to help participants understand the meaning of what God offers them in the sacraments, symbols, and rites of the church. Not only is it expected that a pastor will explain the meaning of worship, liturgy, marriage, Baptism, and the Eucharist, but that a pastor will help people to prepare for meaningful participation in them. Intellectual understanding is one thing, but being ready to receive God himself and what he offers is quite another, and even more highly desired.

It is not difficult to see why this characteristic appears with other activities that foster community. It speaks to the human need to feel included and to be able to understand or participate in what is going on, especially when the meaning of a rite is not self-evident. Few things can make one feel more effectively excluded from a group than observing or being present at a symbolic act or rite that one does not understand. In contrast, one's sense of belonging grows when approaching a familiar and understood rite or activity that is peculiar to a community.

Awareness of Children's Needs (53). The laity placed more value than the clergy did on a ministry that shows special sensitivity to the needs of children. Though a good many priorities precede it in the ranking of the 77 expectations for ministry, this being number 53 in the sequence, Lutherans do value a ministry that shows special sensitivity to the needs of children. It is important that worship be conducted and classes taught in ways that are meaningful for children, but the core of what is desired here is that children be provided with ministry and instruction in whatever ways best serve them. Whether the avenue of ministry is assisting in the training of Sunday school teachers, stressing the importance of Lutheran parochial education, or some other means, Lutherans want children to be regarded as worthy and valued members of the community of faith.

Because the questionnaire items did not provide much opportunity for special emphasis on the particular needs of other age levels, it would not be appropriate to assume that this age group is viewed as being altogether special. It seems reasonable to interpret this emphasis on children's needs partly as a concern that any teaching ministry take into account the instructional needs of the age-group being served.

Ministry that motivates action

The ultimate goal of education is not simply understanding, but also action. Action is both a cause and an effect. It results from and also contributes to a congregation's sense of community. The two characteristics described here speak of a ministry that spreads before congregational members a vision of the part they may take in building community. By living out their community's goals in their own lives, they help to strengthen and perpetuate that Christian community.

Encouraging Responsibility to Means of Grace (5). This highly ranked expectation of ministry is brief, but obviously important. More than four out of five Lutherans said its highest-rated item is either absolutely essential or contributes very much to effective ministry.

Despite its title, the thrust of this ability is not encouraging parishioners to baptize their children, attend the Lord's Supper, and listen to sermons. Rather it consists of encouraging and teaching members to recognize and take up their lifelong responsibilities toward infants baptized in a congregation. It means teaching older Christians to offer intercessory prayer, express interest, provide example, pay attention, give advice, teach, answer questions, trust, and do the myriad other things for children and their parents that are usually considered the role of good, supportive baptismal sponsors. Though it is mentioned by name in none of the items, this ministry skill concerns confirmation too.

Lutherans see appropriate confirmation instruction as not only a matter of several months of individualized or class instruction from the pastor, awesomely important as that is. Even more, it is lifelong acculturation in and to the life and heritage of the Christian community—a process of living constantly in the midst of examples of what it is to be a Christian as seen and felt in the presence of one's friends, neighbors, relatives, teachers, and others. Implied in all of this is that the pastor will be effectively exhorting and encouraging adults (who are models for children) to avail themselves constantly of every means of grace—which is also part of "Encouraging Responsibility to the Means of Grace."

Motivating Faith-Consistent Action (35). In looking for this characteristic in their pastors, Lutherans are asking to be led, prodded, challenged, guided, and exhorted to translate their faith into consistent action. Contrary to all the literature about lay people wanting to occupy comfortable cocoons in the church, Lutherans ask that their pastors help them participate in meeting the needs and concerns of their communities and provide experiences that help them not only to grow spiritually, but also to be creative in applying their faith to their lives.

What Lutherans are implying here is that, when their lives are not consistent with their faith, it may be that they don't know *how*, rather than *what*. "What we want of the church," they are saying, "is some down-to-earth examples. I know I'm supposed to love my neighbor. How does that translate out into how I should relate to the neighbor who is suing me because he says the tree I cut down was his?" Being able to do God's will on earth takes more than a good sense of *ought*. It requires instruction in *how* others at various points in life have been doing it. It requires a chance for experimentation—to try and to fail without being condemned; a place for successful experimentation to be encouraged and shared with others; it requires an active, supportive community.

Emphases and Contrasts

The pattern of preference for this area of ministry resembles that for a pastor whose ministry is spiritually founded (Chapter 1); older Lutherans, people who find the most satisfaction in their participation in congregational life, and people who attend worship every Sunday place the highest value on ministry that creates and sustains congregational community. These three factors—age, satisfying participation, and frequency of worship make the greatest difference; professionals and women also accent some characteristics of congregational community, but either fewer characteristics or with somewhat lesser intensity. There are also certain unique preferences related to church body membership, amount of education, and particular ministry settings.

Age

Younger Lutherans particularly value only one characteristic of this area of ministry, "Fostering Congregational Gospel Community" (23); it is the only one they rate higher than older Lutherans do. This is consistent with a pattern throughout this project: younger Lutherans generally place higher priority on aspects of ministry that support or contribute to Christian community in the form of close, candid interpersonal relationships. Therefore it is not surprising that here they show greater appre-

Table 5. Groups that place higher value on Area IV, "Community Through Word and Sacraments."

	all professionals	less educated	older	LCMS	women	weekly attendance	high participation/ satisfaction
community building							
11 Creating Sense of God's Family					HH	HH	HH
23 Fostering Congregational Gospel Community	H		LL				
59 Open, Evaluative Stance	HHH						
building people							
10 Communicating Grace and Forgiveness	HH		HH	L (vs. LCA)	H	HH	HH
36 Personal Approach in Worship	HH		HH		HH	H	HH
18 Relational Preaching and Worship Leading	L	H	HHH	H (vs. LCA)	H	H	HH

(continued on next page)

(Table 5 continued)

	all	professionals	less educated	older	LCMS	women	weekly attendance	high participation/ satisfaction
providing instruction								
15 Relating Biblical Faith to Everyday Experience				HH		H		
20 Explaining Sacraments and Rites				HH		H	HH	HH
53 Awareness of Children's Needs	L		HHH	HH	H (vs. LCA)			HH
motivating action								
5 Encouraging Responsibility to Means of Grace						H		HH
35 Motivating Faith-Consistent Action							H	

As compared with Lutherans' average rating (or contrasting groups specifically listed):

HHH = much higher
HH = higher
H = slightly higher
L = slightly lower
LL = lower
LLL = much lower

ciation for a characteristic that requires pastors to become a part of the daily life, work, and play of their people, helping congregations be places of friendship and support, enlivened by the gospel spirit of freedom and love. What is surprising is that younger Lutherans emphasize only one characteristic here.

The special concerns of older Lutherans for congregational community are somewhat different. They showed greater interest in warm and personal worship experiences than in finding gospel community in the broad range of congregational activities. In comparison with Lutherans as a whole they placed less value on that which is personal and relational in worship, and placed *much greater* emphasis on the contribution of "Relational Preaching and Worship Leading" (18) and *somewhat greater* emphasis than is typical of Lutherans on "Personal Approach in Worship" (36). Being generally more concerned about all three characteristics of "building people," they were also generally more concerned about ministers' "Communicating Grace and Forgiveness" (10).

In addition, older Lutherans emphasize pastoral teaching and instruction. They placed additional importance on "Relating Biblical Faith to Everyday Experience" (15), "Explaining Sacraments and Rites" (20), and "Awareness of Children's Needs" (53). Even when we adjusted the data for the fact that most older Lutherans tend to be less-well educated, we still found the same general pattern: the older the person, up to age 65, the greater the likelihood of increased enthusiasm for pastoral teaching, instruction, and activities that build people up.

Participation and attendance

Those Lutherans who find major satisfaction in their participation in congregational activities placed greater-than-typical priority on seven of the eleven characteristics of this area. Those seven are related to all four of the categories of this area of ministry, but do not include "Fostering Congregational Gospel Community" (23) and "Open, Evaluative Stance" (59) in the category of community-building, "Relating Biblical Faith to Everyday Experience" (15) as part of providing instruction, or "Motivating Faith-Consistent Action" (35) in motivating to action. One might think that these active people in congregations would be more concerned than most that pastors exhort and encourage the participation of others, but not so.

Those who attend worship weekly are slightly more than typically concerned about "Motivating Faith-Consistent Action" (35), plus five of the same characteristics that the most satisfied participants look for. The three characteristics they are *most* concerned about here lie at the very heart of this area of ministry: "Creating Sense of God's Family" (11),

"Communicating Grace and Forgiveness" (10), and "Explaining Sacraments and Rites" (20).

These two elements—satisfaction in participation, and regular attendance—are closely related to the values people place on a sense of community in a congregation.

Professionals vs. the laity

The laity and professionals agree on the importance of five of these characteristics; but one can expect professionals to be more sensitive to four others, and lay people to two. Professionals accented "Open, Evaluative Stance" (59), "Communicating Grace and Forgiveness" (10), "Personal Approach in Worship" (36), and "Fostering Congregational Gospel Community" (23). In fact, professionals were the only ones especially concerned about "Open, Evaluative Stance" (59), and they placed the highest additional priority that they gave to any characteristic in this area upon that stance. The laity, on the other hand, placed a somewhat greater accent on the importance of "Relational Preaching and Worship Leading" (18) and "Awareness of Children's Needs" (53). These two emphases are not in conflict, however. The professionals were accenting the importance of doing those very things that are likely to provide what lay people most want to receive and experience.

Seminary students (one subgroup of professional ministers) differed from the laity by being less interested in "Relational Preaching and Worship Leading" (18), but they were more interested in "Fostering Congregational Gospel Community" (23) and slightly more interested in "Motivating Faith-Consistent Action" (35). These tendencies correspond with what many researchers found youth were concerned about when these seminary seniors were teenagers: that adults practice what they preach. Since several of the items in "Motivating Faith-Consistent Action" refer to pastors' helping and exhorting middle-aged Christians, one might expect *all* younger Lutherans to rate it slightly higher, but that is not the way it turned out. Perhaps it is because this characteristic presents not just action but *faith-consistent* action that seminarians alone, rather than all younger Lutherans, gave it additional emphasis.

Women

Men have no special appreciation for any of these characteristics. Women placed slightly higher priority on four—"Communicating Grace and Forgiveness" (10), "Explaining Sacraments and Rites" (20), "Encouraging Responsibility to Means of Grace" (5), and "Relating Biblical Faith to Everyday Experience" (15). Women accented even more strongly two characteristics that stress the warmly personal and the familial—

exactly what is stereotypically identified with the feminine—"Personal Approach in Worship" (36) and "Creating Sense of God's Family" (11).

Less educated

Lutherans with less formal education were slightly more concerned about "Relational Preaching and Worship Leading" (18) and "Awareness of Children's Needs" (53). More of them want sermons that speak of sin and one's need for Christ and more of them want worship services where God's presence is felt. Also significant is the fact that the less educated look to the church for help in meeting the needs of their children, because the church's programs for children and youth have often favored children of the best-educated.

Church body differences

The primary pattern of differences between church bodies in this area exists between the Lutheran Church–Missouri Synod and the Lutheran Church in America. While members of the LCA placed added emphasis on the importance of people experiencing God's graciousness and forgiveness in whatever form that might take (10), members of the LCMS gave higher priority to pastors' inspiring joy and a sense of God's closeness through "Relational Preaching and Worship Leading" (18). They also placed added importance on "Awareness of Children's Needs" (53). These two accents are consistent with what the LCA and LCMS have historically emphasized. Church bodies that formed the LCA were inclined to emphasize the importance of making the Christian faith understandable and relevant to people in whatever environment or situation they found themselves. The LCMS has historically supported parochial schools (a part of the characteristic related to children's needs) and shown evangelical concern for bringing the Christian witness to individuals in correct, traditional language and symbols. But LCMS members accent here not only the support of parochial schools, but also a pastor's function as teacher, and therefore as a direct participant in parochial education.

Ministry-situation

Apparently, at least some of the time, people put more value on what is especially needed in their own settings. Those in congregational settings, where whole families—including numbers of children—are part of the membership, generally put greater emphasis on the need for a pastor's "Awareness of Children's Needs" (53). In other types of settings—the military, educational institutions, hospitals and homes, and the like— whole families are usually less well represented, and the need for creating a community of the household of faith is likely to be greater and to require more conscious effort. In keeping with this, persons from non-congregational settings expressed a slightly greater desire for "Fostering Congregational Gospel Community" (23).

Reflections

It is a pity that the word *community* has become so widely and so variously used as to endanger its capacity to convey what exists in this set of characteristics. In common usage the word has a variety of connotations, and strictly denotes little more than living or being together. But the community we see described here is something much more than an easy, cozy togetherness. It is a relationship with bones, muscle, and teeth. It is a relationship full of active verbs: *building, instructing, motivating, encouraging, helping, challenging, emphasizing, creating, correcting.* "Community Through Word and Sacraments" describes a body of persons becoming, learning, and acting by means of their relationships with God and each other, and in the process rediscovering their primary identity.

Within congregational community, as nowhere else, we can see ourselves primarily in our baptismal identity—as children of God, as members of the household of faith. In every other relationship of life we are viewed in other ways. We are social beings, consumers, citizens, winners, losers, sexual beings, bosses, or helpers. Only within the community of a congregation do we have our primary identity reaffirmed as at our baptism—as princes and princesses, adopted but nevertheless true children of the King of the Universe.

"The family of God" is a phrase both regularly and aptly used to describe congregational community. But with its consistent use, or because of the kind of use it gets, the burden of meaning becomes the *family* of God. There is nothing wrong with that. But to understand it only in that way is to miss the magnificence and wonder of the incredible kinship expressed: the family of *God.* One layman, weary of his pastor's overencouragement of warm, personal relationships within the congregation, observed, "I don't come to church looking for my 'family.' I have several quite satisfactory circles of friends among my colleagues and others whom I know socially. What I find in church is a reminder and an experience of who I am and can become by the grace of God. Along with these other folks whom I don't know very well I am, and am becoming, a son of the Most High God. *That* kind of reminder and possibility I can't find anywhere else."

The church has received from God the gift of ministry. In order for that gift to be received as it is intended, both ordained and lay ministers must be fully involved and respected in their own roles. Community is completely realized only when respect for the two is kept in balance, not polarized, and when neither one is subordinated to the other—when they move in concert, not competition.

There is potential for imbalance in both directions. A *clergy elitism* would hold that ministry is really only for pastors, and that they are aided in their ministry by those lay people who support what they are doing in the congregation and outside it. Lay people, in this view, have no valid ministry of their own. A *lay elitism* would regard ministry as given by God to the whole people of God, who only for the sake of convenience and efficiency ordain some of their number to proclaim the gospel in Word and sacraments and administer the work of the church. In this view of the church, clergy are seen as rising from and receiving their authority only from congregations, or the priesthood of believers, but not directly from God.

The proper balance in this matter is relatively easy to see, and it appears from our data that Lutherans can (in their minds, at least) successfully integrate the ministry of the laity and the clergy, recognizing the importance of both. But understanding this balance and integration is easier for many than acting on it. Part of the function of congregational community is not only to speak about but to symbolize the complementary and integrated functions of the ministry of the laity and clergy.

Pastors symbolize the presence and significance of the ministry of the laity, for example, when church bulletins are liberally sprinkled with the names of people engaged in ministries of various kinds, when groups of persons (church school teachers or youth workers, for instance) are periodically recognized within worship services, and when intercessory prayers are offered for the ministry that some individual or group is carrying out.

Lay people symbolize their recognition and respect for the ministry of the clergy when they seek pastors' insights, ask for advice or cautions on a given plan, seek the benefit of their experience, ask for their theological perspective on particular decisions, ask that they share some of their special knowledge or training with some of the laity, show enthusiasm for their continuing education, and, above all, expect from them God's word of forgiveness.

The ministry of the priesthood of all believers and the ordained public ministry of Word and sacraments must be kept in complementary perspective. Once they are out of balance, the ramifications spread in all directions, and true Christian community erodes.

Fullness of Christian community demands more than the gentle, caring acts of encouraging, complimenting, cooperating, and appreciating. It demands that we wrestle with tough, disagreeable, disturbing issues, and in that process reveal our weaknesses, failures, fears, and sins—that we become vulnerable to one another so we can help, confront, admonish, forgive, and thus show that we care for each other. In such community, Bible study will not focus exclusively on the beauties of the 23rd Psalm, but will also raise uncomfortable questions and issues that people meet and try to deal with alone in daily life. "As a Christian, how do I deal with the employee who has done well for two years, but whose drinking is now affecting his work? If I decide I must, is it un-Christian to fire him?" "I'm in the business of selling hardware. Does Christianity have anything to say to what I do, other than asking me to be fair with people and pleasant to them?" "We know about the zero population growth thing, but we like children and want a big family. Is it Christian to have, or not have, children?"

Christian community implies that when we are open in this way to one another we can then offer one another forgiveness, acceptance, and support in living through problems that may be beyond solution. This kind of self-revealing, vulnerable living-out of the law and gospel creates new people in a way that no congregation can if it lives only on the dressed-up, superficial, Sunday-best surface of life. If groups within the church are willing to take the risk of knowing and understanding one another thoroughly, willing to reveal that they face questions to which no one has answers, they may find that they have come to a new understanding and experience of community.

If we had been designing this book according to our own logic rather than shaping it to follow the areas of ministry identified by Lutherans as they answered the questionnaire, there wouldn't be both a chapter on congregational community and one on liturgical leadership. Since both deal with aspects of Christian worship, they would have been presented together. Our reflections on preaching and leading worship have therefore been divided between these two chapters. Some of them are here, and some are in Chapter 10. Their origins may be in either chapter, or both.

The division that appears in the book, however, illustrates the very thing we want to make one observation about. Lutherans apparently make a mental division between the more formal, aesthetic, dignified, impersonal liturgical aspects of worship and the more warm, personal, communal, contemporaneous preaching and teaching which larger numbers value more highly. There are, therefore, a series of issues over which anyone planning and conducting worship is pulled in opposite directions. Some pastors and congregations consistently favor one direction over the other. Our data imply that the most useful and community-sustaining worship will occur when attention is paid to *both* halves of a series of contrasting elements.

The first set of contrasting elements that need equal attention is an emphasis on the transcendent presence of God, in contrast with a sense of the human community that gathers in that presence. To help individuals be conscious only of the presence of God, without reminding them of the community of which they are a part, is to move from the category of corporate worship to the category of private worship—which is not the same thing at all. On the other hand, to encourage consciousness only of one another, without an accompanying sense of God's presence, is to lose that which reminds worshipers of their primary identity as God's children.

A second pair of opposites is the tension that exists between appreciation of the long and revered tradition of the church and the pressure to be creative, innovative, and relevant. To move all the way toward one and discard the other is to lose something extremely important. There is power, when one is singing a hymn text from the 6th century or praying a 12th century collect, in remembering that the people of God—thousands upon thousands of them—in a variety of places and circumstances over hundreds of years have been nourished and sustained by these words. To discard them as no longer relevant smacks of the presumption of a 16-year-old who is certain that he or she knows all there is to learn about life. But it is no wiser to cling to the tried and traditional without leaving room for innovation and the release of the creativity that is present now. To do that would be to rob ourselves of that which is more immediately relevant and to deny the ever-new expressions of God's creative Spirit.

A third of the pairs of apparent opposites that must be kept in creative balance is the inclusion of that which is carefully prepared and planned along with the freedom to be creative or spontaneous within worship services in response to the demands or promptings of the moment. We believe that pastors and lay leaders who respect their congregations and callings will put much time and effort into planning worship. They will pay attention to the use of language and the appropriateness and aptness of illustrations. They will prepare. But they will also take the freedom to depart from the prepared script when the situation calls for it.

Our view is that the most appropriate worship atmosphere and most lively congregational worship and community will exist where both pastor and people worship and live with one foot in Chapter 6 and one in Chapter 10.

Component characteristics: Chapter 7

From central to peripheral

32 Responsible Group Leadership
27 Promotion of Mutuality
31 Effective Administration
24 Sharing of Congregational Leadership
25 Creative Use of Conflict
40 Respect for Proper Procedures
39 Redemptive Forthrightness
16 Development of Interpersonal Trust
41 Encouragement of Expression of Disagreement
57 Innovative Style of Leadership

In order of Lutheran ranking

16 Development of Interpersonal Trust
24 Sharing of Congregational Leadership
25 Creative Use of Conflict
27 Promotion of Mutuality
31 Effective Administration
32 Responsible Group Leadership
39 Redemptive Forthrightness
40 Respect for Proper Procedures
41 Encouragement of Expression of Disagreement
57 Innovative Style of Leadership

Making Ministry of Administration

The tone of voice in which some pastors pronounce the word *administration* makes it sound like profanity. The tone identifies it as representing all that the speaker abhors, avoids, puts off, and hopes will some day fall off the bottom of the pastoral priority list.

Our study presents evidence that younger pastors hold this view more strongly than older pastors, and seminary students more strongly still. Perhaps it takes years of experience with administration for its true nature to become clear. When that takes place, pastors no longer see administration as a task divorced from the real work of ministry, but germane to it; somewhere along the road pastors realize that the word carries ministry within it: ad-*ministra*-tion.

It may be that some of the aversion to administration also stems from too narrow a view of it. The scope of this feature of ministry is much broader and more complex than the letter-writing and record-keeping that probably looms in the foreground of the popular image of administration. When one views this area of ministry as most Lutherans see it, an effective ministry of administration emerges as having far less in common with the drudgery of the desk-bound clerk than with the scope and nature of the work of an orchestral conductor.

An orchestra, warming up before the conductor arrives, bears certain similarities to some congregations. The total effect is of energized chaos; there are a lot of good things going on, but without unity or direction. There are a few virtuoso performances here and there, an occasional duet, and a lot of earnest working away without reference to anyone else—all of which may produce dissonance and discomfort for both performers and observers. It requires the skills, understandings, talents, and rapport with the orchestra of a good conductor to bring order from chaos, and to give direction to that energy.

The same kind of leadership is required of a pastor in a typical congregation, if there isn't going to be a powerful lot of chaos. Lutherans rank this area of ministry as fifth in importance, which causes it to fall into the lower "contributes very much" range of importance for effective Christian ministry. Congregations vary, of course, in their need for administrative direction; many have seemed to fare remarkably well during interims without pastoral leadership. But when this happens, the congregation may be operating on the lingering effects of past leadership, as an orchestra can continue for some time, even after the conductor steps away from the podium. But that independence is short-term. Every congregation can benefit by having a pastor who can identify the superabundance of talent, energy, and dedication present and guide it into basically harmonious joint ministry. Even the finest orchestras, staffed with individually-accomplished concert artists, require direction under a wisely wielded baton if their efforts are to materialize in a faithful and inspired rendering of the score.

Of the many things a good orchestral conductor knows and does, there are three that Lutherans want of their pastors as leaders and administrators in congregations: (1) they want a pastor to have skill like a conductor's ability in reading and interpreting a musical score, that is, to be able to work within a framework or structure; (2) they want a pastor who knows that discord is not to be shunned, but to be investigated and sensitively dealt with; and (3) they want a pastor who, like a conductor, knows how to facilitate individual efforts and channel energies to produce a mutually-desired result.

Operating within structures

An orchestral director knows how to read a musical score, does so, and generally directs the orchestra in keeping with it. He or she knows that structures are disciplines that help, not boundaries that imprison. Of the ten characteristics that make up this area of ministry, three have to do with the capacity of a pastor to operate within a stated framework or structure. These are "Sharing of Congregational Leadership" (24), "Respect for Proper Procedures" (40), and "Innovative Style of Leadership"

(57). Pastors possessing these three characteristics show sensitivity to the contexts within which they work, are comfortable with a certain amount of "given-ness" in congregational situations, and yet have interest in broadening the base from which congregations work—they are able to write new arrangements of the score.

Sharing of Congregational Leadership (24). A section entitled, "The Pastor as Leader" appeared in the original questionnaire to which the 5000 Lutherans responded. When one seminary president examined this section he concluded that its items did not describe leadership at all. Why? Because, he said, they do not describe a pastor as being where the buck stops—the one taking final responsibility for things.

In the concept of leadership that this characteristic describes (and, indeed, in this whole area of ministry), leadership does not take the form of being a final arbiter or prime decision maker. Lutherans don't want a pastor who unfurls plans and programs like an enormous banner under which everyone is expected to rally. They expect a pastor to share responsibility with lay leaders by helping them become adept at developing strategies and making decisions themselves. In this sense of shared leadership, a player-coach of an athletic team might provide a better analogy to a pastor's role than an orchestral conductor.

There are, in fact, times when lay people may appropriately teach pastors, helping them to be sensitive to the existing customs and traditions of a congregation and to be aware of (though not irrevocably bound by) relevant decisions that have been made in the past. In decision making, a pastor with this kind of leadership style takes initiative in the form of providing facts people need for making decisions, or showing how to establish long-range goals or develop an overall parish strategy. The central message of this characteristic is that a pastor should neither take over nor abandon leadership, but share it with the members of the congregation. One item received the highest rank among professionals of all the items in the characteristic, and second highest among all Lutherans: "Shares leadership with lay leaders chosen by the congregation."

The mutual ministry to be carried out in partnership with the laity includes such specifics as setting long-range goals together, employing time-saving administrative procedures, evaluating the success of current programs in meeting parish needs, and making informed use of parish and community records in planning. The laity and clergy agreed on the need for a pastoral administration that provides a sound basis for mutual decision making. What is implied, but not stated in the characteristic, is the possibility that in congregations where certain lay persons are vocationally trained in goal-setting and planning, they may provide leadership in ministry by sharing this special expertise with pastors and other lay people.

Respect for Proper Procedures (40). Pastors who exhibit this characteristic accept normal channels of procedure as one of the givens of ministry. They accept the discipline of parliamentary procedure and see that areas of responsibility and chains of command are clarified for all concerned. Respect for procedures means also that pastors will press the governing boards of congregations to establish fair policies and practices for their employees so that there, too, clearly stated procedures can be adhered to with integrity. They will help congregations evaluate how they treat their employees and think through policies that go beyond the single rule that what is the least and cheapest is best. Such pastors will also observe professional courtesies such as informing neighboring pastors if members of their congregations seek them out for ministry.

Innovative Style of Leadership (57). Some Lutherans lean toward innovation, and others toward leaving things as they are. Demonstration of awareness, courtesy, and respect does not demand that one never initiate change. Orchestral conductors sometimes rearrange scores. Though they do not place quite so high a priority on this characteristic as on others in this area of ministry, 69% of Lutherans say that a pastor's search for new patterns or styles of organizational life in a congregation and the church at large "contributes quite a bit" or "contributes very much" to ministry. They place equally high priority on bringing members of minority groups into positions of leadership, and they appreciate a pastor's effort to enlarge a congregation's cultural interests. Some will doubt the appropriateness of pastors' spending part of their time as "ministers of culture," especially if viewed as art for art's sake. But others will affirm that any investment that makes the message of the church more comprehensible to the modern mind is a good investment of time.

Before going further with this chapter, you might find it useful to reflect on your own ability to work within structures. On the left, check the column that indicates what is true for you. On the right, check what you wish you could do better—and might, with some training or guidance.

Checklist on working within structures

Doing well				*Want to improve*	
yes	*no*			*yes*	*no*
		Shares leadership with lay leaders chosen by the congregation.			
		Knows and uses parish and community records and data in program building.			

Evaluates how well the congregation's programs are meeting the people's needs.

Accepts the discipline of parliamentary procedure in formal meetings.

Clarifies areas of responsibility and chains of command in administrative matters.

When possible, clears with neighboring clergy before ministering to their members.

Presses governing board of congregation to establish fair policies and practices for employees.

Works to enlarge the cultural interests of the congregation.

Works for new patterns or styles of organizational life in the church.

Brings minority people into positions of leadership.

Dealing with discord

The issue of remodeling was up for a decision at a church business meeting. Following the report of the long-range study committee, a number of speeches were given echoing the committee's recommendation of the proposed project. Little opposition was voiced. But when the ballots were counted, the project was resoundingly defeated. This was obviously a church where unspoken rules of behavior prevented the open expression of disagreement, but did not prevent disagreement from existing, or from having a final and bitterly felt effect.

An important move toward bringing order out of chaos, whether one is a conductor or pastor-administrator, is to deal with discord and work toward getting people in tune with one another. Three of the characteristics that form this area of ministry relate to the practice of deliberately exposing tensions and points of disagreement so that they can be dealt with. These are "Encouragement of Expression of Disagreement" (41), "Redemptive Forthrightness" (39), and "Creative Use of Conflict" (25).

"Encouragement of Expression of Disagreement" (41). This set of items concentrates on Lutherans' desire for pastors to help people feel free to express their opinions, knowing they will be heard and their expressions respected. A pastor who exhibits these characteristics not only allows others' opinions to be heard, but ferrets them out, asks people to express

their opinions if they have not done so, and creates opportunities especially designed to help people air their differences.

Since general observation would make it seem that people frequently operate on the assumption that disagreement within the church is sinful and to be avoided at all costs, it is a pleasant surprise that Lutherans say this characteristic "contributes very much" to effective ministry. Most Lutherans want church members to feel that it is all right to disagree with their pastor. Further, they want their pastors to "Discourage the use of stereotyped sex roles in assigning responsible positions within the congregation." Such a stance opposes pastors whose regular counsel to appointing committees is to make sure that people selected to work together "are compatible, since, of course, we wouldn't want any uncomfortable situations." Though the items in this characteristic encourage the expression of disagreement, there is no hint that constant sniping or incessant haggling over every detail is either healthy or welcome.

Redemptive Forthrightness (39). Creating the conditions for others to express disagreement is not to be an easy out for pastors who are personally uncomfortable about confrontation. This characteristic makes that point eminently clear.

On the average, Lutherans place almost as high priority on pastors' speaking directly and redemptively with persons about their errors and estrangements as they do on encouraging the expression of disagreement within the church. But this characteristic does not consist only of forthrightness; it involves being *redemptively* forthright. This means speaking directly and kindly with those who are delinquent in churchgoing, attending Communion, or making contributions. It means being constructive when making evaluations of the church staff, and communicating honest judgments to them.

This note of redemptive and reconciliatory concern is further demonstrated by the item, "Acts as mediator between parents and estranged young people." To take this one task as a major focus could exhaust a pastor's reserves of courage and lovingkindness. But the presence of this item here shows that both candor *and* the search for reconciliation are essential ingredients of a ministry of administration.

Creative Use of Conflict (25). This characteristic speaks of the pastor's role in opening lines of communication between differing groups in order to help them move beyond anger to constructive action.

Shortly after World War II one of the authors was present at an international conference of youth leaders sponsored by the Lutheran World Federation. During the second evening the meeting broke down under a sharp exchange of strongly voiced but differing opinions. Norwegians, still smarting from the German occupation, opposed the Germans' position.

Indian and African leaders, conscious of being the "have nots," took issue with the apparently affluent and successful Americans. Jan Kooiman, then a university student from Holland, compared the event with a number of other international conferences he had attended. "In every one," he said, "we had experiences of conflict like this. I've noticed, however, that where there is a common bond of faith, the people move toward each other and try to resolve their differences. When that bond is lacking, the chasm usually widens as days progress."

Conflicts, which characterize every human organization, usually surface along the lines of old resentments and unresolved hurts. To be surprised when they occur in the church is to expect people in congregations not to be human. A pastor who deals effectively with discord is no doubt as interested in unity as other people, but refuses to buy the false appearance of unity at the price of silence and unresolved problems. Such a pastor wants to speak and to hear the truth spoken in love, and to move toward real understanding and effective action.

You may want to complete the personal checklist on dealing with discord which follows. On the left, check what is true for you. On the right, check what you want to improve.

Checklist on dealing with discord

Doing well			Want to improve	
yes	no		yes	no
		Shows skill in moving people from anger to creative action.		
		On controversial issues, concentrates on helping all to understand the issues.		
		Shows ability to offer an opposing view without attacking the person.		
		When he or she sees the need, is not afraid to confront individuals privately with their sins.		
		Acts as mediator between parents and estranged young people.		
		Shows skill in training and evaluating staff.		
		Personally confronts individuals whose gossiping is damaging others.		
		Speaks kindly but directly with parishioners who are delinquent in churchgoing, communion attendance, and giving.		

Working toward harmonious action

The first two sets of characteristics that make up this area that we are calling "Making Ministry of Administration" deal with a sensitivity to structures and an ability to handle discord. But these two alone will not produce much in the way of desired results. A third facet of administrative ability is what enables congregations to move, within existing structures and beyond the barriers of discord, to orderly, harmonious, person-respecting action. The four characteristics that describe this move toward significant accomplishment are "Responsible Group Leadership" (32), "Development of Interpersonal Trust" (16), "Promotion of Mutuality" (27), and "Effective Administration" (31).

Responsible Group Leadership (32). Resolving conflict is a good thing, but minimizing the incidence of conflict over time is perhaps even better. This characteristic, central to the meaning of the whole area of pastoral administration, outlines an administrative sophistication that finds pastors seldom called on to stamp out fires because they have done such a good job of fire prevention. Responsible group leadership centers in the capacity to anticipate where conflict may arise and to intervene before it becomes heated or destructive. It also involves postponing decisions until the heat of emotional conflict has dissipated, and describes the pastor who serves as arbitrator rather than taking sides on an issue.

The characteristic shows itself in a pastor's effort to tie innovations to the recognized needs of a congregation, and to seek broad and informed congregational support before making detailed plans for new projects. It is reflected in the direct and positive way in which a pastor deals with a person who must be removed from the staff of a church. A carefully thought-through approach to each of these situations minimizes the chance of its resulting in bitter feelings.

Encouraging individual responsibility is a subtle art and represents the final facet of this characteristic. In part it is accomplished through developing among church members a sense of responsibility for the financial support of the congregation, by means of both preaching and example. It is also encouraged by the pastor who carefully chooses the right persons for specific tasks and, having oriented them to the tasks, gives them freedom to carry them out in their own ways.

Development of Interpersonal Trust (16) and *Promotion of Mutuality (27).* The development of an atmosphere of mutual trust and respect is an important part of the administrative function, as Lutherans outline it. The first of this pair of characteristics gives a very short and specialized description of pastors who develop feelings of trust and confidence between themselves and members by taking the time to know parishioners well, and by going the further step of seeking out those who are discontented to hear their story. The second characteristic draws a broader picture but plays on the same theme—ideas expressed both by pastors and people in an atmosphere of trust, freedom, and respect. Respect, indeed, is a thread that runs through all of the items in this characteristic. Promoters of mutuality try to include more members in decision making, relate to other staff members in ways consistent with their own theology, are careful to explain to affected groups why changes are being made, and cause people to feel needed in the ongoing work of their parishes.

A careful look at these two characteristics indicates that Lutherans believe one of the most valuable tools of the successful pastor-administrator is the creation of an atmosphere of candid openness and respect. It is not surprising that Characteristic 6, "Loving Devotion to People" (described in Chapter 2), correlates significantly with both of these administrative qualities.

Effective Administration (31). Some church people who work in the business world think wistfully about how their congregations could be run. During the week they employ sophisticated and effective business procedures in the handling of money and staff, and know these could enhance the good stewardship of God's resources in the church. Some pastors, on the other hand, become nervous when such people talk about efficient business procedures. They are perhaps uncomfortably aware that their own lack of administrative training or sophistication is showing, or are perhaps fearful that the church may lose its reliance on God's providence. Lutherans are here giving a reminder that God's church is both divine and human. Because the church is human, it needs efficient organization. Because it is divine, it must rely on God's Holy Spirit. To ignore one and rely wholly on the other would be to reduce the ability of the church to fulfill its mission.

"Effective Administration" presents a description of efficient administrative procedures employed within the context of Christian stewardship. Three of the items describe activities that promote open communication: being accessible to any other staff members employed by a congregation, facilitating communication between a congregation and its church body, and soliciting ideas from members. The other five items relate to employment of good stewardship in handling the resources of energy, finances, possessions, and time—both in a pastor's personal life and on behalf of a congregation.

You may wish to fill out a checklist for this group of characteristics. As with the previous checklists, on the left, check what is true for you. On the right, check those items on which you wish to improve.

Checklist on working toward harmonious action

Doing well			Want to improve	
yes	no		yes	no

Often anticipates where conflict may arise among members.

Discourages groups from making decisions in the heat of emotional conflict.

On occasion will bring conflict out into the open in a constructive way.

Lets others "run the show" when they are in charge.

Takes time to know parishioners well.

Seeks out discontented persons in the congregation to try to understand their complaints.

Develops a feeling of trust and confidence between self and members.

In conflict situations lets people know where he or she stands in a way that does not alienate them.

Works to broaden the base of participation in the decision-making process of the congregation.

Points out the values implied in alternatives the congregation is considering when making decisions.

Allows persons freedom in carrying out assigned responsibilities.

Helps people to know what changes are being made and why they are recommended.

Causes people to feel they are needed in the ongoing work of the parish.

Is easily accessible to staff.

Invites and solicits ideas from staff members.

Administers with a sense of stewardship the monies and properties assigned to his or her care.

Keeps improving own management and business skills.

Shows skill in managing church funds (e.g., establishing budgets, raising funds, employing good accounting procedures).

Emphases and Contrasts

Who cares most about administration? In a typical congregation, one can expect young people, with their enthusiasm and optimism, not to be nearly as concerned as older people, and lay people not to be quite as convinced as professionals of the need for it. Beyond that, the more educated will probably be slightly more excited about three aspects of administration. Satisfied pillars of the church and seminarians will likely each emphasize the relevance of one aspect, while seminarians join with laity to considerably underemphasize another. Among church bodies, members of the Lutheran Church–Missouri Synod (LCMS) rather than the Lutheran Church in America (LCA) can be expected to be somewhat more ready to applaud one practice sometimes included in church administration. We will look at the less extensive contrasts first.

Variation among churches

Though differences among members of the three Lutheran church bodies are relatively scarce in this study, one exists here. Members of the LCMS showed greater appreciation than members of the LCA for "Redemptive Forthrightness" (39). This greater openness to ministry that confronts people with their sins shows that Missouri Synod members tend to think of a pastor's functions as including that of guide or disciplinarian. This fits with that synod's historic emphasis on the Office of the Keys. Members of the LCMS are, on the average, likely to be more accepting of ministers who present themselves as the authorities in matters of sin and grace—but not necessarily in matters of parish administration. Though we report a difference by church body in this area of ministry, we feel impelled to point out that the difference exists for only *one* of a total of ten aspects of administration. On the other nine there is no important difference.

What's important to satisfied lay leaders

People whose participation in congregational life is a major source of satisfaction especially appreciate pastors who recognize the authority of lay leaders and cooperate with them. These core members gave a

Table 6. Groups that place higher value on characteristics of Area V, "Making Ministry of Administration."

	older	clergy	more educated	seminary seniors
24 Sharing of Congregational Leadership	HHH	H		
40 Respect for Proper Procedures	HHH	H		LL (vs. other professionals)
57 Innovative Style of Leadership	HHH	HH		
41 Encouragement of Expression of Disagreement		HH	H	
39 Redemptive Forthrightness	HH	H		
25 Creative Use of Conflict	HH	H		
32 Responsible Group Leadership	HHH	H	H	
16 Development of Interpersonal Trust		H		H (vs. laity)
27 Promotion of Mutuality	HH	HH	H	
31 Effective Administration	HHH			

As compared with Lutherans' average ratings (or other groups specifically listed):

HHH = much higher
HH = higher
H = slightly higher
L = slightly lower
LL = lower
LLL = much lower

slightly-higher-than-average rating to "Sharing of Congregational Leadership" (24).

An appreciation that comes with education

The more educated joined the clergy at three points of emphasis. They placed slightly-higher-than-average value on "Responsible Group Leadership" (32), "Promotion of Mutuality" (27), and "Encouragement of Expression of Disagreement" (41). The common element here appears to be the value educated members place on engaging in give-and-take on an equal plane with their pastors and with other members when decisions or conflict are to be worked out.

Contrasting views of laity and clergy

The laity are not as convinced of the importance of administrative skill as clergy are. The only criterion that clergy did not especially stress is "Effective Administration" (31). A reading of the items revals that it consists mostly of clearly business-oriented tasks, which study after study shows that ministers tend to dislike.

One segment of the clergy—seminary seniors—showed themselves to be different from the rest of the clergy, and from older Lutherans. Along with other young people generally, they placed a much-lower-than-average value on "Respect for Proper Procedures" (40). On this point the youth of most seminary seniors is apparently more influential than seminary education and whatever other influences transform lay people into clergy.

The perspective from experience

Church members who have reached their later years placed higher value on all but two of these administrative practices. One is a characteristic that older Lutherans may see as threatening, "Encouragement of Expression of Disagreement" (41), and one they may see as too personal, "Development of Interpersonal Trust" (16). Most older Lutherans instead accent more clearly religious and pious practices, and those that reinforce traditional ways of doing things. To illustrate, they rated "Respect for Proper Procedures" (40) very much higher than the Lutheran average. The next greatest discrepancy between older Lutherans and the Lutheran average was on "Responsible Group Leadership" (32). One place where older Lutherans broke with their pattern of reinforcing the importance of doing things "according to the book" was in rating "Innovative Style of Leadership" (57) much higher than the Lutheran average. But even there, what they are saying is, "Yes, we are open to innovation and change if normal channels and procedures are followed."

Since they placed high value on "Creative Use of Conflict" (25), but not on "Encouragement of Expression of Disagreement" (41), it is clear that they see value in conflict as long as it is eventually resolved constructively. But they have scant enthusiasm for purposely opening and clarifying points of tension and disagreement merely in the interest of complete openness and candid clarity.

Of the 10 characteristics of this area of ministry, "Development of Interpersonal Trust" (16) was generally rated highest as contributing to effective ministry, with professionals and especially seminary seniors placing the very highest value on it. "Innovative Style of Leadership" (57) was, on the average, given the lowest rating, with younger lay people appreciating it least. Nine of the ten practices were judged on the average to contribute "very much" to efficient administration. Only "Innovative Style of Leadership" (57) was, on the average, judged to contribute "quite a bit" to effective Christian ministry as a whole.

The kind of parish administration that Lutherans generally expect and appreciate from their pastors is more like that of an orchestral conductor or player-coach than it is that of a chief executive. Pastors who view parish activities predominantly as their own programs to be carried out by the laity, after they alone have devised and proposed them, are not likely to be well received. But pastors who view the development and execution of parish programs as a joint effort (or largely as decision making, work, and ministry of the laity in which pastors participate by providing counsel, conflict-resolution, coordination, and integration) are likely to be well received and respected. A medium to low profile, participatory style of leadership is likely to be generally most effective in Lutheran congregations—especially when pastors recognize that efficient administration is also ministry.

Reflections

Whether they like the idea or not, pastors cannot help administering. They may do it badly or well, but they all administer. When a conflict arises, pastors choose whether to mediate, take over and settle, or quietly escape. The choice defines the administrative style, but pastors cannot *not* administer. Money comes into and flows out of congregations. Pastors' involvement or noninvolvement with that flow of resources reveals administrative style. Points of decision arise in the church, and whether a particular decision is to buy more mimeograph paper or to take on a new staff member, the style of a pastor's involvement in that decision is *administrative*. People call on the phone, asking, "Who do you think ought to handle this matter?" There is no way to escape the ministry of administration. All pastors have are choices among methods of carrying it out.

Sources of avoidance

We began this chapter by acknowledging that many pastors denigrate and avoid the administrative work of ministry. It is sometimes instructive to look at the reasons why people avoid things, because within those reasons there often lies an implied corrective that needs no further explanation. We think of two possible reasons why pastors avoid the study and practice of administration.

The first is that many believe administrative work is outside their proper theological and pastoral functions, that it is work that can, and therefore should, be done by people who are not pastors, and that pastors should reserve their time and energies for those things that only pastors are trained or ordained to do. To be concerned about the possibility of frittering away one's energies on nonessentials is wise. However, a pastor who avoids administration on those grounds may be substituting a stereotype, a caricature, of administrative activity for the real thing. Stereotypes have their uses. They sometimes provide a kind of mental abbreviation that enables us to think quickly or make on-the-spot judgments about things. But when a stereotype or caricature is regularly and seriously treated as if it were the whole thing, we operate on false premises. Unfortunately, many pastors may hold in their minds a caricature of the administrator's role: a round-shouldered, desk-bound clerk, doing little more than shuffling papers, answering phones, and checking off lists. If they substitute this caricature for the spectrum of person-serving activities that constitute the whole of real administration in the church (or anywhere else), and then reject this narrow image, they may also reject and devalue the larger whole that is so essential to the ministry of the church.

A second possible reason for avoidance (and one less comfortable to see in oneself) is that an administrator does not play the role of a star performer. Administration does not offer the ego satisfaction of addressing carefully-prepared golden words to 900 people at a time. An administrator, instead, fills the role of facilitator: a worker behind the scenes, negotiator, helper of others, and sharer of leadership. An administrator often works alone or with a very few people at a time—arranging, meeting, thinking through, mediating, explaining, applying creative thought. It is a ministry of service.

A gospel-tinged administration

Because theology has implications for group relationships as well as for individual relationships, the gospel has implications for administra-

tion. The way Lutherans connect the items of this area of ministry indicates that they see a close relationship between certain elements of
leadership style. They value a church where the gospel is not only
preached but experienced in a redemptive community. There can be a
ministry of gospel-informed and gospel-shaped administration within a
congregation, as is shown by items such as these:

"Has an understanding of conflict as it relates to own theology."
"Relates to members of staff in manner consistent with own theology."
"Engenders a sense of community where members are concerned for
each other."
"In a conflict situation, makes sure opinions of the minority are heard."

The data from this study imply that if the gospel is to be not only the
message of the church but the *style of its life* together, as well, the tasks
of administration must be taken seriously. One way of taking them seriously would be for a pastor and church council together to take a careful look at the administrative and decision-making process as it works in
that congregation. Using insights from this chapter—or perhaps the checklists—they might together evaluate their style as a leadership team. They
might ask questions such as the following: How do our administrative
practices relate to our understanding of the gospel? What does this do to
people within our congregation? Does it open up to them greater opportunities for freedom and responsibility in the gospel? Does it give them
greater opportunity for being part of the people of God? Does it tend
to cut them off, hem them in, and provide a hierarchical, legalistic style
of leadership? (For example, do we hold congregational meetings where
the overriding desire for a quick, smooth meeting make it clear that asking difficult questions or suggesting different ideas is not really wanted—
implying that gospel talk about sharing ministry decisions responsibly
together is just talk, and not to be taken seriously? On the other hand,
do we so emphasize or demand the participation of everyone at every
point that people begin erroneously to believe they can't trust decisions
made by others in the congregation unless they were in on them?) Does
our administrative style offer members opportunity to take responsibility
commensurate with their gifts?

To pick up one possible direction the discussion of that last question
might take, such a group might begin to consider how well their congregation or pastor is facilitating the total ministry of their people, taking
seriously the desire and ability of members to minister when they are not
within the walls of the church or engaged in a clearly-identified churchly
function. This kind of administrative inquiry would identify the capacity
of the pastor to see members of the congregation as peers in ministry,

possessing expertise and in fact doing ministry in fields outside the church. A series of examples in which real people are offering such ministry may serve to illustrate:

• A clinical psychologist not only thinks of and carries out her work as part of her own life's ministry, but is available as a resource to the pastor in working with difficult counseling problems.

• A bank trust officer is able to counsel another church member not only as regards the financial soundness of various investments or bequests, but also in terms of the potential for Christian stewardship in those financial options.

• A middle-aged woman in a congregation has been observed to have an insightful, supportive way of dealing with young people that has been a major force in keeping many of them interested in church throughout their high school years. Though she does not work with the formally-structured youth program, she is asked to meet periodically with youth workers to share her observations and intuitive skills.

• A coordinator of volunteers at a hospital works regularly with the pastor, giving help in filling a particular volunteer spot, but also offering insights on ways of working with volunteers—information any pastor can well use.

A ministry of administration that results in more and more relationships of this kind may not show up in an annual statistical report, but would surely be working toward the increase of effective ministry in and to the world.

Christians dealing with conflict

Though this is not the place for a full-blown discussion of conflict management, perhaps some comment may be worthwhile, since conflict (acknowledged or unacknowledged) is so surely a part of all life together, including life within the church, and the way it is handled is viewed as so important by Lutherans.

Like the whole field of administration, conflict management is not a field one can successfully avoid. Instead, one develops one style or another for dealing with it. As with administration, a favorite method is avoidance—pretending that conflicts are not there, sweeping them under the rug, and keeping them out of sight. Informal meetings where the real decisions are made but which occur outside the official meetings, telephone diplomacy, and other such devices are standard tools of conflict-avoiders.

The first step toward more effective conflict management may be a straight look, by pastors and lay members, at how conflict is customarily managed in their congregations. The goal of such a step would be to discover more effective and more Christian ways of dealing with differences. Too often personal habits and group traditions of long standing have become so much second nature that people no longer realize what they are doing.

In learning to play tennis, one learns early to use the racket to hit the ball, not clout an opponent over the head. In dealing with conflict, it is similarly important to learn to attack a problem, in search of a solution, but not directly to attack another Christian who is on the opposite side of a question. Most of us don't realize how often we attack one another when we differ. It is important to recognize that those who are on the opposite side of a question are not less Christian for opposing us. Being Christian doesn't necessarily mean being on a particular side of a question. Having recognized this, the challenge then becomes, How do I affirm my Christian opponents' faith and self-esteem at the same time that I take the opposite side of an issue?

One church has developed a method of deciding on budget and program priorities that moves in this direction. Its structure eliminates the necessity to vote no on anyone's proposal. On a given Sunday afternoon, all those who want to promote a particular project for the coming year prepare displays, booths, or other explanatory material. After all presentations have been viewed, members vote by volunteering contributions of time and money to those projects they choose. The governing body of the church then puts into operation those projects for which sufficient resources of money and time are available. Sponsors of other, unsuccessful projects can make another and perhaps more persuasive presentation the next year. No sponsor is made to feel permanently defeated or rejected.

Though this plan is not without its possible flaws, it illustrates the point that there are fresh ways of structuring necessary decision making in congregations that get the job done and at the same time work toward preserving every member's self-esteem and general goodwill.

Implications for denominational leaders

The nourishing of pastoral skills in this area could be materially aided by leaders of denominational judicatories. The sponsorship of district-wide seminar experiences on the relation of the gospel to creative organizational development or administration in parishes might have two effects. Such experiences might have an immediate effect on the pastors who attend, and an accompanying effect on the work and worship of the congregations represented. They might also have long-range effect in that the sponsorship of such seminars would underline the importance church leaders accord a gospel-shaped administration. It has a powerful effect on the group life of churches in their care when denominational administrators acquire and internalize an understanding of how the gospel relates to individuals working with groups, and when they demonstrate those understandings as they deal with the pastors in their charge.

Component characteristics: Chapter 8

From central to peripheral

In order of Lutheran ranking

Ministry of Counseling

Over the period of a month, most pastors are in contact with people struggling under a variety of burdens and stresses. Some pastors might deal with all of the following in a single day:

- a man trying to decide whether a job promotion makes it worthwhile to uproot his family and move to another state.
- an unmarried college girl who is pregnant and trying to decide about abortion.
- a young man who feels shut out of his high school group, church group, and family.
- a dedicated church member who is angrily questioning God's justice in allowing the death of her son.
- a drug-dependent young man who wants to talk about whether he should continue living with his current girlfriend.

When pastors meet people like these, they are confronted with the raw, bleeding edges of life, pleading for them to do something to ease the suffering. As one pastor put it, "An endless parade of pain knocks at my door, comes to my study, and calls me in the middle of the night." Another added, "Yet there is no time when I have the kind of opportunity to communicate the gospel that I have when I am with a hurting person who has confidence in the help I can provide, or that God can provide through me."

It is significant that the New Testament word for ministry, *diakonia*, carries the primary meaning of "serving the needs of people." During his ministry, Christ conveyed the gospel both by the life-giving word of instruction and by an immediate and concrete ministry of healing. In his ministry, bodily healing and salvation from sin were inextricably linked. It should not be surprising, therefore, that Lutherans place considerable importance on ministry that deals sensitively and helpfully with those wounded spirits who seek personal healing within the Christian church.

The rating Lutherans gave to this feature of ministry was sixth in a list of ten, but its distance in perceived value from either "Making Ministry of Administration" (rated 2.65) or "Community Through Word and Sacraments" (rated 2.76) was very small, indeed. As a total area, it still achieved an overall rating (2.66) of "contributes very much" to effective ministry.

Though Lutherans see counseling as important, they do not see it as a separate area of ministry in quite the same way as members of many other churches do. This four-characteristic feature of ministry, in fact, represents a rather loose-knit grouping. Mathematical analysis of Lutheran perceptions makes it nearly as sensible to assign two of these characteristics—"Empathetic Aid in Suffering" (42) and "Enabling and Perceptive Counseling" (17)—to the ministry area "Reaching Out with Compassion to Community and World" described in Chapter 9. It would be equally valid to assign the other two characteristics—"Intentional Counseling" (46) and "Gracious Availability" (21)—to the area of ministry described in Chapter 1. This means that although Lutherans recognize theologically-based counseling and guidance as a distinct area of ministry, they also see it as closely involved with two other areas of ministry—pastors' witness to their own faith, and the church's outreach to the community and world.

What characteristics are a part of Lutherans' expectations of those who offer this healing ministry? There are four of them, each describing a different facet of ministry to wounded and struggling spirits.

Enabling and Perceptive Counseling (17). The counseling skills described in this characteristic come in two parts, the ability to understand the needs of those who come for help, and the ability to offer—or recommend—the kind of help needed. Lutherans want pastors who can quickly understand what a person's counseling needs are, even when the troubled one may not be entirely clear about them. They want pastors who can distinguish between a crisis situation and one where long-term help is required, and who arrange counseling help appropriate to that need.

They value an ability to listen sensitively—to hear feelings as well as words. They value pastors who respect people's freedom to choose a course of action even when they would choose another. They appreciate an intuitive sense that knows when to move gently with persons who are hurting, when to offer help simply by being present, and when to encourage grieving persons to talk about their grief.

Evidence of the high regard people have for this set of counseling skills is found partly in its rank—17th out of 77—and partly in the ratings given to individual items that make it up. Sixty-two percent considered it "absolutely essential" that a pastor "In counseling, addresses a problem with honesty and reality"; 50% rated "When conversing with a person, listens for feelings tones as well as words" as "absolutely essential"; and 49% gave that rank to "Counsels in a way that respects a person's freedom to choose own course of action."

The key words connected with this counseling skill are *understanding, sensitivity, warmth,* and *support.*

Gracious Availability (21). "And there was my mother, dying in the hospital, and I called the pastor, and he didn't even come!" This, in the eyes of many Lutherans, would be a cardinal sin for any pastor to commit. The neglect of persons in need reflected in the item "Rarely, if ever, visits the sick or shut-ins," was rated by Lutherans as *hindering* effective ministry *quite a bit.* Lutherans generally placed high priority on pastors' responding graciously when called for help, even at inconvenient times. Almost half (47%) considered it "absolutely essential" to an effective ministry that a pastor go immediately to minister to members in crisis situations.[1]

The issue is not only availability, but graciousness. Lutherans' description of this characteristic underlines the value of a pastor's calming presence when ministering in places such as hospital emergency units, funeral homes, and nursing homes. The description includes the same calming, hope-inspiring presence that causes those who are fearful of

---

1. Remembering the high value Lutherans put on a pastor's commitment to family, it becomes clear that no pastor can achieve perfection in all aspects of ministry. Some characteristics are at particular moments mutually exclusive. Some pairs, like "Commitment to Family" and "Gracious Availability," must be kept somehow in acceptable balance. In dividing the 24 hours in a day, a pastor cannot be available at all times to everyone who asks *and* make and keep a significant commitment of time to his or her family. Pastors must exercise judgment in individual situations, and the decision need not always tip in the same direction nor be consistent with the last similar decision. Similarly, there are other opposing characteristics that call for exercise of judgment. A pastor cannot over the same period of time exhibit "Exclusive Devotion to Congregational Concerns" (66) and such a community-oriented characteristic as "Ecumenical Openness" (58)—to be described in Chapter 9. The need for good judgment applied to individual situations, often involving the rejection of one of two desirable alternatives, continues throughout one's ministry.

death to feel less anxious. Calm graciousness is also hoped for when pastors explain why a request that conflicts with denominational policy cannot be granted—such as when a woman, though not a member of the Missouri Synod, requests that the Masonic Order participate in her husband's funeral. This quality of graciousness is more of an attitude or spirit than a specific action, and is particularly valued in any situation that is tense, stressful, or tragic. The hope is that pastors can be "little Christs" to the suffering, leaving with them the benediction of God's Spirit and life-giving Word.

Empathetic Aid in Suffering (42). Experienced counselors often warn beginners about the dangers of becoming emotionally involved with other people's troubles to such a degree that counselors accept them as their own. When counselors take on the pain and responsibility of another's suffering, they then hamper their own ability to engage in all other varieties of ministry, and usually without appreciably helping the original sufferers. But involvement is a matter of degree. Some degree of participation in the suffering of others is necessary in order to develop a bond of understanding that allows for dialog and easing of burdens through assurance that someone else knows and cares. This characteristic describes a sensible and sensitive involvement with others in the relief of suffering. Not only does the description include pastors' attempts to learn from those who are suffering and from the terminally ill, but also their knowledge of, and ability to marshal other resources in the community when needed.

A single important item relates to the willingness and ability to seek out people who have struggled through a particular problem to help others who are now facing that problem. This item may point to an area of service which does not receive the attention it deserves in many counseling ministries (see "Reflections," p. 158).

Intentional Counseling (46). In another research study involving 47 denominations, the Readiness for Ministry Project, it was found that people usually perceive counseling in two distinct ways. As a result, there were two sets of counseling characteristics. One set consisted of the qualities required of any good counselor, whether Christian or not. The other set included characteristics that involve using the language and symbols of faith when sharing one's beliefs or interpreting experiences in light of the Christian faith. In the responses of pastors and seminary students in that study, few combined the two sets of characteristics. Most indicated they would provide counseling of either one type or the other.

In this study, Lutherans made it clear that they want pastors to counsel in both ways—though, admittedly, they give greater value to "Enabling and Perceptive Counseling" that is sensitive to persons' needs for sympathetic understanding and warmth, a characteristic that has theological content only implicitly.

This characteristic, ranked 46th out of 77, focuses on the hoped-for ability to manifest one's theology and share one's faith without imposing either on counselees. This is a fine art. Some pastors make sure they never convey their own convictions to counselees. Some who mainly employ the reflective (or nondirective) style of counseling consider it best not to share their faith at any time in the counseling process. But most lay people, when involved in a counseling relationship, want to know in theological terms where their pastor stands.

Lest the lower rank of 46 seem to minimize this accent in pastoral counseling, it may be helpful to note how many viewed the following items as contributing "very much" or being "absolutely essential" to an effective counseling ministry. One out of two deemed it highly important that a pastor "Presents a theological position on matters such as divorce, abortion, suicide, amnesty," and "Uses counseling approaches that are expressions of Lutheran theology." Two out of three value a pastor who "In counseling, shares own beliefs without forcing them on a person." It is quite evident that people want to know what pastors believe and think about issues confronting them.

Communication of Life-Related Theology (8): A reprise. This characteristic, which has already been described and dealt with as we discussed the area of Lutheran distinctiveness (Chapter 3) could very well have been assigned, on the basis of mathematical evidence, to this area of ministry. Though it correlated slightly better with the area in which it was originally discussed, it also showed a strong relationship to counseling. Lutherans want pastors who have the skills of counseling, but they also want this counseling to be founded on clearly-thought-through theological positions related to people in their own situations. They want pastors who can convey these theological understandings in ways that lay persons can understand. Such understanding and clarity must be informed partly by what books, professors, and classroom discussion can bring, and partly by what lay people share of what they have learned from life's experiences. The ultimate pastoral counselor, in the view of Lutherans, would be a theologically-informed co-seeker and co-learner with those who, in the midst of their suffering, seek the will of God for them.

Emphases and Contrasts

Do chaplains give highest value to counseling? Strangely enough, chaplains and others ministering in therapeutic settings do not appear to value

Table 7. Groups that place higher value on characteristics of Area VI, "Ministry of Counseling."

	professionals	more educated	older	women
17 Enabling and Perceptive Counseling	HHH	HHH		HH
21 Gracious Availability		LL	HHH	HH
42 Empathetic Aid in Suffering	HH			
46 Intentional Counseling	LL	HH		

As compared with Lutherans' average: HHH = much higher
HH = higher
H = slightly higher
L = slightly lower
LL = lower
LLL = much lower

this area of ministry any more highly than parish clergy do. In fact, the importance Lutherans in various types and settings of ministry place on counseling ministry hardly varies. Neither are there systematic differences that can be credited to frequency of church attendance, satisfaction from congregational participation, church body, income, region of the country, or size of congregation.

Do graduating seminary students favor this ministry? Seminary seniors gave lower priority than others to both "Gracious Availability" (21) and "Intentional Counseling" (46). Their de-emphasis of both these aspects of ministry seems consistent with other practices for which their enthusiasm is not high. For students to accord less importance to these two is consistent with their lesser appreciation for several of the characteristics treated in Chapter 1, "Personal Faith, Spiritual Depth," which is the area to which "Gracious Availability" and "Intentional Counseling" are very closely related (see p. 152). The seniors' de-emphasis of "Gracious Availability" seems, additionally, quite compatible with the especially high value they place on family commitment, since availability to one's own family and to one's parishioners sometimes presents conflicts.

Do clergy value counseling more than the laity? Professionals gave higher priority to "Empathetic Aid in Suffering" (42), which is the central characteristic in this ministry area, and to "Enabling and Perceptive Counseling" (17), and lower priority to "Intentional Counseling" (46). But the two groups did not differ significantly in the value they placed on "Gracious Availability" (21).

Do well-educated people put greater emphasis on counseling? Education has some relationship to ratings given these characteristics. The more highly educated showed much more appreciation for the counseling skills and expertise represented in "Enabling and Perceptive Counseling" (17). The less well-educated gave higher priority to "Gracious Availability" (21), indicating a definite desire that their pastors be present with them in time of trial or difficulty. This should dissuade pastors from any notion that their presence may generally be less welcome among those whose formal educational background is more limited than their own.

Is age a factor? Older Lutherans favored "Intentional Counseling" (46) just as they accorded greater importance to many of the characteristics of Area I, "Personal Faith, Spiritual Depth." Younger Lutherans gave much lower priority to "Gracious Availability" (21), perhaps because they are less likely to need or to have had experience with this kind of help.

Did women's evaluations differ from men's? Women, more than men, look to their pastors for a calming graciousness (21) and for the counseling expertise of Characteristic 17. Their greater appreciation for pastoral counsel than men express may be a reflection of the tradition that males should be independent and self-sufficient, particularly in the presence of other men.

Reflections

Christians do not suffer less than other people. Their faith does not shield them from personal failure, severe disappointment, physical or emotional illness, or separation from or loss of people they love. (In fact, a Christian who is sensitive to the pain of others, as Christians frequently are, probably suffers *more* than non-Christians.) The blithe "He'll take all your burdens away" school of thought to the contrary, Christians fall heir to as many troubles and as much human pain as other mortals. The difference comes in that Christians have opportunity to view suffering, when they experience it, through a different set of lenses.

Lutherans imply this point of view in the way they speak of the role of the church and pastors in dealing with suffering. Counseling, for them, is one means of witnessing to the faith in the world with suffering individuals. For Lutherans this is not a separate, easily compartmentalized, specialty. They generally believe that dealing with suffering is part and parcel of the life we are called to live, and that in loving our neighbors as we love ourselves, we rejoice with those who rejoice and weep with those who weep. The weeping is as legitimate an activity as the rejoicing.

Regarding laity

Lutherans see this attitude toward suffering as so much a part of the ministry and witness of the church that they responded with considerable emphasis to the item that suggests the involvement of lay people in helping others who are suffering.

If we are to draw the conclusions suggested by two pieces of evidence from our research, this co-ministry of sufferers is an avenue of ministry that is much underused, in terms of both supply and demand. A *Study of Generations* found a majority of Lutheran adults saying they would be willing to help others if called on. In this study, three out of five reflect that it would contribute very much or be absolutely essential to their congregation's ministry to have a ministry that "Engages people who have struggled through a problem to help those now facing the same kind of problem." Whether that help takes the form of Alcoholics Anonymous, of widowed or divorced persons helping others now going through the same experiences, or of parents of troubled or handicapped children meeting together, there is apparently considerable willingness to be helpful to others in Lutheran congregations. It might be of great aid to countless people if pastors took this expressed willingness in hand to marshal it toward greater employment of the ministry of the laity. (As additional evidence that the characteristics of ministry do not stand pure and disconnected from one another, though recognition of this avenue of ministry comes as part of a counseling characteristic, its translation into practice requires the administrative skill described in Chapter 7.)

Regarding seminaries

We mentioned in Chapter 3 that Lutherans do not isolate the role of theologian and thinker to the degree that members of many other denominations do. For Lutherans, the doing of theology is seen as necessarily pervading all ministerial activities. Somewhat comparably, we learned from the ATS Readiness for Ministry Project that most denominations, especially the more mainline denominations, identify counseling as a very distinct, separate, and much more precisely detailed area—a specialty, if you please. For them it amounts to something more like techniques that might be expected of a clinical psychologist or professional marriage counselor—but relatively devoid of theological reference or description. As we mentioned earlier in this chapter, Lutherans seem to have difficulty thinking of counseling without mixing it in with a variety of other areas of ministry such as "Personal Faith, Spiritual Depth," "Reaching Out with Compassion to Community and World," and "Critical Awareness of Lutheran Heritage and Theology." It is interesting to speculate why this difference exists. Are Lutherans here showing a naivete that will dissipate with the years ("as the Lutheran church enters the 20th century," as some might put it)? Does this reveal a lack of perceptiveness that cannot distinguish important scientific counseling skills and techniques from the rest of ministry? Or are Lutherans showing a sophistication which other denominations in time may achieve?

When a suffering person confronts a minister, the big question is, "Why is this happening to me?" This is an appropriate question for Christians to ask. Both C. S. Lewis (in his classic book *The Problem of Pain*) and Leslie Weatherhead (in *The Will of God*) deal with Christian perspectives on suffering. They do not treat suffering as a problem in counseling, except peripherally. They treat it as a matter that must be dealt with from the deepest roots of one's understanding of who God is and who human beings are.

We believe Lutherans have here caught hold of something profoundly true, and that they have done so because of their conviction that every area of ministry must be perceived and executed with theological sensitivity (see Chapter 3). We believe that counseling must be done within the context of Christian faith—that pastoral counseling *should* involve the language of faith, *should* bring in the resources of faith in confronting a problem, and that pastoral counselors *should* help Christian sufferers wear the special lenses that begin to enable them to see their problems in the context of the love, power, and grace of Almighty God.

Whether or not we are right, this is the way Lutherans view counseling at this time. Seminaries who prepare people to do pastoral counseling, as well as seminarians themselves, should be aware of the synthesis of the purely "secular" skills of counseling with the theological foundations of pastoral care that Lutherans value. It appears to us that many programs, even though separated from seminary communities, are successfully integrating pastoral theology with the skills and techniques proper to all good counseling. Yet there is a related question that occurs to us: For learning seminarians, where are the models—people who counsel from this base of the Christian faith, who have successfully achieved the synthesis, and who communicate that synthesis in the way they lecture, counsel, and relate to students? Such people cannot be quickly trained, if they are not present. Those who live a successful blend of the two are likely found as gifts, not built to order. But the desire of Lutherans to see this blend of counseling expertise and clear grounding in faith should be taken into account as seminaries choose faculties and construct curricula, whether on or off campus.

One of the items in the area of Lutheran distinctiveness (Chapter 3) is "Increases own theological competence through research and study." Part of the research and study toward improvement of theological competence that Lutherans are looking for in their pastors is deep enough involvement with large enough numbers of lay people so that they develop and can share theological understandings of all kinds of issues and problems of daily living. One is almost left with the impression, though it is no more than implicit in these data, that lay people are looking for the kind of interaction with their pastors that will allow both to learn theology, and, as well, more about *how* to theologize, how to *do* theology. This may present a challenge to bringing the intimate depth, honesty, and reality of private counsel, as in a pastor's study or even private confession, into group discussions, classes, and the larger arena of parish education. This challenge would be not only for congregations, however, but also for seminaries. Just as teachers often teach as they have been taught, so clergy often pastor as they have been shepherded. Such problem and issue-centered interaction and reflection might not be the best stewardship of many a professor's time, but it might be possible to use congregations, church agencies and institutions, parish pastors and other specialists as adjunct classrooms and faculty—both for the education of seminarians and for the continuing education of pastors beyond present internships and contextual education programs.

Use of the Appendix C checklist for the four characteristics of this area of ministry might be useful, as in other areas, for pastors who want to evaluate their own strengths and weaknesses in ministering to persons under stress, or want to know the perceptions of others. We suggest that those evaluating their skills by this means look at the results of the checklist wholistically, from the perspective of all four characteristics (as Lutherans in general do), rather than in light of only one or two of special interest.

Component characteristics: Chapter 9

From central to peripheral

62   Assertive Civic Leadership
47   Community Bridge Building
44   Initiation of Community Services
51   Prophetic Concern for the Oppressed
56   Active Concern for the Oppressed
48   Integrative Ministry
64   Openness to Civil Disobedience
49   Equipping for Community Service
58   Ecumenical Openness
55   Co-Ministering to the Distressed and Alienated
60   Balanced Acceptance of Theological Diversity
54   Broad Intellectual Stimulation
45   Candid Christian Humanness
37   Use of Broad Knowledge

In order of Lutheran ranking

37   Use of Broad Knowledge
44   Initiation of Community Services
45   Candid Christian Humanness
47   Community Bridge Building
48   Integrative Ministry
49   Equipping for Community Service
51   Prophetic Concern for the Oppressed
54   Broad Intellectual Stimulation
55   Co-Ministry to the Distressed and Alienated
56   Active Concern for the Oppressed
58   Ecumenical Openness
60   Balanced Acceptance of Theological Diversity
62   Assertive Civic Leadership
64   Openness to Civil Disobedience

9

Reaching Out with Compassion to Community and World

It is fair to say that Lutherans have consistently agreed on an individual-works-of-mercy approach to alleviate human suffering. They have not shown as much agreement when it comes to social reform. Differences have been even more pronounced when the objective has required cooperative work with other religious organizations, as well as "secular" groups such as community agencies and government, to enhance social, economic, and political situations.

In his thesis, "The History of a Developing Social Responsibility Among Lutherans in America," a study covering the years 1930 to 1960, Lloyd Svendsbye observed:

> Lutherans in America have generally been described as a group lacking a vital social consciousness and a sense of corporate responsibility, except for the area of institutional welfare. They have been depicted as quietistic supporters of the status quo, rather than as a group interested in social reform. This portrait has, by and large, been correct.[1]

1. Lloyd Svendsbye, "The History of a Developing Social Responsibility Among Lutherans in America from 1930-1960, with Reference to the American Lutheran Church, the Augustana Lutheran Church, the Evangelical Lutheran Church, and the United Lutheran Church in America" (doctoral thesis, Union Theological Seminary, 1966), p. 1.

In recent decades, however, Lutherans have shown growing awareness that Christian service includes more than individual works of mercy. There is a new awareness, especially among clergy, that the teachings of Jesus can and should be applied to society—to its economic structures and social institutions—in order to serve the needs of the suffering and oppressed, and, ultimately, the needs of all people.

The collision of the assumptions of the past with the new interest in social involvement became evident in the replies of Lutherans to our questionnaire on ministry. Among the laity, almost two in five (38%) agreed with the statement, "Clergy should stick to religion and not concern themselves with social, economic and political questions." Seventeen percent even thought it "highly important" that clergy adopt this stance. But 44% of the laity disagreed, saying that such a stance hinders an effective ministry. Of these, 21% believed that it "hinders very much."

A similar split in opinion appeared in lay people's responses to the item, "Remains generally uninvolved in civic (governmental) activities." Almost half (47%) viewed such a position as contributing to an effective ministry, but three in ten (29%) saw it as hindering. On this question 25% of the laity said that such noninvolvement "contributes little or nothing."

Given these differences in enthusiasm, one would scarcely expect Lutherans, in ranking the areas of ministry, to give top rank to a ministry of active social involvement. They did not. The area of ministry described in this chapter ranks seventh among the ten areas measured. Lutherans view it only as "contributing quite a bit" to effective ministry, and there is a perceptible break between the rank given this set of characteristics and the one given the next higher, "Ministry of Counseling," which followed close on the heels of "Making Ministry of Administration" and "Community Through Word and Sacraments." All three were viewed as "contributing very much."

Although they rank it as somewhat less important than most others, Lutherans know what this area of ministry is; they can identify it clearly. This is the most cohesive set of characteristics of all 10 areas of ministry. The 14 characteristics intercorrelate more strongly than those in any other area, partly because people have very definite, though often divided, opinions about them.

The following is a profile of "Larry," a pastor who illustrates this feature of ministry as described by Lutheran responses to the questionnaire statements:

Politically, Larry is an activist.

Organizationally, he is involved, working through structures to better the conditions of the oppressed or those who are unjustly treated. He prefers the political approach over a one-to-one approach that ministers to the immediate needs of individual people or families.

Theologically, Mark 2:15-17 is writ large in Larry's life. He is a scourer of the highways and hedges of life, and spends a good deal of time with publicans, sinners, and all kinds of the downtrodden. He is a Good Samaritan who has taken up full-time patrolling of the road to Jericho, focusing on those who lie wounded in the shadows along the roadside.

Intellectually, he is omnivorous. He is well-informed on current events and local power structures, knowledgeable about how systems work and don't work, about who's getting hurt and why, and what should be done about it.

Socially, Larry is a consummate "includer," not so much for reasons of jollity and friendship, but because his view of community is so firmly ingrained that distinctions between people, while sometimes valuable, seem most of the time irrelevant. Though he is capable of recognizing, appreciating, and even capitalizing on the strengths of individual differences, he does not respect them as presenting real barriers to communication, cooperation, or ministry. Confronted with the kind of wall that customarily separates people from one another, Larry breaks through the wall, or builds a stile.

For Larry, walls shouldn't exist between the church and the rest of society, between the affluent and the poor, between denominations or individual congregations, between members of different professions, between Jews and Christians, between prisoners and the free, between races, between clergy and laity, or between the advantaged and the disadvantaged. One other wall doesn't get much notice from Larry, either. When this tireless mover and shaker sits down to relax—to see a movie or play or to read—he doesn't see why his reading, viewing, or attending ought to be restricted to demonstrably theological fare. He sees a wide variety of material as of interest and germane to his task of ministry, which is social and political, and set in the larger community and world.

Though Lutherans view the 14 characteristics of this area as being related to one another, there is considerable difference in their perceptions of how much each contributes to an effective ministry. As the more-highly-favored end of the continuum is Characteristic 37, "Use of Broad Knowledge," and at the least-favored end, Characteristic 64, "Openness to Civil Disobedience." In very general terms, the more desired characteristics are those that describe a pastor as knowledgeable about the problems of community and world, an educator, an enabler, and even one actively effecting racial and cultural integration. But the more in-

volved a pastor becomes in political action, direct service to the oppressed, or in aggressive attempts to change social structure, the less
enthusiasm Lutherans show.

The characteristics of this area of ministry fall into two general categories—"Personal Perspective," which includes 6 of the 14 characteristics,
and "The Pastor in Action," which includes the remaining 8.

Personal perspective: Wide-angle world view

Those who would reach out with compassion to the downtrodden, dis-
enfranchised, and losers of the world need a wide range of interests.
Not only should they be comfortable in a world full of diversity, but
should show a preference for that kind of world. Those who consider
taking on the reform or reorganization of society and involving other
people in that task need a special kind of personal perspective—a wide-
angle world view, and a way of forming open circles that take others in.

Such people have need of near-encyclopedic knowledge. They need to
be endlessly curious, be constantly learning, and be at ease with am-
biguity, disappointment, struggle, and even with accepting help in whatever form it presents itself. They need to be interested in people who are
different from themselves, even to the point of cherishing those differences.

Broad Intellectual Stimulation (54). Pastors described here are curious and alert, always seeking intellectual stimulation and acquiring
knowledge. They give evidence of this tendency by working with other
professional people as colleagues, attending retreats and seminars, reading widely, attending plays and movies, and keeping up with develop-
ments in relevant fields (such as counseling).

Significantly, three out of five (60%) Lutherans consider it highly
important that pastors work with members of other professions as colleagues. The same number of lay people (60%) believe it is important
that pastors show confidence in their own intellectual ability. All this
adds up to say that Lutherans see professional ministry as requiring
intellectual acumen along with piety of spirit.

Use of Broad Knowledge (37). The second desired component in the
world view of community-outreach pastors is an intentional effort to acquire a broad background of knowledge related to church and faith.
When pastors go out into the community, Lutherans prefer that they be
well-informed, with a firm grasp on the historical position of the Lutheran
church as well as on social and religious factors that affect the current
local situation. Lutherans want pastors to *work* at being well-informed.
Furthermore, "Works at further development of pastoral skills" was iden-

tified by 52% of all Lutherans as being "absolutely essential" to effective ministry. An additional 37% believed that it "contributes very much."

Candid Christian Humanness (45). The third characteristic in this set describes a quality of humanness that contradicts the stereotype of a pastor's being a tower of strength, fully delivered from all doubt and temptation. Part of the Lutheran view of activist pastors is that they be human and admit that humanity; that they acknowledge their struggles with doubt, worry, disappointment and temptation, and that they be willing to seek others' help as they strive to discern God's will for them. Strange as it may seem to some, 34% of the laity said it is "absolutely essential" and 35% said it "contributes very much" to effectiveness when pastors openly admit to times of struggle over personal faith.

Personal perspective: Enthusiastic includer

The next three characteristics describe a theological and philosophical stance of openness that plays the theme of general inclusiveness.

Integrative Ministry (48). A *Study of Generations* reported that Lutherans are 99% white, and primarily of European origins. Is there, indeed, a desire among these people of Scandinavian and Germanic background that pastors work actively for a racially integrated community and church? Would they truly welcome people from other ethnic and cultural backgrounds?

What people say in reply to survey questions and what they later actually do may not be the same. But if expression of an ideal is significant (and we think it is), then the following is eminently noteworthy. Most of the laity take a positive stance on an integrating ministry. The numbers below indicate the percentage of lay people who considered each item "absolutely essential," "contributing very much," or "contributing quite a bit" to effective ministry:

"Encourages all classes of people to join the congregation" (90%)
"Works toward racial integration in the community" (61%)
"Works for racially integrated congregations" (51%)

On the basis of these responses, race appears—for Lutherans—to present somewhat more of a barrier than class, and the enthusiasm for racial integration wanes when some contemplate its occurring in their own congregations.

Ecumenical Openness (58). The items that form this characteristic describe a pastor who participates in ecumenical projects with ministers of other denominations, fosters cooperative activities with other Lutheran congregations, and is open to experimenting with new liturgical forms and educational methods.

Balanced Acceptance of Theological Diversity (60). This characteristic goes a step beyond the kind of cooperative activity described in the previous one (58) to acknowledging that theological diversity is not only a fact, but is legitimate. Pastors exhibiting this theological stance encourage members to acknowledge each other as belonging to the body of Christ, even though they hold divergent theological views. Just how much or what is meant by "theological diversity" is not specified, though some items of this characteristic refer to distinctions among various denominations and to contrasting emphases on preaching the gospel, working to improve the material well-being of people, and openness to pentecostal or charismatic renewal. That pastors have some openness to diversity as something appropriate within the church is desired by most Lutherans and deemed essential for leadership in a community ministry. One half (49%) of all Lutherans viewed this acceptance as "absolutely essential," and an additional 33% said it "contributes very much" to effective ministry.

The pastor in action: Working through structures

The first five of this set of eight characteristics describe the variety of ways in which pastors become *personally* involved in the larger community. The other three center on pastors' efforts to *equip others* to be active in the community and the world.

Community Bridge Building (47). When "Larry," our example for this area, encounters a wall, he builds a stile. The facet of ministry described here is one that brings diverse groups of people together and helps them work in an atmosphere of mutual trust and cooperation to improve their own situation. It is a ministry of reconciliation that works toward unity and the elimination of whatever divides and separates people from one another.

Initiation of Community Services (44). "Originates, locates, requests, stands behind, works"—these are the opening words in some of the items that comprise this characteristic. They speak of the avenues through which pastors take initiative in the community. This characteristic speaks of a person who begins with an awareness of what a community needs, and from that awareness takes steps to see that services are established to meet those needs. The characteristic is one that appears frequently in the pages of the New Testament, where it is said that Christ "went about doing good." It includes such efforts as working to improve community services to the mentally retarded, emotionally disturbed, aged, and children, as well as convincing employers to hire the physically handicapped and rehabilitated convicts, alcoholics, and drug addicts.

Assertive Civic Leadership (62). Although this characteristic is central to the meaning of this area of ministry, it is not a characteristic that most

Lutherans enthusiastically welcome in pastors. This kind of leadership means a pastor's participation in political action that seeks to correct what is unfair and unjust. It means the possibility of pastors running for public office, taking positions on controversial community issues, exerting pressure on public officials to see that people are treated justly, or working for freedom of choice in housing. Pastors who do this are acting on the assumption that political matters are a rightful concern of the church.

The laity differed sharply in their reactions to some of the items in this characteristic. Forty-nine percent opposed the idea of their pastors' running for public office. However, only 7% objected to "Participates vigorously in community services as a private citizen." Moreover, 25% would consider such involvement as being "absolutely essential" or "contributing very much" to a congregation's mission.

Openness to Civil Disobedience (64). Of all the characteristics in this area of ministry, Lutherans have the least enthusiasm for this one. Pastors who fit this characteristic are willing to make direct attacks on the legal system. If they perceive laws to be unjust or morally wrong, they organize efforts to change the laws, participate in lawful protest, or will, if necessary, disobey with risk of arrest. About a third of Lutheran lay people believed a willingness to risk arrest in protest would hinder ministry, and were opposed to a pastor's disobeying a law as a means of protest. Bearing witness against injustice in today's world, for many Lutherans, is difficult to view as Christian service, particularly if it involves breaking existing laws.

Prophetic Concern for the Oppressed (51). This characteristic identifies compassion for people and a prophetic concern for the poor as the motivating forces for involvement in community life. Its high correlation with the other four in this group indicates that, for Lutherans, community involvement should be more than do-gooding. It should represent a *theologically based* desire to show compassion toward people usually condemned or discriminated against, to bring liberation to the oppressed, and to provide prophetic leadership in the community. Such leadership was considered highly important ("contributes very much" or "absolutely essential") by 48% of the laity and professionals.

The pastor in action: Training others for outreach

Three characteristics relate to a pastor's ministry of equipping others for ministry, encouraging and enabling others to serve. The first two of the three, "Equipping for Community Service" (49) and "Active Concern for the Oppressed" (56), lean more toward focusing the attention of congregations on the connections that exist between themselves and local and world needs. The third, "Co-Ministry to the Distressed and Alienated" (55), describes a pastoral approach that sees to it that this kind of ministry is carried out.

Equipping for Community Service (49). This characteristic describes a ministry that is devoted to sensitizing people to needs, helping them to evaluate their own goals and values, conveying a theological understanding of how God works through institutions, and encouraging the laity to see themselves as capable of ministry in the community—all, in short, that is needed for lay people to engage in a thoughtful community ministry.

Active Concern for the Oppressed (56). This characteristic, too, is educational in tone. However, several of its items begin with phrases like "makes individuals aware," "raises the awareness," and "raises members' level of sensitivity." Pastors exhibiting this characteristic strike a prophetic note. They combat racism and prejudice with facts and information. They exhort; no doubt they sometimes offend. The aim of the kind of ministry suggested here is that members be led to seek justice for others. The specifics of the characteristic that are mentioned are world poverty, racism, prejudice, and oppressed people—but the characteristic's meaning goes beyond these to imply concern with other areas of injustice and denial of opportunity. The oppressed need not be those commonly viewed as minorities, and oppression may not always appear in expected forms.

Co-Ministry to the Distressed and Alienated (55). The third characteristic of this trio describes a ministry more actively involved in seeing that ministry occurs. Specific mention of those to be helped includes single parents, unmarried parents, retirees, isolated persons, the suicide-prone, the divorced, the sick, and members of estranged families. The method of ministry is personal—pastors may lead groups of such persons, may arrange for lay persons to be involved individually or in groups with such persons, or may organize groups of lay people to give emergency help wherever special need occurs. The verbs introducing the items are activist: *leads, provides, makes contacts, helps, involves, establishes.*

How many Lutherans want such an emphasis? Here is how both the laity and professionals responded to the item, "Sees that groups are trained to carry out specialized ministries (rehabilitation, crisis intervention, legal and medical aid, financial counsel, etc.)":

"absolutely necessary"	7%
"contributes very much"	27
"contributes quite a bit"	36
"contributes somewhat"	23
"contributes little or nothing"	7
"hinders ministry"	1

Emphases and Contrasts

With many of the 77 characteristics of ministry, we found very little difference between the opinions of professional ministers and of the laity. But on the matter of carrying a vital social consciousness into action in the world outside the confines of congregations, there were many contrasts. Clergy saw considerably more value than the laity in 10 of the 14 characteristics of this area of ministry. The differences were particularly great for "Prophetic Concern for the Oppressed" (51) and "Equipping for Community Service" (49).

One of the possible messages of this discovery, for seminarians about to graduate and serve parishes or for parish pastors, is that they should be neither surprised nor irritated if they find that the enthusiasm of most lay people will not match their own for either educational endeavors or personal action aimed at combating prejudice in their congregations and communities. In rating all eight of the characteristics described in the first two categories of this chapter—"The Pastor in Action: Working Through Structures" and "The Pastor in Action: Training Others for Outreach"— clergy showed greater tendency than the laity to recognize them as valuable parts of Christian ministry.

Church body

Knowing Lutherans' status as clergy or laity is the most useful information in helping to predict the level of their enthusiasm for outreach into community and world. The next most useful thing to know is the name of the Lutheran body they belong to. Svendsbye's study (quoted at the beginning of this chapter) found that development of social responsibility between 1930 and 1960 was most characteristic of church bodies now included in the LCA.

Members of the LCA placed higher or much higher value on six of the characteristics in this chapter, with members of the LCMS consistently giving lower value: "Community Bridge Building" (47), "Initiation of Community Services" (44), "Assertive Civic Leadership" (62), "Active Concern for the Oppressed" (56), "Ecumenical Openness" (58), and "Balanced Acceptance of Theological Diversity" (60). The last-mentioned characteristic, "Balanced Acceptance of Theological Diversity," is the one on which the greatest disparity in rating occurs. Members of the ALC sometimes sided with members of the LCA on a characteristic, sometimes sided with LCMS members, and sometimes stood about halfway between (see Table 8). But on Characteristic 54 both LCMS and LCA members appreciated a pastor who shows evidence of interest in "Broad Intellectual Stimulation," differing from ALC members, who rated it lower.

Table 8. Groups that more highly value the characteristics of Area VII, "Reaching Out with Compassion to Community and World."

	professional	LCA	younger	women	more educated	participation/ satisfaction
working through structures (action)						
47 Community Bridge Building	HH	HH (with ALC vs. LCMS)				
44 Initiation of Community Services	HH	HH (vs. LCMS)			H	
62 Assertive Civic Leadership	HH	HH (vs. LCMS)	HH		HH	
64 Openness to Civil Disobedience	HH		L		HH	
51 Prophetic Concern for the Oppressed	HHH			H		H
training others (action)						
49 Equipping for Community Service	HHH					
56 Active Concern for the Oppressed	HH	HH (with ALC vs. LCMS)				
55 Co-Ministry to the Distressed and Alienated	HH					H

(continued on next page)

(Table 8 continued)

	professional	LCA	younger	women	more educated	participation/satisfaction
wide-angle view (perspective)						
54 Broad Intellectual Stimulation		H (with LCMS vs. ALC)				
37 Use of Broad Knowledge						
45 Candid Christian Humanness	HH					
inclusiveness (perspective)						
48 Integrative Ministry	HH					
58 Ecumenical Openness		HH (vs. LCMS)	HH	H		
60 Balanced Acceptance of Theological Diversity		HHH (vs. ALC and LCMS)				

As compared with Lutherans' average rating (or with groups specifically listed):

HHH = much higher
HH = higher
H = slightly higher
L = slightly lower
LL = lower
LLL = much lower

Younger Lutherans

If research never proved that things are approximately the way you think they are, we would have trouble believing the research. And if research always proved that things are exactly the way you expect them to be, we would all fall asleep over it. Fortunately, this research does neither. It goes on for a period of time—as the rest of life does—unfolding just about as one would expect it to. Then, suddenly, it presents a surprise. Considering the political activism and liberal stance of many young people, especially during the '60s, it is not surprising that younger Lutherans show special interest in a pastor's providing "Assertive Civic Leadership" (62) and "Ecumenical Openness" (58). But what is unexpected is that young Lutherans showed slightly *less* interest than their elders in "Openness to Civil Disobedience" (64). Research presents information, but often no explanation. We don't know why youth shy away from civil disobedience.

Women

Women are slightly more likely than men to hope for a ministry that includes "Initiation of Community Services" (44) aimed at meeting the needs of special groups in the community, "Prophetic Concern for the Oppressed" (51), and "Ecumenical Openness" (58). The flavor of all three of these is compassion, understanding, and openness, but that is also the flavor of several other characteristics in this area of ministry which women *do not* seem to value more than men. Why these three are valued highly and not others is unclear.

Education

At the bottom of the range of preference in this area of ministry come "Assertive Civic Leadership" (62) and "Openness to Civil Disobedience" (64)—the two most militant of the characteristics. Lutherans as a whole said only that they "contribute somewhat" to effective ministry. More-educated Lutherans accorded this kind of ministry a slightly higher rating, but the difference was slight.

Participation-satisfaction

One might expect regular attenders at worship who also find deep satisfaction in congregational activities to place higher value on a ministry of Christian service to outsiders. However, few differences appear between the irregular-attending-dissatisfied Lutherans and the regular-attending-satisfied ones. The latter group placed slightly higher value on "Prophetic Concern for the Oppressed" (51) and "Co-Ministry to the Distressed and

Alienated" (55), both of which have a slight relationship to the works-of-mercy approach historically connected with Lutherans.

Reflections

Putting the history of Lutheran response to the suffering world aside, what can we say about Lutherans *now?* In placing their response to this area of ministry low on their list of priorities (seventh), are they showing evidence of a renewed quietism, a movement back to the position more typical before the turbulent '60s and earlier? Or conversely, are Lutherans showing evidence of steady progress toward a position of radical social activism? The answer to both questions is no. Both statements are too extreme and too simplistic.

Lutherans generally view practices of ministry oriented to the community and world as being most effective to the degree that they are moderate, considerate, use present structures, develop trust, and the like —and are not highly aggressive, violent, intolerant, and insistent on specific political and social goals. Most see the more hard-nosed, tough political activism as a less effective way of doing ministry than moderate political and social action.

But Lutherans *are* interested in action. They typically see pastoral action, congregational action, and church body action as being more effective than talking about, helping others to see the need for, being open to, or taking a cooperative stance with others in the alleviation of human suffering.

What this adds up to is a continued growth in social conscience, even from the situation described by Svendsbye in 1960:

> In the last few decades, however, several significant changes have taken place so that the attitudes and actions relating to social issues on the part of many Lutheran individuals and groups can no longer be portrayed by the usual phrases. Gradually, a new sense of social responsibility has emerged, new understandings concerning social issues have developed, and new patterns for social action have evolved. Some of these new emphases stand in sharp contrast to the past tradition.[2]

Yet Lutherans still will not support every attempt at social reform or search for social justice. There are methods that are too violent, too disruptive, and too blatantly political for the comfort or approbation of most of them. The issue for Lutherans is not so much, any longer, one of *whether or not.* The issue, instead, is one of *method*—how shall it be done? The preferred role is still, among Lutherans, principally that of the Good

---

2. Svendsbye, "History," p. ii.

Samaritan rather than the fighting politician. There always has been and still is a great deal of relatively quiet charity and philanthropy flowing out of Lutheran hands and pockets. There continues to be great interest in looking after matters of social welfare and education. There is a lesser, but growing, acknowledgment that it is appropriate for the institutional church to become involved in the struggle to reform social structures, but the acceptable style is by moderate, "reasonable" methods.

A second argument presented in Svendsbye's "History of Social Responsibility Among Lutherans" is that development of a broadening sense of social responsibility seems to have arisen chiefly from nontheological factors. He wrote:

. . . social responsibility appears to have developed primarily in response to particular social forces such as the depression of the '30s, the war of the '40s, and the racial tensions and threats of nuclear annihilation of the '50s. . . . To say it differently, theology does not seem to have played the major role in the development of a broader social responsibility. . . . To say this is not to assert that theology had no influence whatsoever. But it is to assert that the major impetus appears to have been social rather than theological.[3]

Our discoveries about Lutherans from this study generally support this view. Despite the presence of some theological content in this area of ministry, such as the note of theological exploration sounded in "Prophetic Concern for the Oppressed" (51), the major motivations for concern for the world appear to be more firmly based in historical and social forces than in theology.

What does this information add up to in terms of practical action for graduating seminarians or parish pastors? In the first place, it is important to know where people generally are—a whole congregation as well as individuals or groups within it. There is great variation among people in their enthusiasm for any ministry to the world's suffering. There is, additionally, equally great variation in how those with enthusiasm want to go about offering that ministry.

Whether one's hope is to change hearts and enthusiasms or to make use of the willingness and enthusiasm that is there, it will be useful to know how the believers of a particular congregation view ministry to the community and world. As a means of assessing the shape of this willingness, one might make use of the items of "Appendix C" related to Area VII, "Reaching Out with Compassion to Community and World" (p. 236). In using these with groups of lay people, an appropriate introduc-

---

3. Svendsbye, "History," p. 486.

tory statement for each item might be, "It is important that the ministry of this congregation. . . ." (This altered introductory statement will cause most items to be usable in a checklist except for those in "Candid Christian Humanness" [45] and "Ecumenical Openness" [58], which are stated so as to relate clearly to individuals.)

If the results of our study truly indicate what is present in most Lutheran congregations, pastors and lay leaders should be prepared to find more than usual willingness to take an active role in aggressive social ministries, particularly among those people who are already most satisfied with their participation in church activities. Most such satisfied participators gave slightly higher ratings to the items of two characteristics —"Co-Ministry to the Distressed and Alienated" (55) and "Prophetic Concern for the Oppressed" (51).

One of the common complaints of lay people, particularly the more talented and capable, is that too many church activities and too much church-related service is "Mickey Mouse"—not really significant. But when the tasks are as challenging as directly helping others in times of illness and trouble, carrying out specialized ministries of rehabilitation, being trained for crisis intervention, providing legal or medical aid, or offering financial counsel, lay people find the deep satisfaction in co-ministry that they are looking for. Unpublished data from A Study of Generations suggest that this deep satisfaction will encourage not only further participation but additional support of their church. (The data referred to showed that Lutherans with the strongest sense of belonging, of being accepted by other church members, and of finding satisfaction in their own participation were also the best stewards.)

What all this suggests to us is that pastors make a mistake if they expect and ask too little of their lay co-workers because they sense apathy. That apathy may be due to not providing enough opportunity and training for lay people to carry out truly challenging, significant ministries of mercy and action that concretely meet human need outside the congregation in the larger community and world.

Component characteristics: Chapter 10

From central to peripheral
63 Liturgical Orientation
33 Effective Speaking
52 Balanced Liturgical Judgment

In order of Lutheran ranking
33 Effective Speaking
52 Balanced Liturgical Judgment
63 Liturgical Orientation

Informed Leadership
of Liturgical Worship

The story of this area of ministry is quickly told. To begin with, it is composed of only three rather brief characteristics. In the second place, along with the area of ministry described in Chapter 9, it occupies a relatively low-ranking spot in the hierarchy of Lutheran preferences. This is not so much because it doesn't matter to people, but because Lutherans differ so much about it. Finally, it represents what may seem to be the area most limited in scope—it covers only what happens in most Lutheran churches between the hours of 9 A.M. and noon on Sundays.

Although the area of corporate worship—what happens on Sunday mornings—is a very limited area of ministry, it is very important. It is the most public area and the one best known to anyone with any degree of familiarity with the Christian community, and therefore the area on which people have the most definite ideas.

Lutherans hold two views of worship. For some, worship primarily means community and sharing with other members of the family of God, regularly highlighted by a meal together—the Lord's Supper. For others, worship is primarily a mystical relationship with a transcendent God in the setting of a sanctuary where one is not so much aware of others as of God's presence. These differing concepts of the meaning of worship

179

result in divisions as to the form it should take, as illustrated in comments like these:

"I've never been able to get much out of repeating the same ritual week after week. My mind wanders. I don't hear what I'm saying, and it gets to be just a bunch of words going by. I like prayers to have current and immediate meaning, and I like the service to be different each time. Then it's interesting and holds my attention."

"I really appreciate the universal nature of the liturgy. When I'm away from home, or when we've moved, it's like coming home to attend church and hear familiar hymns and liturgy."

"I want a worship service where I can meditate, where nothing interferes with the mood. I like liturgy that is simple and that moves smoothly. I don't like artificial exercises like turning around and speaking to the people around me. From the time I meet the usher until the time I leave, I want a quiet, worshipful atmosphere, where I can be conscious of God."

"The best parts of worship are the parts that are different. I like the sermon to shake me up and give me a new way of looking at things. I like to learn new hymns, and I don't see why organ music is the only kind we ever have. Lots of people play other instruments well, and I think they should be able to use their gifts in worship—it would mean a lot to us and to them, too. I think worship should be exciting and personal. Too often I feel as if I'm going to fall asleep."

Lutherans differ in attitudes toward the content, conduct, and even the importance of worship. In *A Study of Generations* it was reported that 60% of all Lutherans agreed that one of the most important aspects of Christianity is the liturgical service of public worship. Yet only 30% said that the more formal and highly liturgical the service, the more meaning it has for them. And 60% said they prefer variety rather than the same order every Sunday. Fewer than 60% of all Lutherans reported being "very" or "quite" inspired by their worship services. To some readers, being inspired or not through worship may seem inconsequential, but *A Study of Generations* provided evidence to the contrary. Lutheran youth, ages 15-18, who did not feel part of a friendship group in the church, and *who were not inspired by the worship services*, were the most disappointed with the church as a whole of all Lutheran young people. How youth feel about the Sunday morning worship service is one of the two best predictors of how they will feel about the whole church.

Lutherans identified a total of 12 characteristics associated with worship. Nine of them fell into the area of congregational community, discussed in Chapter 6. The other three formed this separate group. In general, these were given a lower rank than those that appear in Chapter 6.

The three characteristics in this area all point to a formal type of service and relate to pastoral skills and practices appreciated and applauded by only some Lutherans. These are "Effective Speaking" (33), "Balanced Liturgical Judgment" (52), and "Liturgical Orientation" (63). While for some Lutherans this area of ministry is very important, for many others these characteristics (especially the latter two) are viewed as relatively inconsequential or even something of a hindrance to an effective ministry.

Effective Speaking (33). To the extent that there is agreement in this area, it lodges here. Given the generally low rank accorded this area, this characteristic was the clear winner in popularity. A pastor who exhibits these skills is the one of whom people say, "When he is before a congregation at worship, he knows what he's doing." Timidity and tentativeness are not valued here. Such pastors speak clearly and distinctly enough to make themselves well heard when reading and preaching. They deliver sermons in a sufficiently vivid and lively way so as to hold their hearer's interest. Further, their prayers and meditations are not obviously top-of-the-head, spur-of-the-moment improvisations, but show depth of experience and knowledge of the spirit and meaning of prayer. As these pastors lead their congregations in worship, it is evident that they have form, substance, and skills of delivery well in hand.

Balanced Liturgical Judgment (52). This characteristic speaks of an attitude of attention and care devoted to preparation and celebration of worship services. Such pastors would be careful to see that the traditions of the church year are observed, would have a liturgically informed opinion on hymns and other music appropriate to particular occasions, and would be so attuned to, and at home in, the spirit of corporate worship that they would behave with both dignity and concern for people, even in handling the occasional disturbances that may occur during worship.

Liturgical Orientation (63). Pastors described here place a high priority on the aesthetics of worship. Such pastors will see that the paraments, vestments, and all appointments being used are appropriate for the time in the church year. For them, the service is not unlike a dinner honoring a special guest, where one takes note of how the table is set and the guests are seated. In both situations, details communicate a message and such pastors want a fitting and appropriate message to be conveyed. They see themselves first and foremost as liturgists. Among Lutherans, 21% considered it highly important that their pastors be primarily worship oriented. The same number (21%) considered ministry hindered when pastors see themselves primarily as liturgists.

Table 9. Groups that place higher value on the characteristics of Area VIII, "Informed Leadership of Liturgical Worship."

	older	laity	less educated
33 Effective Speaking	HHHH	HH	HHHH
52 Balanced Liturgical Judgment	HHHH	HH	
63 Liturgical Orientation	HHHH	HHH	HHH

As compared with Lutherans' average rating: HHHH = very much higher
HHH = much higher
HH = higher
H = slightly higher

Emphases and Contrasts

Those who are most pleased when pastors are good liturgists, preachers, and over-all worship leaders are those who are older, less well-educated, and with incomes less than $15,000 a year. Younger, better-educated Lutherans whose family incomes are above $15,000 a year will more frequently be among those least concerned about these matters.

An interesting division of labor (or phenomenon of cooperation, if you prefer) occurred as this area of ministry was defined and its value determined. All three of the characteristics were *defined* by the responses of clergy; it was their perceptions of the individual items that caused these groups of items to form. However, lay people *rated* every item in this area of ministry higher—often considerably higher—than professional ministers. This is unusual, since the general tendency throughout the questionnaire was for professionals to provide somewhat higher ratings than the laity. Here we see the reverse of what we reported in Chapter 9.

There clergy showed a markedly higher enthusiasm for ministry that reaches actively into the community and world, and we suggested that clergy should not be surprised if their own enthusiasms are not echoed in lay people. In this area of ministry we find that lay people set greater store on good preaching and an emphasis on liturgy than clergy do. Therefore pastors should not be surprised if occasional liturgical slips or several hastily-prepared sermons in a row turn out to be disturbing to a number of lay people.

Reflections

The message is that lay people want pastors to *care* about worship. They make here a plea for good preaching and for worship services prepared with intelligence and conducted with clarity.

The reputation of preaching, particularly among clergy, has of late fallen on less than the best of times. There are those who declare that the day of preaching has passed. Others take the more moderate view that, though preaching may be with us to stay, it is no longer legitimate to spend a great deal of time and effort on it—that there are other pastoral tasks that more effectively do the work of ministry.

The attitudes arise from several sources. The first is likely the (welcome) de-emphasis in educational circles on the value of lecture as *the* teaching tool, and an increased emphasis on discovery by the student through discussion, experimentation, or structured experiences. The attitudes probably also rise in part from the emphasis of the late 1960s on action versus words. Certainly there are fewer great pulpit orators nowadays than there have sometimes been. Whether that is a cause or effect of the general tendency to downgrade the importance of preaching, we are not prepared to say.

But we swim upstream against the prevailing attitude. Preaching, in our view, *is* effective, and how it is done *does* matter. For one thing, preaching is not lecturing. It is not primarily the conveyance of factual information or knowledge. Preaching is admonition and a declaration of good news. It is the subject of God's promise: "My Word shall not return to me void." We fear that those who believe preaching has lost its effect are depending too much on easily perceived, clearly documented, and readily countable results as their index of effectiveness. Preaching, in our view, is something that must be done, and done well, as part of a whole and rounded ministry. Its effectiveness is not a matter for pastors alone to judge; instead, it depends in major part on the work of the Holy Spirit and whatever receptiveness exists among the hearers.

Our study tells us that many lay people are swimming upstream, too.

They have not given up on the value of preaching as a means of changing minds and lives. The magnitude of the discrepancy in this area of ministry between the ratings of laity and those of the clergy is greatest on this point—on the importance of effective, articulate, and interesting preaching and speaking. Being able to hold the interest and attention of one's hearers while preaching is what the laity value most in this area, followed closely by an ability to read aloud clearly and distinctly.

There is a sense in which pastors' preaching and liturgical skills need to be even more sharply honed than in the past. We have before us the constant example of the expertly-delivered announcement on radio and TV, with words precisely spoken and arranged so as to communicate meaning efficiently. People *expect* a corresponding clarity of thought and speech in pulpits. When pastors are being compared (perhaps albeit unconsciously) with the likes of Walter Cronkite and Charles Kuralt, they cannot afford to be slipshod and stumblingly offhand.

In addition, the general educational level of Lutherans is rising, and with it the expectation that sermons will contain meaty, well-thought-out arguments about the actions of God in life. Sermons that have a single point and are filled out with one jolly and amusing illustration after another simply won't do. Lay people expect something with protein in it.

There is an old book that, if we remember correctly, is titled, *Thirty Minutes to Wake the Dead.* It is about preaching, and the title still applies. Given the increasing competition for people's thinking time today, we do not believe we can afford to make anything less than the best use of the time we have to raise people's consciousness of God's relationship to them, and to give them a sense of the implications and potential of that destiny. We don't have the leisure of two-hour worship services. We must conscientiously make use of the short time we have to bear the astonishing message that God has invaded history and comes to each of us in daily life, asking what we will do to welcome or resist that invasion.

Our own recommendation is that seminaries consider placing considerably more emphasis on public speaking skills as prerequisites, and on opportunities to maintain and sharpen such skills as part of seminary curricula and extracurricular involvement. Not only homiletics, but techniques of effective public speaking are definitely implied in what Lutherans as a whole, and especially the laity, desire in a minister. Most of the laity place public speaking skills on a par with theological reflection and biblical scholarship.

Next on the list of the laity, after good preaching, is an ability to stimulate a singing congregation and encourage a strong music program, including the appreciation, selection, and use of hymns in such a way that they complement the theme of worship of a given day and compatibly serve pastoral purposes. This does not require ministers to be musicians, but to appreciate quality, recognize psychological impact, and integrate the verbal content of music with the rest of a worship service—or depend on people who can. Though effective preaching and speaking was generally viewed as contributing "very much" to effective ministry as a whole, this appreciation and encouragement of the use of appropriate hymns and good music by a singing congregation was viewed as contributing "quite a bit."

Besides preaching and music, there is liturgy. Liturgy, if it is vain repetition and only that, is indeed deadly dull. We believe time must be taken to teach what the liturgy is and what it is for. It is not surprising that if members were not taught, either as children or as adults, the "what" and the "how to" of participating in liturgy they now do not truly engage themselves in it, but rather let it flow over them unheeded. (It must be recognized, though, that even in such cases liturgy is, we believe, being stored in people's memory for later reference. However, consciously-participating congregations receive other benefits as well.) One pastor we know made a point of teaching and dramatizing for first through sixth graders in Sunday school the meaning of the Christian liturgy, over a period of several months, 12 minutes at a time. "When they came into the service, as they did every few Sundays," he reported, "and the liturgist chanted 'The Lord be with you,' you could hear those little voices producing more enthusiasm and more volume than all the rest of the congregation put together when they replied, 'and with thy spirit.' They knew what they were saying, and they were participating in worship as perhaps only a few of their elders were."

It does not seem to us that children need to be kept out of a service until they can understand it. There is much that can be conveyed in a worship service even when one doesn't understand the language—as those who have attended worship conducted in a foreign tongue can testify. In our own language, none of us knew, the first time we heard it, what an intercontinental ballistic missile was, either. But somehow we all—including the youngest—learned.

Variety is an issue also raised, at least implicitly, in this area of ministry. It is evident that though there are some—about 30% of Lutherans— who are happiest with rigorous adherence to a formal, high-church liturgy, 60% like variety in at least the voluntary portions of the service, and others prefer a service that is free and spontaneous, with a minimum of order that remains the same from service to service. To us this implies that in order to provide attractive opportunity for parishioners to worship, given these diverse preferences, there should be variety not only within given orders of service, but also in types of services scheduled at different times.

In summary, lay people particularly care about worship and how it is led, and about preaching and how well it is done. This will come as welcome news to pastors who believe it is especially true of worship services, as of all things done in the name of God, that they be prepared and done with all the good taste, intelligence, sensitivity, and clarity we can manage.

Final Reflections

The Lutheran Seminarian Project has broadened beyond its original intent. The original purpose was to help seminarians and faculty members know more about the territory of ministry as Lutherans presently experience and view it, and to devise ways of assessing seminarians' strengths and weaknesses, capacities and needs, as they begin to prepare for ministry. But it has become broader in application. This book is about more than professional ministry. A good deal of it adds to our knowledge about all Lutherans. What is presented here is an ideal, as Lutherans see it and either aim for it or avoid it in their personal lives. In the process of presenting their Christian ideal, Lutherans have also revealed their enthusiasms and interests, their areas of resistance or reluctance, their priorities in ministry, and those things certain groups among them especially prize. This information should be of value to any Lutheran, whether lay or clergy, who is interested in ministry, and possibly to non-Lutherans as well.

Our chief purpose in writing this book has been to share what we discovered as a result of our study. We do not think we know all there is to know, either about ministry or about Lutherans, but we have tried to share much of what we have learned. While reactions to this information will vary, we have been bold enough to offer some of our own reflections. Some may raise the question, "Who are you to be offering remedies, suggesting changes, and recommending action?" Yet we know, from past experience, that people want more from us than facts and figures. Our speeches, presentations, and reading of research papers are always followed by requests for us to identify implications, to interpret what we have said, and to suggest possible directions for action. Therefore, beyond summarizing the data available to us (as we have done in the first two parts of each chapter), we have offered reflections that grow from our own experiences, convictions, and understandings. Perhaps our own human (and therefore fallible) interpretations will encourage others to wrestle with the implications of our research on their own.

Some Summary Comments about Differences

Lutherans aren't tremendously different from each other in how they perceive ministry. To be sure, the opinions of any two Lutherans may be quite different, but as one examines the perceptions of large groups of Lutherans, there is a great deal of agreement. Even those groups commonly expected to differ turn out to agree more often than not. Older people usually value certain ministries more highly than younger people. However, the two are not at opposite poles; instead, the enthusiasm of one for certain matters is somewhat higher than that of the other. With a few exceptions, such as in parts of the chapters on dominating influence and liturgical leadership, groups of people differ only by degrees rather than in taking strongly opposing positions. However, once that point is securely made, there are some general observations to make about the remaining differences.

People in the following groups are likely to place different values on some areas of ministry. They are listed in descending order of the likelihood that they will differ:

- Clergy and laity
- Less-educated and more-highly-educated
- Younger and older people
- Men and women
- Members of the major Lutheran bodies: the American Lutheran Church, the Lutheran Church in America, and the Lutheran Church–Missouri Synod
- People who attend worship frequently and those who attend less frequently
- People who derive great satisfaction from their participation in church activities and those who do not gain such satisfaction
- People in various ministry settings

Clergy and laity

Of all the influences on how people view ministry, the most powerful we were able to identify is whether a person is a member of the clergy or laity. The clergy and lay members of a congregation are more likely to perceive ministries as of different value than any other two Lutheran groups. Given the amount of information we had about people who participated in the project, we determined that theological education accounts for almost all of the differences in responses between the clergy and laity. (Some, but fewer, are due to differences in general education.) Something happens in seminary training and experience that causes a person to understand ministry differently from other people. This is not so difficult to understand. One would expect an architect to view architecture differently from the rest of the populace, or a doctor to view health differently from others.

Where lay people and professional ministers agree is on matters of attitude, belief, and such general things as positive approach, loving devotion to people, adaptive self-confidence, and an ability to relate faith to experience and learning to action. Where the clergy rank characteristics higher, those characteristics are usually more specific, and are often *skills* or particular courses of action. The laity and clergy seem to agree on the general objectives or desired effects of ministry—for example, that a sense of God's family be created in congregations, or that there be efficient administration in parishes. What the professionals emphasize more are the particular activities or skills that must be practiced if those goals are to be reached. The professionals put extra stress, for example, on accepting mutual ministry, communicating grace and forgiveness, exuberance for life, promotion of mutuality, redemptive forthrightness, and encouragement of congregational gospel community. If all these ministries are happening in a congregation, then it is likely that a sense of God's family will also be there. On the desirability of that *result*, clergy and lay people agree.

Relatively speaking, lay people really emphasize few things as *more important* to effective ministry than do professionals. In addition to some matters having to do with liturgy and worship leadership, distinctive emphases of lay people tend to be only upon piety, a sense of calling, a few personal qualities, and some matters of style. They show one distinctive point of de-emphasis: they generally see all the characteristics of dominating influence (Chapter 4) as *less* of a hindrance than do clergy in general.

Education

Another source of variation is the one related to differences in education. The more-highly-educated are, in general, less tolerant of counseling that is directive, a ministry that tries to exert an authoritative influence over parishioners, or any tone of exclusiveness, defensiveness, or lack of leadership. Instead, they especially value a pastor who is a scholar, who can reflect theologically on experiences, and can communicate that study and reflection clearly to others. In addition, the highly-educated value a strong personal faith and a ministry of evangelism. This last will come as a surprise to those who assume that, generally speaking, more education tends to result in less respect for spiritual matters.

Lutherans with less formal education not only more easily accept but are more inclined to want ministry that is directive, that firmly and literally adheres to scriptural injunctions, is couched in clearly spiritual language, and exercises its influence openly and directly.

What we may be observing here is two types of piety, different in kind. One may be more intellectually respectable than the other, but we have no assurance that intellectual respectability is the highest good in the sight of God. In being critical of the style of piety of the less-well-educated, one may succeed only in taking that piety from them without substituting anything else. It seems to us that if one tries to produce a radical change in the views of the less-well-educated, without helping them become well-educated theologically, one may serve only to make their faith less secure, cause them to lose respect for the theologically educated, or drive them out of Lutheran churches and into the arms of fundamentalist groups.

Age

The third greatest set of differences in perception of ministry occurs across age gaps. There are many areas in which there is no significant difference. But where there are age-related differences, there is one predominant pattern of variation: the greater the difference in age, the greater the difference in opinion about the importance of a wide variety of ministry practices.

These differences, most of them outlined in the preceding chapters, are primarily along the lines of youth's desire for aggressive action in behalf of the welfare of others, and for a ministry that is sensitive and open— enabling people to experience and participate in a community of warm mutual support. This is consistent with our other youth studies, which generally show that the two essential ingredients for effective youth ministry are personal experiences of *mutuality* and participation in a caring community, accompanied by vision of a great *mission* to be accomplished.

Older people generally put increasing emphasis on nearly all the spiritual foundations dealt with in Chapter 1, all but one characteristic of congregational community (Chapter 6), Lutheran heritage and theology (Chapter 3), and liturgical leadership (Chapter 10). They are more encouraging of ministry that focuses rather exclusively on the specific needs of congregations (Chapter 4). They are harder than youth on behavior unbecoming of the clergy—telling dirty jokes, gambling, being involved in illicit sexual relationships, and the like (Chapter 5).

We believe the church would be the poorer if there were not tension between the particular emphases of the young and of the old, and the education each can offer the other, if they will listen to one another.

Men and women

Although they are not great, there are some differences in the perceptions of men and women as to what aids or hinders ministry. Women are more likely to want a mature person of faith who is approachable, available to help when called, and who will provide a skilled, sensitive kind of counsel. They place greater importance on pastors' being committed to their own families and creating a sense of the family of God in worship. So far the emphasized characteristics are consonant with what might be expected of those who have traditionally carried the nurturing role in society. Women also are more aware of the hindrance to ministry represented by qualities like aloofness, distance, self-isolation, unapproachability, authoritarianism, and self-centeredness.

Is there anything in pastors that men are especially concerned about? Our data showed nothing except that men are slightly more tolerant (or desirous, whichever way you want to interpret these characteristics) of exclusive devotion to congregational concerns and of lack of leadership. We do not know exactly why. The former may be the result of a perspective that employees should devote their attention to the needs of their employers. It may also be related to the greater tendency we found for women to empathize with the needs of oppressed and disadvantaged people who may not be church members. Men's greater tolerance of lack of pastoral leadership may be due to the fact that men are typically less involved in congregational activities.

Church bodies

As we have said before, we did not find members of the three major Lutheran bodies to differ greatly from one another. Contrasts in expectations that are identifiably different among members of church bodies occur primarily between the LCA and the LCMS.

The greater LCA emphasis, true to its history, is upon ministry to the larger community and world through caring for the broad-range, diverse needs of people everywhere. The Lutheran Church–Missouri Synod is obviously not without concern for the larger community and world, but this concern shows itself differently. Within the LCMS, and to some degree the ALC, the larger world concern focuses on what has historically been known as evangelism or world missions. This is not to suggest an either/or mentality in any of the three church bodies, but rather that their emphases tip in slightly different directions. The differences are *not in kind, but only in degree.*

An additional LCMS emphasis, by contrast with both the LCA and ALC, is on all three of the theological characteristics of dominating influence (Chapter 4), and especially on firm adherence to the authority of Scripture as interpreted rather literally and seen as verbally inspired.

There are also slight variations in emphasis among all three church bodies across most of the characteristics of "Personal Faith, Spiritual Depth" (Chapter 1). However, these variations in priority also should not be understood as mutually exclusive of divergent interests, but rather as differences in degrees of emphasis on common concerns.

A Note about Seminary Seniors

The information given at this point should be viewed with some caution, in that it reports on a single group of seminary students—those who were seniors in a particular year. More than for any other group, the picture presented might have been different if we had distributed the questionnaire two years earlier or two years later, though we do not know for sure. While we believe the information we present about seminary seniors is significant, it should be read in light of the singularity of the group from which it was taken.

Of the 77 characteristics of ministry, seminary seniors rated 19 significantly differently from one or more other groups (most frequently, the laity). The predominant direction in which they differed was de-emphasis. They downplayed the importance of 15 characteristics and significantly emphasized the other 4. In their pattern of emphases and de-emphases, the message they convey goes something like this: "Look, we're less concerned than some of you about making sure people believe the right things and express their Christian faith in certain traditional forms of piety, and we're also less intense about issues of theological orthodoxy and diversity. We're less impressed than most of you about the effectiveness of presenting authoritative facts in reducing racism and other forms of oppression. What we are more concerned about is developing a congregational atmosphere of friendship, support, cooperation, love, and freedom—that kind of gospel spirit. We're committed to developing and sustaining a good family life for our spouses and children, and to having good, deep interpersonal relationships with the members of our congregations. We want to help members develop life-styles that are consistent with what they believe as Christians. We are not so likely as some of you to be judgmental about some of the behaviors generally viewed as sinful, or as disqualifying for the ordained ministry. To sum it up, we put less emphasis on Christianity as a set of beliefs and formal actions, and more on Christianity as a way of life—a faith lived out together in gospel community."

Whether this point of view is cause for alarm or rejoicing depends on the reader. It is understandable that seminary seniors show evidence of some differences with other people. They are involved in a unique process —somewhere in the act of changing from lay people into clergy, traversing the perception gap that we have reported as being wider than any other. Sometimes these seminarians' perceptions agree with those of the professional clergy, sometimes with the laity, and sometimes they fall between the two. They are in a position of transition, and show evidence of it.

Concluding Comments on the Nature of Ministry

For the sake of the oversimplification that summary statements demand, this book has presented, in its two major parts, the two important elements in ministry as Lutherans view it: pastoral perspectives (who a minister is) and ministry skills (what a minister does). Of the two, Lutherans clearly declare that a minister as a person is most important. The best testimonies and the best ministries, it would appear, come in the form of persons. God sent his clearest message to the world in the form of a person, and people still see the most-valued ministry as presented in a minister's way of *being*. Skills are involved, of course. To have no skills, or to have some half-perfected ones, is in fact a way of being. But perhaps it is not stretching a point too far to say that one can more clearly see Paul's list of the fruits of the Spirit running through the descriptions of ministry in the early part of the book—love, joy, peace, patience, kindness, fidelity, gentleness, and self-control. These all work powerfully toward effectiveness in ministry when they are present, and in hindering ministry when they are absent. The quality of ministry, the spirit in which it is offered, powerfully influences its effectiveness.

Ministry is shared, interactive, and mutually affecting. It is a solemn thing—a transaction one expects the Holy Spirit to tend with special care —when a congregation calls a pastor, and that pastor accepts a call. Realizing that ministry is shared, both are becoming partners in serving as God's instruments. Realizing that ministry is interactive, they are agreeing to minister together and to one another. Realizing that ministry is mutually affecting, they are agreeing to the possibility of being changed by the ministry that occurs between them. The minister is agreeing to pledge to the congregation perhaps five to ten years of life and professional work, and to permit his or her life and ministry to be affected and shaped by that congregation. The people pledge, in effect, to receive the gifts that the minister brings, and to hear the Word and experience the sacraments administered, and thereby also to be changed.

In the course of our study, we have experienced a fresh sense not only of understanding but of wonder at what is implied in ministry. The more deeply we come to understand ministry, the more thoroughly we are convinced that the offering and the doing of Christian ministry is the work of the whole church, and that all of us serve a variety of functions in ministry. Whatever our roles or gifts, we are sometimes leaders, sometimes teachers, and sometimes enablers of others. We are sometimes in ministry as we listen and sometimes as we honestly speak our firmest convictions. Sometimes we minister by sharing our struggles and frustrations, and sometimes by offering our discoveries. And sometimes, when we least realize that we are doing so, we minister profoundly simply by being present and being who we are.

We are in partnership in ministry. The laity and clergy engage together in ministry to each other and to the world. But the partnership does not end there. The conviction that we are engaged in a partnership of another and more awesome sort has deepened as we have studied the nature and variety of ministry. It has been borne steadily in on us that God's creative power is still at work, as it has been from the beginning of all things. God takes what we offer to one another and to the world in his name—human, self-willed, sinning, and incomplete as all of us are—and uses those blemished offerings to see that his work on earth is done. To join one another and with God in that partnership is to experience the gift and the glory of ministry.

Appendix A

In this listing, the 77 characteristics of ministry are grouped according to the 10 general areas described in this book. The areas are presented in order of their general desirability among Lutherans, Area I being the most desired, and Area X the least. Within each area, the characteristics that make it up are listed *in the order of their rank among all Lutherans*. The rank number is also the number by which it is referred to in the text.

There is usually a range of rank within a given area of ministry. The first-ranked area, "Personal Faith, Spiritual Depth," is composed of nine characteristics ranked from 1st through 34th. It is ranked first because these characteristics, which together describe a particular area of ministry, come out with a higher average rating (3.02) than any other, even though they include some characteristics that are, by themselves, seen by Lutherans as of only middling desirability.

The three columns of numbers on the right represent, from left to right, the ratings given that characteristic by all lay people (Column 1), by all questionnaire participants, both clergy and lay (Column 2), and by all "professionals" (Column 3), i.e., the four categories of clergy: parish pastors, denominational executives, seminary faculty, and seminary seniors. Each number was arrived at by averaging the ratings given to all of the individual items that make up the characteristic.

Meanings of the numbers are as follows:

> 3.51 to 4.00 = *absolutely essential for effective ministry*
> 2.51 to 3.50 = *contributes very much*
> 1.51 to 2.50 = *contributes quite a bit*
> 0.51 to 1.50 = *contributes somewhat*
> −0.51 to −1.50 = *contributes/hinders little or nothing*
> −1.51 to −2.50 = *hinders somewhat*
> −2.51 to −3.50 = *hinders very much*
> −3.51 to −4.00 = *absolutely disqualifying*

Sometimes individual characteristics arose from the replies of clergy only, sometimes from lay people only, and sometimes from the total group. Since it is sometimes useful to know where a given characteristic came from—to know whose perceptions of that characteristic were strong enough to cause it to be expressed in this form—we underline the rating of the group which identified the characteristic. However, in assigning the final rank order of the characteristics, the ratings given by all Lutherans (total group) were used, no matter where the characteristic was originally identified.

		avg. lay rating	avg. Luth. rating	avg. pro. rating
Area I				
Personal Faith, Spiritual Depth				
(Chapter 1)		2.96	3.02	3.08
1	Personal Devotional Life	3.43	3.48	3.53
2	Confidence in Christ's Lordship	3.20	3.25	3.29
7	Pastoral Guidance	3.09	3.06	3.04
9	Christian Example	3.10	3.05	3.01
13	Accepting Mutual Ministry	2.77	3.00	3.22
14	Scripture-Based, Resurrection Faith	2.94	2.99	3.05
22	Ministry as a Calling	2.96	2.90	2.84
29	Evangelism and Mission Concern	2.64	2.79	2.93
34	Pastorally-Oriented Biblical Scholarship	2.55	2.68	2.81
Area II				
A Person for Others				
(Chapter 2)		2.84	2.91	2.97
3	Commitment to Family	3.08	3.22	3.36
4	Nondefensive Integrity	3.06	3.16	3.25
6	Loving Devotion to People	3.04	3.09	3.13
19	Positive Approach	2.91	2.93	2.94
26	Theologically Integrative Reflection	2.80	2.86	2.91
28	Imperviousness to Threat	2.84	2.83	2.81
30	Adaptive Self-Confidence	2.74	2.79	2.84
43	Exuberance for Life	2.28	2.42	2.55
Area III				
Critical Awareness of				
Lutheran Heritage and Theology				
(Chapter 3)		2.49	2.74	2.99

		avg. lay rating	avg. Luth. rating	avg. pro. rating
8	Communication of Life-Related Theology	2.93	3.06	3.19
12	Simul Justus et Peccator	2.79	3.04	3.28
38	Lutheran Confessional Stance	2.35	2.55	2.75
50	Scholarly Openness and Objectivity	1.87	2.29	2.72

Area IV
Community Through Word and Sacraments
(Chapter 6)

		2.70	2.76	2.82
5	Encouraging Responsibility to Means of Grace	3.07	3.09	3.12
10	Communicating Grace and Forgiveness	2.90	3.05	3.20
11	Creating Sense of God's Family	3.03	3.04	3.04
15	Relating Biblical Faith to Everyday Experience	2.89	2.96	3.03
18	Relational Preaching and Worship Leading	3.04	2.94	2.84
20	Explaining Sacraments and Rites	2.95	2.92	2.89
23	Fostering Congregational Gospel Community	2.77	2.89	3.01
35	Motivating Faith-Consistent Action	2.59	2.68	2.77
36	Personal Approach in Worship	2.46	2.64	2.82
53	Awareness of Children's Needs	2.31	2.23	2.16
59	Open, Evaluative Stance	1.73	1.92	2.10

Area V
Making Ministry of Administration
(Chapter 7)

		2.54	2.65	2.76
16	Development of Interpersonal Trust	2.84	2.95	3.06
24	Sharing of Congregational Leadership	2.81	2.87	2.94
25	Creative Use of Conflict	2.78	2.86	2.93
27	Promotion of Mutuality	2.68	2.84	2.99
31	Effective Administration	2.68	2.75	2.82
32	Responsible Group Leadership	2.63	2.74	2.85
39	Redemptive Forthrightness	2.42	2.52	2.62
40	Respect for Proper Procedures	2.32	2.51	2.70
41	Encouragement of Expression of Disagreement	2.26	2.48	2.69
57	Innovative Style of Leadership	1.96	1.98	2.01

Area VI
Ministry of Counseling
(Chapter 8)

		2.62	2.66	2.70

		avg. lay rating	avg. Luth. rating	avg. pro. rating
17	Enabling and Perceptive Counseling	2.77	2.95	3.13
21	Gracious Availability	2.97	2.91	2.85
42	Empathetic Aid in Suffering	2.30	2.45	2.60
46	Intentional Counseling	2.43	2.32	2.21

Area VII
Reaching Out with Compassion
to Community and World

(Chapter 9)		1.90	2.07	2.23
37	Use of Broad Knowledge	2.55	2.60	2.64
44	Initiation of Community Services	2.15	2.33	2.52
45	Candid Christian Humanness	2.10	2.32	2.53
47	Community Bridge Building	2.18	2.31	2.43
48	Integrative Ministry	2.08	2.30	2.51
49	Equipping for Community Service	2.02	2.30	2.57
51	Prophetic Concern for the Oppressed	2.00	2.25	2.49
54	Broad Intellectual Stimulation	2.13	2.19	2.24
55	Co-Ministry to the Distressed and Alienated	2.07	2.16	2.25
56	Active Concern for the Oppressed	1.82	2.09	2.36
58	Ecumenical Openness	1.87	1.96	2.05
60	Balanced Acceptance of Theological Diversity	1.96	1.89	1.81
62	Assertive Civic Leadership	0.97	1.31	1.65
64	Openness to Civil Disobedience	0.63	0.93	1.22

Area VIII
Informed Leadership
of Liturgical Worship

(Chapter 10)		2.27	2.04	1.81
33	Effective Speaking	2.96	2.73	2.50
52	Balanced Liturgical Judgment	2.41	2.25	2.09
63	Liturgical Orientation	1.45	1.14	0.84

Area IX
Not Wanted: Dominating Influence

(Chapter 4)		0.25	−0.19	−0.62

		avg. lay rating	avg. Luth. rating	avg. pro. rating
61	Extreme Adherence to Scriptural Authority	2.00	1.37	0.74
65	Spiritual Talk	1.23	0.81	0.39
66	Exclusive Devotion to Congregational Concerns	0.27	-0.10	-0.46
67	Law unto Self	-0.43	-0.84	-1.25
68	Spiritual Superiority	-0.55	-1.08	-1.61
69	Unbusinesslike Leadership	-1.01	-1.28	-1.54

Area X
Not Wanted: Ministry-Defeating Behaviors

(Chapter 5)		-2.62	-2.59	-2.56
70	Secular Life-Style	-2.33	-2.15	-1.96
71	Self-Centered Isolation	-2.19	-2.22	-2.24
72	Evidences of Insecurity	-2.21	-2.29	-2.36
73	Instability	-2.48	-2.37	-2.25
74	Self-Isolating Behavior	-2.67	-2.66	-2.65
75	Insecure Authoritarianism	-2.81	-2.85	-2.88
76	Undisciplined Living	-3.20	-3.10	-3.00
77	Impersonalness Without Trust	-3.04	-3.10	-3.16

Appendix B

This list presents the 77 characteristics of ministry arranged in descending order, beginning with the one Lutherans consider most highly essential, and ending with the one they believe hinders ministry most. The average Lutheran rating is presented at the right. (In the first year of the project's use in Lutheran seminaries, the characteristics had other numbers, so an "old" number precedes the present rank number.) The characteristics are presented under verbal meanings attached to the numerical ratings from the questionnaire given to 5000 Lutherans.

As you can see, the first 65 of the 77 fall into the category of contributing at least somewhat, with the majority—the first 41—considered to "contribute very much" to effective ministry. Differences in average ratings are often no more than hundreths of a point. The ranks of characteristics 23 and 28, for instance, are separated by only .05. For a few (Characteristics 16 and 17, or 29 and 30, for example) the difference in the rank order was determined only by thousandths of a point. In these cases the characteristics are, in effect, tied for the same rank, so that it is not wise to make too much of the fact that one characteristic has a higher rank than its immediate neighbors unless you have first looked at the differences in number ratings.

You will also notice that most of the characteristics toward the top of the list are very close in rating. In general, differences in rating are greater toward the bottom of the list.

An asterisk beside a characteristic means that in participating seminaries, during the school year 1977-78, these characteristics were assessed in entering students through the Lutheran Seminarian Project.

old no.	new no. and rank	meas. 1977		average Lutheran rating

Absolutely Essential
(3.51 to 4.00)

(no characteristics)

Contribute Very Much
(2.51 to 3.50)

old no.	new no. and rank	meas. 1977	characteristic	average Lutheran rating
35	1	°	Personal Devotional Life	3.48
72	2	°	Confidence in Christ's Lordship	3.25
41	3	°	Commitment to Family	3.22
42	4	°	Nondefensive Integrity	3.16
2	5		Encouraging Responsibility to Means of Grace	3.09
43	6	°	Loving Devotion to People	3.09
20	7	°	Pastoral Guidance	3.06
26	8	°	Communication of Life-Related Theology	3.06
36	9		Christian Example	3.05
1	10	°	Communicating Grace and Forgiveness	3.05
3	11		Creating Sense of God's Family	3.04
73	12	°	Simul Justus et Peccator	3.04
37	13		Accepting Mutual Ministry	3.00
25	14	°	Scripture-Based, Resurrection Faith	2.99
65	15	°	Relating Biblical Faith to Everyday Experience	2.96
54	16		Development of Interpersonal Trust	2.95
21	17	°	Enabling and Perceptive Counseling	2.95
66	18		Relational Preaching and Worship Leading	2.94
44	19	°	Positive Approach	2.93
4	20		Explaining Sacraments and Rites	2.92
22	21	°	Gracious Availability	2.91
38	22		Ministry as a Calling	2.90
64	23		Fostering Congregational Gospel Community	2.89
56	24	°	Sharing of Congregational Leadership	2.87
57	25	°	Creative Use of Conflict	2.86
27	26		Theologically Integrative Reflection	2.86
55	27		Promotion of Mutuality	2.84
45	28	°	Imperviousness to Threat	2.83
11	29	°	Evangelism and Mission Concern	2.79
74	30		Adaptive Self-Confidence	2.79
58	31		Effective Administration	2.75
76	32	°	Responsible Group Leadership	2.74

old no.	new no. and rank	meas. 1977		average Lutheran rating
7	33		Effective Speaking	2.73
28	34		Pastorally-Oriented Biblical Scholarship	2.68
6	35		Motivating Faith-Consistent Action	2.68
5	36		Personal Approach in Worship	2.64
30	37		Use of Broad Knowledge	2.60
29	38		Lutheran Confessional Stance	2.55
60	39		Redemptive Forthrightness	2.52
61	40	°	Respect for Proper Procedures	2.51

Contribute Quite a Bit
(1.51 to 2.50)

59	41		Encouragement of Expression of Disagreement	2.48
23	42		Empathetic Aid in Suffering	2.45
46	43		Exuberance for Life	2.42
14	44		Initiation of Community Services	2.33
39	45	°	Candid Christian Humanness	2.32
70	46		Intentional Counseling	2.32
12	47		Community Bridge Building	2.31
16	48		Integrative Ministry	2.30
13	49		Equipping for Community Service	2.30
31	50	°	Scholarly Openness and Objectivity	2.29
69	51	°	Prophetic Concern for the Oppressed	2.25
67	52		Balanced Liturgical Judgment	2.25
8	53		Awareness of Children's Needs	2.23
32	54		Broad Intellectual Stimulation	2.19
24	55		Co-Ministry to the Distressed and Alienated	2.16
15	56		Active Concern for the Oppressed	2.09
62	57		Innovative Style of Leadership	1.98
9	58		Ecumenical Openness	1.96
68	59		Open, Evaluative Stance	1.92
71	60		Balanced Acceptance of Theological Diversity	1.89

Contribute Somewhat
(0.51 to 1.50)

33	61	°	Extreme Adherence to Scriptural Authority	1.37
17	62	°	Assertive Civic Leadership	1.31
10	63		Liturgical Orientation	1.14

old no.	new no. and rank	meas. 1977		average Lutheran rating
18	64	°	Openness to Civil Disobedience	0.93
40	65		Spiritual Talk	0.81

Contribute/Hinder Little or Nothing
(0.50 to –0.50)

19	66	°	Exclusive Devotion to Congregational Concerns	–0.10

Hinder Somewhat
(–0.51 to –1.50)

63	67	°	Law unto Self	–0.84
34	68		Spiritual Superiority	–1.08
77	69		Unbusinesslike Leadership	–1.28

Hinder Quite a Bit
(–1.51 to –2.50)

47	70		Secular Life-Style	–2.15
48	71	°	Self-Centered Isolation	–2.22
50	72		Evidences of Insecurity	–2.29
49	73		Instability	–2.37

Hinder Very Much
(–2.51 to –3.50)

75	74	°	Self-Isolating Behavior	–2.66
51	75	°	Insecure Authoritarianism	–2.85
52	76		Undisciplined Living	–3.10
53	77		Impersonalness Without Trust	–3.10

Absolutely Disqualifying
(–3.51 to –4.00)

(no characteristics)

Appendix C

In Chapters 2 and 7 of this book, checklists are offered as a means of helping individuals think through their own tendencies in a particular area, or to get information from others about themselves. Since this appendix lists all the individual items that make up the 77 characteristics discussed in this book, there is checklist material here for any or all of the characteristics of ministry.

A checklist can be used:

- As a personal checklist
- As a means toward goal setting
- As a way of offering information to others
- As a way of asking for evaluation of yourself from others
- As part of a group discussion of the ministry of your congregation

When the items are to be used as a checklist, the introductory question is, "About myself, this item is. . . ." or "About Person X, this item is. . . ." Then check the appropriate column for each item. To use the items for goal setting, circle the number of each item which represents an area of desired change or improvement.

The list of items, in its entirety, is fairly exhaustive. There are a number of modifications or abbreviations of the list you might consider in rating yourself or seeking ratings from others. If you want as full a rating as possible on only a few characteristics, you will probably ask for ratings on every item. If you want ratings on a large number of characteristics, use only the first three items of each of your chosen characteristics. In each characteristic, these three are the ones most central to the whole meaning of the characteristic. You might choose to work on one area of ministry at a time, using the checklist only for that area. Or, if you want to cover all the areas of ministry, you might choose only two characteristics from each area for rating purposes, choosing characteristics on the basis of what you have read about them or their importance to you.

It would be possible, though it would give you a less accurate reading, to rate yourself or be rated on the basis of the characteristic name and description only, not using the individual items.

———————◆———————

Some people have interests or questions that will carry them beyond the text of the book. For them, this appendix offers a fruitful area for study. It presents in condensed form much of what is presented in the descriptive part of each chapter, along with some additional information.

Here the areas of ministry are presented in order of their general desirability among Lutherans, beginning with the most-desired Area I and finishing with the least-desired Area X. Within each area, the characteristics that make it up are listed in the order of their rank among all Lutherans. Each characteristic is listed by number and name, followed by a description of its central meaning and all of the items that make it up. The items are listed in the sequence of their centrality to whatever it is that is the essence of that characteristic—its *meaning* (see the discussion of "raisin-ness" on pp. 18-19).

It is important to note that, although the areas of ministry and the characteristics are ranked (and numbered) in the order of their importance to ministry, the numbers given to the *items* have *nothing* to do with rank. *Item numbers indicate only the sequence in which they appeared in the original questionnaire* and are included here as a means of easy identification for group discussion.

Numbers to the right of each page show the rating given to each characteristic, and to each individual item, by laity, by professionals, and by all Lutherans.

One of the best ways to understand a given characteristic is to read the items that comprise it without looking at its name or description, and then to try to form your own description and assign a name of your own making. The titles and descriptions given here were assigned by the research team in consultation with a panel of representatives from a number of Lutheran seminaries, and were modified on the basis of further suggestions from seminaries during the early use of this information. However, your own titles and descriptions may come closer than ours to your own understanding of the meaning.

There are a number of other ways in which this information could be studied. One possibility, if your focus is on laity, would be to locate the three highest-ranked items in a given characteristic and the three lowest-ranked items as the laity rated them, to see what understanding that conveys. Another possibility is to note which characteristics are more highly rated by professionals than by laity. Your own interests will best dictate the use you make of the information.

	avg. lay rating	avg. Luth. rating	avg. pro. rating	very true	somewhat true	not true

Area I
Personal Faith, Spiritual Depth
(Chapter 1)

Characteristic 1
Personal Devotional Life   3.43   3.48   3.53

Use of prayer, Word, and sacraments that shows a profound sense of dependence on God's sustaining, guiding, and redeeming activity.

		avg. lay	avg. Luth.	avg. pro.
386	Acknowledges own sin and confesses this to God.	3.54	3.65	3.75
382	Uses Scripture as a source of spiritual nourishment.	3.35	3.41	3.47
387	Spends time daily in private prayer and meditation.	3.30	3.28	3.25
389	Lives with a sense of daily forgiveness.	3.21	3.39	3.56
366	Shows sensitivity to the leading of the Holy Spirit.	3.24	3.30	3.36
361	Believes the gospel he or she preaches.	3.77	3.83	3.89
365	Receives Holy Communion regularly.	3.57	3.59	3.60
355	Shows the mission of Christ to be first in own life.	3.42	3.38	3.34

Characteristic 2
Confidence in Christ's Lordship   3.20   3.25   3.29

Confidence in ultimate outcomes based on belief in the kingdom of God in Christ, reflected in hope, zeal, and sense of freedom.

		avg. lay	avg. Luth.	avg. pro.
380	Expresses profound hope because of a belief in kingdom of God.	3.39	3.39	3.40
379	Acknowledges personal need for continued growth in faith.	3.34	3.41	3.47
377	Expresses desire for all to recognize the lordship of Christ.	3.16	3.14	3.13

	avg. lay rating	avg. Luth. rating	avg. pro. rating	very true	somewhat true	not true
378 Approaches life as one who believes the forces of good are greater than the forces of evil.	3.16	3.05	2.94			
357 Holds that in the midst of serious problems, God is at work.	3.40	3.45	3.50			
373 Lives with a sense of freedom in the gospel.	2.77	3.07	3.38			
335 In teaching, relates God's activity to everyday life and happenings.	3.17	3.21	3.25			

Characteristic 7
Pastoral Guidance   3.09   3.06   3.04

Guidance of others to sharpened
consciousness of God's forgiveness
and present power as well as to
heightened personal commitment.

266 Leads people to recognize ways God may be working in their lives.	3.11	3.06	3.01			
262 Leads people to deepened spiritual growth and commitment.	3.18	3.22	3.25			
271 Helps people use the resources of faith in coping with personal problems.	3.16	3.20	3.24			
260 When counseling, may sometimes confront person with the need to believe.	2.91	2.73	2.54			
249 Counsels on matters of wrongdoing with the intent of conveying the assurance of God's forgiveness.	3.06	3.10	3.14			

Characteristic 9
Christian Example   3.10   3.05   3.01

Exemplary personal life manifested
in generosity, a joyous attitude,
and a life of high moral quality.

		avg. lay rating	avg. Luth. rating	avg. pro. rating	very true	somewhat true	not true
393	Sets a Christian example that people in the community respect.	3.48	3.29	3.10			
391	Provides a personal witness to the gospel by own generosity.	2.76	2.87	2.99			
385	Demonstrates the joyous character of the Christian life.	3.11	3.10	3.09			
390	Behaves morally in a way that is above reproach.	2.96	2.86	2.76			
392	Spouse is a companion in the faith.	3.17	3.13	3.10			

Characteristic 13
Accepting Mutual Ministry   2.77   3.00   3.22

Gospel freedom of spirit to accept the ministry of others and to be engaged in intercessory prayer for other people.

397	Accepts the ministries of another pastor or Christian friend.	2.74	2.98	3.23			
398	Goes about work in a way that reflects the liberating power of the gospel.	2.95	3.14	3.33			
396	Actively engages in intercessory prayer on behalf of others.	2.63	2.87	3.11			

Characteristic 14
Scripture-Based, Resurrection Faith   2.94   2.99   3.05

Firm conviction that the Scriptures are normative in matters of faith and that the resurrection of Jesus Christ is a historical event.

| 293 | Treats the Bible as the norm in matters of faith. | 3.06 | 3.22 | 3.39 | | | |
| 299 | Affirms with conviction the historical resurrection of Jesus Christ from the dead. | 3.36 | 3.40 | 3.44 | | | |

	avg. lay rating	avg. Luth. rating	avg. pro. rating	very true	somewhat true	not true
305 Own beliefs are not easily swayed by opposing views.	2.40	2.36	2.32			

Characteristic 22
Ministry as a Calling 2.96 2.90 2.84

A sustaining sense of ministry as a call of God, which opens the way to a spirit of cooperative, unselfish service and to commendation of the ministry to young people.

	avg. lay rating	avg. Luth. rating	avg. pro. rating
363 Views the call or appointment to a parish, once accepted, as a calling of God.	3.16	3.12	3.08
360 Appears to be sustained by a sense of God's call when the going gets rough.	3.20	3.17	3.14
364 Accepts guidance and counsel of ecclesiastical superiors willingly.	2.78	2.66	2.53
369 Interprets the decision to enter the ministry as a personal call from God.	3.19	2.87	2.55
370 Encourages selected young people to consider the ministry as a vocation.	2.56	2.50	2.45
368 Is at peace with himself or herself.	3.11	2.97	2.82
371 Acknowledges own inability to arrive at major decisions without deep prayer and thought.	2.54	2.51	2.48
359 Serves others willingly with or without public acclaim.	3.17	3.22	3.28
358 Expresses appreciation for the personal support and edification given by the congregation.	2.93	3.06	3.20

Characteristic 29
Evangelism and Mission Concern 2.64 2.79 2.93

Commitment to an evangelism and service outreach that is evidenced

	avg. lay rating	avg. Luth. rating	avg. pro. rating	very true	somewhat true	not true

by actively involving the congregation in local and worldwide efforts to reach all with the gospel.

158 Organizes evangelism programs that involve the congregation in witnessing for Jesus Christ in the community.	2.17	2.36	2.55			
131 Seeks to bring everyone to know God's love in Jesus Christ.	3.42	3.35	3.28			
127 Stimulates congregation to interest and support for world missions.	2.33	2.56	2.78			
146 Speaks and acts as one concerned about reaching others with the gospel.	3.30	3.37	3.43			
159 Urges members to respond to critical needs in the world through sacrificial giving.	2.00	2.30	2.61			

Characteristic 34
Pastorally-Oriented Biblical Scholarship

	avg. lay rating	avg. Luth. rating	avg. pro. rating	very true	somewhat true	not true
Pastorally-Oriented Biblical Scholarship	2.55	2.68	2.81			

Thorough and continually renewed knowledge of Scripture and theology that is applied to current pastoral issues.

326 Is informed on the scriptural and theological background of the current charismatic movement.	2.09	2.25	2.42			
327 Demonstrates knowledge of Scripture.	3.48	3.48	3.49			
325 In private study, uses original languages (Greek or Hebrew) to clarify biblical passages.	1.37	1.61	1.84			
318 Presents a theological basis for the mission of the church.	2.62	2.85	3.08			
300 Gives evidence of continued and thorough study of the Scriptures.	3.28	3.36	3.43			

	avg. lay rating	avg. Luth. rating	avg. pro. rating	very true	somewhat true	not true
340 Shows skill in finding theologically sound solutions to pastoral problems.	2.47	2.55	2.62			

Area II
A Person for Others
(Chapter 2)

Characteristic 3 **Commitment to Family**	3.08	3.22	3.36			

An attitude of responsibility towards the family in relation to the congregation, both with respect to sharing time and the handling of confidential material.

491 Schedules regular time to be alone with family.	3.03	3.20	3.38			
463 Treats spouse with same care as given parishioners.	2.90	3.00	3.11			
486 Spouse keeps confidential information to self.	3.33	3.46	3.59			
482 Keeps commitments to own children as consistently as professional appointments.	3.05	3.20	3.35			

Characteristic 4 **Nondefensive Integrity**	3.06	3.16	3.25			

Lack of defensiveness concerning one's limitations and mistakes, relationships with other clergy, and the necessity to keep promises.

494 Recognizes own emotional and physical limitations.	3.09	3.22	3.34			
493 Relates warmly and nondefensively to ministers who are either predecessors or successors.	2.89	2.94	2.98			
497 Says willingly, "I don't know,"						

		avg. lay rating	avg. Luth. rating	avg. pro. rating	very true	somewhat true	not true
	regarding problems beyond own experience or competence.	3.15	3.31	3.47			
496	In embarrassing situations can laugh easily, even at self.	2.94	3.01	3.08			
492	Maintains personal integrity despite pressures to compromise.	3.15	3.28	3.41			
495	Acknowledges own mistakes to church council.	2.72	2.80	2.89			
490	Spouse is sympathetic and committed to minister's vocation.	3.10	3.10	3.09			
489	Works independently without prodding or supervision.	3.02	3.12	3.22			
487	Keeps own word—fulfills promises.	3.56	3.59	3.63			
491	Schedules regular time to be alone with family.	3.03	3.20	3.38			

Characteristic 6
Loving Devotion to People   3.04   3.09   3.13

Disciplined, sensitive, open devotion to the personhood and welfare of all people.

465	Generally finishes what he or she starts.	3.12	3.08	3.04			
469	Demonstrates honest affection for other people.	3.14	3.21	3.28			
470	Works cooperatively with superiors.	3.01	2.98	2.94			
458	Accurately senses the concerns and needs of people.	3.13	3.20	3.28			
460	Is open to learning from other people through their criticism or suggestions.	3.04	3.17	3.30			
467	Manifests a pastoral heart by an accepting and affirming approach to people.	2.88	3.12	3.36			
468	Does not avoid tasks of ministry that he or she does not enjoy.	2.97	2.95	2.94			
459	Takes time to listen to own children.	3.41	3.45	3.48			

		avg. lay rating	avg. Luth. rating	avg. pro. rating	very true	somewhat true	not true
461	Converses easily with the opposite sex.	3.00	3.02	3.04			
471	Relates well to people of varied cultures.	2.87	2.84	2.82			
466	Makes eye contact with people to whom he or she is talking.	2.96	3.02	3.08			
474	Shows a good balance of seriousness and humor.	3.01	3.02	3.02			

Characteristic 19
Positive Approach   2.91   2.93   2.94

A positive attitude towards tasks, relationships, or people that are potentially unpleasant, distressing, or threatening.

468	Does not avoid tasks of ministry that he or she does not enjoy.	2.97	2.95	2.94			
470	Works cooperatively with superiors.	3.01	2.98	2.94			
484	Remains positive and constructive toward cantankerous members.	2.78	2.83	2.88			
493	Relates warmly and nondefensively to ministers who are either predecessors or successors.	2.89	2.94	2.98			

Characteristic 26
Theologically Integative
Reflection   2.80   2.86   2.91

Ability to integrate theology, experience, and a broad base of information by reflecting on their significance.

| 301 | Learns from experiences by reflecting on their significance. | 2.63 | 2.84 | 3.05 | | | |

	avg. lay rating	avg. Luth. rating	avg. pro. rating	very true	somewhat true	not true
302 Demonstrates combination of both thinking and doing.	3.00	3.08	3.17			
320 Teaches and preaches from a broad base of information.	2.93	2.87	2.82			
313 Is clear about the theology that guides and informs own ministry.	3.10	3.18	3.27			
316 Speaks knowledgeably about subjects outside theology without being a bore.	2.36	2.31	2.27			

Characteristic 28
Imperviousness to Threat — 2.84 2.83 2.81

Lack of vulnerability to threats implicit in open opposition, change, negative experience, or persons exhibiting diverse life-styles.

	avg. lay rating	avg. Luth. rating	avg. pro. rating	very true	somewhat true	not true
484 Remains positive and constructive toward cantankerous members.	2.78	2.83	2.88			
481 Expresses honest opinions in the face of opposition.	3.16	3.12	3.09			
483 Accepts the risk involved in change.	2.71	2.91	3.10			
480 Is not disturbed by people whose life-styles differ from own.	2.71	2.68	2.66			
485 Helps others see the best in people.	3.02	2.97	2.93			
475 Bounces back after negative experiences.	3.03	3.06	3.10			
479 Responds to heated arguments without raising voice.	2.62	2.51	2.39			
488 Accepts comfortably the discrepancy between status and income and those of some other professions.	2.70	2.52	2.34			

	avg. lay rating	avg. Luth. rating	avg. pro. rating	very true	somewhat true	not true
Characteristic 30 **Adaptive Self-Confidence**	2.74	2.79	2.84			

Neither accentuating self nor being unduly impressed or intimidated by others while adapting well to new situations.

462 Does not draw attention to self.	2.30	2.40	2.49			
476 Adapts well to new situations or circumstances.	2.96	2.98	2.99			
464 Is neither afraid nor overly impressed by people in the congregation who are "success symbols."	2.95	2.99	3.05			

Characteristic 43 **Exuberance for Life**	2.28	2.42	2.55			

Acceptance of own sexuality and the adventure of exploring friendships, new possibilities, new ideas and cultures.

478 Pastor and spouse have personal friends in congregation with whom they share life's experiences.	1.91	1.92	1.94			
473 Is usually eager to try out new possibilities.	2.42	2.50	2.59			
477 Encourages members to value diversity of cultures, personal experiences, ideas, etc.	2.36	2.51	2.67			
472 Shows positive acceptance of own sexuality.	2.45	2.73	3.02			

	avg. lay rating	avg. Luth. rating	avg. pro. rating	very true	somewhat true	not true

Area III
Critical Awareness of
Lutheran Heritage and Theology
(Chapter 3)

Characteristic 8
Communication of Life-Related
Theology — 2.93, 3.06, 3.19

Communication evidencing an
approach to human problems of
varying complexity that is char-
acterized by clarity of thought
and theological competence.

	avg. lay rating	avg. Luth. rating	avg. pro. rating
291 Own statements of belief reflect careful thought and evaluation.	3.10	3.19	3.29
290 Explains complex issues in understandable terms.	3.01	3.06	3.12
292 Shares a theology that fits the real needs of people experiencing stress.	2.95	3.08	3.21
297 On difficult moral issues, takes into account extenuating circumstances as well as spiritual points of view.	2.62	2.80	2.98
296 Increases own theological competence through research and study.	3.00	3.17	3.34

Characteristic 12
Simul Justus et Peccator — 2.79, 3.04, 3.28

Realistic awareness of own motiva-
tions, inadequacies, and sinfulness
balanced with awareness of congre-
gational needs, sources of help,
and one's own sainthood in Christ.

381   Shows sufficient awareness of

	avg. lay rating	avg. Luth. rating	avg. pro. rating	very true	somewhat true	not true
own inadequacies to know when help is needed.	2.88	3.05	3.22			
388 Balances personal interests and activities with the needs of congregation.	2.88	2.93	2.97			
356 Sees self as both sinner and saint.	2.61	3.13	3.65			

Characteristic 38
Lutheran Confessional Stance   2.35   2.55   2.75

A personal theological stance that reflects a Lutheran confessional position not held rigidly or in a way that ignores insights from biblical scholarship.

298 Makes the Lutheran Confessions own personal confession without feeling obligated to every nondoctrinal detail.	2.08	2.37	2.65			
314 Interprets the authority of Scripture as being in the gospel message.	3.02	2.91	2.80			
315 On controversial issues, shows sensitivity to the relationship between Scripture and traditions of the church.	2.32	2.48	2.65			
353 Interprets Scripture using tools of biblical scholarship.	1.98	2.44	2.90			

Characteristic 50
Scholarly Openness and Objectivity   1.87   2.29   2.72

An openness to learn from lay persons and biblical scholarship that includes commitment, yet not being bound by tradition or a moralistic concept of Scripture.

| 341 Learns theology also from lay persons. | 2.05 | 2.44 | 2.84 | | | |

		avg. lay rating	avg. Luth. rating	avg. pro. rating	very true	somewhat true	not true
345	Though committed to the Lutheran heritage is free to criticize it.	1.55	2.11	2.66			
349	Applies Scripture to persons and society in nonmoralizing way.	1.88	2.17	2.46			
353	Interprets Scripture using tools of biblical scholarship.	1.98	2.44	2.90			

Area IV
Community Through
Word and Sacraments
(Chapter 6)

Characteristic 5
Encouraging Responsibility to
Means of Grace   3.07   3.09   3.12

Encouraging congregation to accept
its responsibility to nurture and
affirm faith received in Baptism.

118	Helps people recognize their responsibilities to infants baptized in the congregation.	2.73	2.77	2.82			
79	Teaches the meaning of Baptism and the Eucharist.	3.24	3.33	3.41			
78	Provides opportunities for all age groups to affirm their faith.	3.23	3.17	3.12			

Characteristic 10
Communicating Grace and Forgiveness   2.90   3.05   3.20

Belief and activity that stimulates
in others the awareness of the
judgment, forgiveness, and grace of
God.

		avg. lay rating	avg. Luth. rating	avg. pro. rating	very true	somewhat true	not true
59	Enables people to sense the gift of forgiveness God conveys through his Word.	3.39	3.51	3.62			
62	Confronts both the unchurched and members with the gospel message.	2.89	3.09	3.29			
77	Considers professional ministry to be a means of making God's grace known to people.	3.08	3.16	3.23			
76	Emphasizes the opportunities of walking in the power of one's baptism through daily repentance.	2.53	2.70	2.87			
53	When preaching, places self, as much as hearers, under God's judgment and grace.	3.11	3.29	3.47			
71	Treats Christian day school teachers as co-ministers in the gospel.	2.40	2.56	2.73			

Characteristic 11
Creating Sense of God's Family   3.03   3.04   3.04

In worship and the Lord's Supper helping people experience the confident, joyous sense of being a witnessing family of God and a community of faith.

68	Helps people experience the Lord's Supper as a joyous celebration.	3.23	3.17	3.12			
69	Helps people feel confident in sharing their faith with others.	3.07	3.05	3.03			
80	Creates a sense of the congregation as the family of God in worship.	3.03	3.08	3.14			
90	Leads worship in a way that encourages a sense of being a community of faith.	2.78	2.83	2.87			

	avg. lay rating	avg. Luth. rating	avg. pro. rating	very true	somewhat true	not true
Characteristic 15 **Relating Biblical Faith to** **Everyday Experience**	2.89	2.96	3.03			

Sensitive, theocentric interpreting, teaching, and drawing attention to God's Word and person in contemporary life.

		avg. lay rating	avg. Luth. rating	avg. pro. rating
44	Presents the Word of God in terms clearly understandable to the modern mind.	3.37	3.48	3.57
49	When teaching, is able to keep students interested.	3.16	3.01	2.85
43	Instills in members a friendliness and openness to newcomers.	3.23	3.12	3.00
46	Uses biblical insights to guide people in making ethical or moral decisions.	2.64	2.84	3.02
47	When he or she is through preaching, you are conscious of Jesus Christ.	3.25	3.24	3.23
50	Guides people by relating the Scriptures to their human condition.	2.74	3.01	3.25
45	Usually explains changes introduced into worship.	2.60	2.64	2.67
48	Helps people determine current educational needs in the congregation.	2.11	2.25	2.38
42	Preaches with authority and conviction.	3.16	3.17	3.18
41	Is actively involved in equipping laity for choices they must make in their daily lives.	2.61	2.86	3.12

Characteristic 18 **Relational Preaching and Worship** **Leading** 3.04 2.94 2.84

	avg. lay rating	avg. Luth. rating	avg. pro. rating	very true	somewhat true	not true

Inspiring joy and awakening evangelical need and awareness of God's closeness, through preaching and worship leading.

73 Leads worship in a manner that inspires joy.	3.12	3.04	2.97			
72 Has clear goals when teaching.	3.13	3.10	3.08			
82 Leads worship in a way that helps people feel the closeness of God.	3.34	3.09	2.84			
64 Preaches sermons that awaken listeners to their sinfulness and need.	2.55	2.52	2.49			

Characteristic 20
Explaining Sacraments and Rites   2.95   2.92   2.89

Attempting to increase the significance of sacred occasions by seeing to it that participants understand the meaning of what God offers them.

52 Helps people prepare for participation in Holy Communion.	2.93	2.84	2.74			
61 Explains the meaning of worship and liturgy.	2.76	2.66	2.56			
79 Teaches the meaning of Baptism and the Eucharist.	3.24	3.33	3.41			
60 Meets with engaged couples to help them prepare for Christian marriage.	2.90	2.87	2.84			

Characteristic 23
Fostering Congregational Gospel Community   2.77   2.89   3.01

Developing a congregational sense of mutual friendship, support,

		avg. lay rating	avg. Luth. rating	avg. pro. rating	very true	somewhat true	not true
	cooperation, love, freedom, and gospel spirit.						
98	Creates an atmosphere in the congregation that is enlivened by the gospel spirit of freedom and love.	2.90	3.04	3.17			
97	Becomes a part of the daily life, work, and play of the people served.	2.45	2.62	2.79			
56	Helps congregation be a fellowship where people can find friendship and support.	2.96	3.01	3.06			
	Characteristic 35 **Motivating Faith-Consistent Action**	2.59	2.68	2.77			
	Teaching and preaching so as to awaken the consciousness of people of all ages to new ways of respond- ing to life's challenges, consis- tent with their faith.						
115	Challenges middle-aged adults to make their life-style con- sistent with their faith.	2.14	2.40	2.66			
116	Helps families to participate as units in the needs and concerns of the community of which they are a part.	2.09	2.27	2.45			
112	Treats each age group, includ- ing youth, as part of the congregation, not as a pro- grammatic appendage.	3.22	3.21	3.19			
105	Teaches and preaches in a way that leads people to act.	3.12	3.15	3.18			
119	Worship (liturgical celebra- tions) under his or her lead- ership has dignity even when new or experimental.	2.64	2.61	2.59			

		avg. lay rating	avg. Luth. rating	avg. pro. rating	very true	somewhat true	not true
102	Provides opportunities within the congregation for personal growth and spiritual enrichment.	2.92	2.99	3.06			
108	Provides educational experiences to help middle-aged adults deal with various phases of family life.	2.13	2.23	2.33			
74	Helps the congregation keep in touch with disinterested and alienated members.	2.45	2.59	2.73			

Characteristic 36
Personal Approach in Worship   2.46   2.64   2.82

Preaching and leading worship in ways that are warmly personal and empathetic.

92	Preaches as one who has experienced the problems of living out the Christian life.	2.72	2.92	3.12			
90	Leads worship in a way that encourages a sense of being a community of faith.	2.78	2.83	2.87			
96	Celebrates worship in a way that is personal yet reverent.	2.92	2.87	2.82			
87	Preaches funeral sermons that acknowledge personal grief.	1.43	1.94	2.45			

Characteristic 53
Awareness of Children's Needs   2.31   2.23   2.16

Communicating awareness of children in the manner of leading worship for them, teaching them, and showing concern about their home and school environment.

| 51 | Conducts worship in a way that is meaningful for children. | 2.76 | 2.61 | 2.46 | | | |

		avg. lay rating	avg. Luth. rating	avg. pro. rating	very true	somewhat true	not true
91	Teaches small children effectively.	2.83	2.53	2.23			
88	Affirms with conviction the importance of Lutheran parochial schools.	1.00	0.84	0.68			
106	Calls regularly on members of the church in their homes.	2.09	2.36	2.63			
75	Assists Sunday school teachers in teaching effectively.	2.85	2.82	2.79			

Characteristic 59
Open, Evaluative Stance   1.73   1.92   2.10

Readiness to receive ministry of
others, including evaluation of
preaching, worship leading, and
understanding of doctrine.

84	Provides for group discussion of the sermon.	1.30	1.47	1.64			
85	Tries to determine where people are in their understanding of Christian doctrine.	2.21	2.47	2.72			
89	Engages groups in evaluating services of worship.	1.40	1.55	1.70			
86	Instills in congregation an openness to ministries from Christians in other parts of the world.	2.03	2.19	2.34			

Area V
Making Ministry
of Administration
(Chapter 7)

Characteristic 16
Development of Interpersonal Trust   2.84   2.95   3.06

	avg. lay rating	avg. Luth. rating	avg. pro. rating	very true	somewhat true	not true
Approach to parishioners on an individual basis that both conveys and inspires trust.						
678 Takes time to know parishioners well.	2.81	2.96	3.12			
680 Seeks out discontented persons in the congregation to try to understand their complaints.	2.56	2.64	2.73			
679 Develops a feeling of trust and confidence between self and members.	3.16	3.24	3.33			
Characteristic 24 Sharing of Congregational Leadership	2.81	2.87	2.94			
Congregational leadership that effectively shares responsibility and creates a sense of team through providing facts laity need for making decisions; helping lay leaders set long-range goals based on needs, and using evaluation and the thinking of many to make decisions.						
672 Knows and uses parish and community records and data in program building.	2.61	2.66	2.72			
671 Employs administrative procedures that make for teamwork and efficient use of time.	2.97	3.01	3.05			
670 Meets with lay leaders to set goals consistent with their mission and potential.	3.13	3.19	3.25			
676 Learns the traditions and customs of the local congre-						

		avg. lay rating	avg. Luth. rating	avg. pro. rating	very true	somewhat true	not true
	gation before suggesting change.	2.85	3.00	3.16			
696	Considers an overall parish strategy before planning individual projects.	2.66	2.75	2.83			
694	Shares leadership with lay leaders chosen by the congregation.	2.97	3.13	3.29			
691	Anticipates building and program needs through long-range planning.	2.52	2.56	2.60			
674	Promotes activities which build a sense of parish family.	2.98	3.04	3.11			
692	Has an understanding of conflict as it relates to own theology.	2.61	2.71	2.82			
684	Evaluates how well the congregation's programs are meeting the people's needs.	2.87	2.96	3.04			
695	In group discussion, stimulates many, not just a few, to participate.	2.95	2.95	2.95			
690	Attempts to find the real reasons why people drop out of church.	3.10	2.99	2.87			
682	Encourages groups to think seriously about why their group should continue to exist.	2.25	2.39	2.54			

Characteristic 25
Creative Use of Conflict   2.78   2.86   2.93

A skill in using conflict constructively that helps people come to understand both sides of an issue and then move to creative action.

		avg. lay rating	avg. Luth. rating	avg. pro. rating	very true	somewhat true	not true
681	Shows skill in moving people from anger to creative action.	2.70	2.76	2.82			
685	On controversial issues, concentrates on helping all to understand the issues.	2.86	2.93	2.99			
683	Shows ability to offer an opposing view without attacking the person.	2.78	2.88	2.98			

Characteristic 27
Promotion of Mutuality   2.68   2.84   2.99

Working with people in ways that make for mutuality because they encourage freedom of expression, participatory democracy, communication, and self-esteem.

		avg. lay rating	avg. Luth. rating	avg. pro. rating	very true	somewhat true	not true
716	In conflict situations lets people know where he stands in a way that does not alienate them.	2.70	2.87	3.03			
727	Works to broaden the base of participation in the decision-making process of the congregation.	2.65	2.79	2.93			
689	Points out the values implied in alternatives the congregation is considering when making decisions.	2.59	2.69	2.79			
714	Presses governing board of congregation to establish fair policies and practices for employees.	2.27	2.41	2.54			
710	Relates to members of staff in manner consistent with own theology.	2.46	2.72	2.97			
722	Allows persons freedom in carrying out assigned responsibilities.	2.68	2.86	3.03			

	avg. lay rating	avg. Luth. rating	avg. pro. rating	very true	somewhat true	not true
717 Helps people to know what changes are being made and why they are recommended.	2.97	3.06	3.15			
711 Causes people to feel they are needed in the ongoing work of the parish.	3.10	3.20	3.29			
744 Has thought through own unique role as minister.	2.67	2.93	3.19			

Characteristic 31
Effective Administration   2.68   2.75   2.82

Management skills in employing resources of time, funds, staff ideas, information and energy to the best advantage.

	avg. lay rating	avg. Luth. rating	avg. pro. rating	very true	somewhat true	not true
729 Exemplifies good stewardship in handling of own personal resources (energy, finances, time).	2.61	2.70	2.80			
738 Is easily accessible to staff.	2.68	2.83	2.97			
740 Facilitates communication of information and resources between church body and congregation.	2.70	2.74	2.78			
730 Invites and solicits ideas from each staff member.	2.68	2.83	2.98			
726 Administers, with a sense of stewardship, the monies and properties assigned to his or her care.	2.70	2.86	3.03			
739 Keeps improving own management and business skills.	2.52	2.59	2.66			
742 Structures calendar so there is time to meet primary responsibilities.	2.85	2.97	3.09			
734 Shows skill in managing church funds (e.g., establishing						

	avg. lay rating	avg. Luth. rating	avg. pro. rating	very true	somewhat true	not true
budgets, raising funds, employing good accounting procedures).	2.68	2.48	2.28			
736 Plans with enough flexibility to meet emergencies when they arise.	2.70	2.74	2.78			

Characteristic 32
Responsible Group Leadership   2.63   2.74   2.85

Skill in relating to people that
resolves or facilitates healthy
conflict, engenders mutual support,
and encourages individual responsi-
bility within the congregation.

720 Often anticipates where conflict may arise among members.	2.40	2.54	2.68			
719 Recruits and orients the most qualified persons for a particular task.	2.58	2.67	2.76			
718 Teaches a sense of responsibility for the financial support of the congregation.	2.89	2.95	3.02			
723 Intervenes in group conflict before it becomes destructive.	2.81	2.84	2.87			
721 Discourages groups from making decisions in the heat of emotional conflict.	2.84	2.86	2.88			
686 Is direct and positive in dealing with a staff member whose services must be terminated.	2.63	2.72	2.82			
675 On occasion will bring conflict out into the open in a constructive way.	2.64	2.78	2.91			
698 Seeks adequate congregational support before planning individual projects.	2.63	2.70	2.77			

	avg. lay rating	avg. Luth. rating	avg. pro. rating	very true	somewhat true	not true
731 Lets others "run the show" when they are in charge.	2.41	2.70	2.98			
693 Ties innovations to the needs of the congregation.	2.33	2.52	2.71			
673 Arbitrates rather than takes sides in a discussion.	2.87	2.83	2.79			
688 Engenders a sense of community where members are concerned for each other.	2.54	2.77	2.99			

Characteristic 39
Redemptive Forthrightness — 2.42 — 2.52 — 2.62

Ability to speak directly and redemptively with persons about their errors and estrangements.

	avg. lay rating	avg. Luth. rating	avg. pro. rating	very true	somewhat true	not true
746 When he or she sees the need, is not afraid to confront individuals privately with their sins.	2.24	2.38	2.52			
747 Acts as mediator between parents and estranged young people.	2.57	2.60	2.63			
745 Shows skill in training and evaluating staff.	2.64	2.64	2.64			
715 Personally confronts individuals whose gossiping is damaging others	2.14	2.38	2.63			
733 Speaks kindly but directly with parishioners who are delinquent in churchgoing, communion attendance, and giving.	2.53	2.62	2.71			

Characteristic 40
Respect for Proper Procedures — 2.32 — 2.51 — 2.70

Consistent observation of institutional and professional courtesies and proper procedures.

		avg. lay rating	avg. Luth. rating	avg. pro. rating	very true	somewhat true	not true
713	Accepts the discipline of parliamentary procedure in formal meetings.	2.35	2.40	2.44			
706	Clarifies areas of responsibility and chain of command in administrative matters.	2.46	2.63	2.80			
705	When possible, clears with neighboring clergy before ministering to their members.	2.18	2.60	3.03			
714	Presses governing board of congregation to establish fair policies and practices for employees.	2.27	2.41	2.54			

Characteristic 41
Encouragement of Expression of
Disagreement   2.26   2.48   2.69

*A sensitivity to the importance of
letting differences of opinion be
expressed, as shown by deliberate
efforts to oppose role stereotypes
and by helping people voice their
disagreements.*

703	Helps others feel it is all right to disagree with a minister.	2.04	2.42	2.80			
699	Discourages use of stereotyped sex roles in assigning responsible positions within the congregation.	2.12	2.30	2.48			
709	Does not gloss over differences among people to give the impression of unity.	2.10	2.39	2.68			
700	In a conflict situation, makes sure opinions of the minority are heard.	2.81	2.90	2.99			
708	Creates opportunities for						

	avg. lay rating	avg. Luth. rating	avg. pro. rating	very true	somewhat true	not true
people to air their differ-ences.	2.23	2.37	2.52			

Characteristic 57
Innovative Style of Leadership   1.96   1.98   2.01

Initiative in expanding the cultur-al horizons, organizational style, and leadership constituency of the congregation.

687 Works to enlarge the cultural interests of the congregation.	2.01	1.89	1.77			
741 Works for new patterns or styles of organizational life in the church.	1.90	2.02	2.14			
735 Brings minority people into positions of leadership.	1.96	2.04	2.11			

Area VI
Ministry of Counseling
(Chapter 8)

Characteristic 17
Enabling and Perceptive
Counseling   2.77   2.95   3.13

Skill in aiding persons under stress to work through serious problems and doing so with per-ception, sensitivity, and warmth that is freeing and supportive.

285   Avoids overcommitment by
distinguishing between crisis

		avg. lay rating	avg. Luth. rating	avg. pro. rating	very true	somewhat true	not true
	intervention and long-term help.	2.08	2.42	2.76			
282	Ministry to another in need is not dependent upon a hoped-for religious response.	2.24	2.49	2.76			
277	Shares the feelings of persons in trouble without taking on their tensions or problems.	2.75	2.89	3.05			
272	Counsels in a way that respects a person's freedom to choose own course of action.	2.89	3.09	3.29			
267	When conversing with a person, listens for feeling tones as well as words.	2.98	3.19	3.41			
280	Demonstrates understanding of the counseling needs of persons distressed with emotional, marital, or sexual problems.	2.88	3.03	3.19			
269	Will at times convey warmth and concern for a grief-stricken person by quietness and physical presence.	2.97	3.10	3.23			
284	Has thought through ways to help dying persons and their families.	2.87	2.91	2.95			
275	Moves slowly and softly with people who are hurting.	2.77	2.88	2.98			
259	Brings persons in touch with professional help they may need.	2.87	3.07	3.26			
258	Encourages the bereaved to talk through their grief.	2.60	2.90	3.20			
263	In counseling, addresses a problem with honesty and reality.	3.49	3.49	3.49			
261	Helps persons weigh the consequences of different courses of action.	2.66	2.86	3.06			

	avg. lay rating	avg. Luth. rating	avg. pro. rating	very true	somewhat true	not true
Characteristic 21 **Gracious Availability**	2.97	2.91	2.85			
Responding immediately with calming graciousness in situations that are tense, stressful, or tragic.						
257 Gives calm, rational explanation when a request contrary to denominational regulations cannot be granted.	2.74	2.67	2.59			
256 Responds graciously when called for help at an inconvenient time.	3.03	2.94	2.85			
289 Appears at ease while ministering in hospital setting, emergency unit, funeral home, mental hospital, home for handicapped, nursing home.	3.17	3.06	2.96			
273 Goes immediately to minister to members in crisis situations.	3.05	3.09	3.13			
264 After visiting with him or her, persons fearful of death and dying often feel less anxious.	2.87	2.80	2.72			
Characteristic 42 **Empathetic Aid in Suffering**	2.30	2.45	2.60			
Capacity for empathetic participation in others' suffering, while offering or seeking out resources to ease suffering or need.						
247 Tries to learn the meaning of suffering from a person who suffers.	2.10	2.34	2.58			
246 Engages people who have struggled through a problem to help those now facing the same kind of problem.	2.41	2.48	2.55			

		avg. lay rating	avg. Luth. rating	avg. pro. rating	very true	somewhat true	not true
251	Helps a terminally ill patient deal with the question of shortening or prolonging life through rejecting or accepting medical care.	2.22	2.35	2.49			
252	Makes maximal use of resources provided by church-related colleges, hospitals, welfare agencies, etc.	2.48	2.63	2.78			

Characteristic 46
Intentional Counseling   2.43   2.32   2.21

Manifesting but not compelling
specific values and beliefs while
seeking theologically based solu-
tions to personal problems of
counselees.

250	Tries to assist counselees in achieving a solution to all personal problems presented.	2.30	1.91	1.51			
248	In counseling, shares own beliefs without forcing them on a person.	2.92	2.86	2.80			
317	Uses counseling approaches that are expressions of Lutheran theology.	2.21	2.19	2.18			
333	Presents a theological position on matters such as divorce, abortion, suicide, amnesty.	2.28	2.31	2.36			

Area VII
Reaching Out with Compassion
to Community and World
(Chapter 9)

Characteristic 37
Use of Broad Knowledge   2.55   2.60   2.64

	avg. lay rating	avg. Luth. rating	avg. pro. rating	very true	somewhat true	not true

*A broad knowledge base from which
information is drawn when seeking
to help people clarify beliefs,
to show understanding, or to teach
ethical decision making.*

322 Knows the historical circumstances that shaped creeds and confessions of the Lutheran church.	2.96	2.74	2.52			
329 Is conversant with the polity and policies of own church body.	2.73	2.77	2.80			
321 Stimulates people to clarify their religious beliefs.	2.71	2.81	2.91			
324 Reflects an awareness of current affairs reported in newspapers and periodicals.	2.41	2.54	2.66			
323 Shows understanding of people who express interest in other religions of the world.	2.39	2.34	2.28			
330 Works at further development of pastoral skills.	3.16	3.29	3.42			
331 Acknowledges the heritage and current contribution Jews provide to an understanding of Christianity.	2.17	2.23	2.30			
332 Teaches processes by which one can arrive at ethical decisions.	2.21	2.33	2.46			
312 Evaluates current trends in theological thought.	2.21	2.31	2.41			

Characteristic 44
Initiation of Community Services   2.15   2.33   2.52

*Sensitivity to the needs of
special groups in the community,
especially the neglected, condemned,
suffering, and alienated, as
evidenced by involvement in seeing
that their needs are compassionately met.*

		avg. lay rating	avg. Luth. rating	avg. pro. rating	very true	somewhat true	not true
150	Works to improve community services to such persons as mentally retarded, emotionally disturbed, aged, etc.	2.46	2.54	2.62			
153	Originates activities which consider youths' interests and awaken their enthusiasm.	2.88	2.77	2.66			
155	Shows compassion and understanding of people usually condemned by society.	2.39	2.63	2.88			
157	Locates people to whom to refer individuals not helped by community agencies.	2.07	2.34	2.60			
152	Gives public expression to own concern for the well-being of the whole community.	1.98	2.26	2.55			
149	Stands behind community efforts to fight for justice for all people.	2.16	2.36	2.56			
151	Requests members to hire such disadvantaged people as the physically handicapped and rehabilitated convicts, alcoholics, and drug addicts.	1.44	1.72	1.99			
148	Makes members aware of how the congregation is ministering to the community.	2.33	2.46	2.59			
166	Wins the respect and cooperation of society's outcasts.	1.65	1.93	2.22			

Characteristic 45
Candid Christian Humanness   2.10   2.32   2.53

*A quality of humanness evidenced by
a willingness openly to acknowledge
the ambiguities of life, the
struggles of faith, the disappoint-
ments of ministry, and to seek
God's thoughts in the thinking of
other Christians.*

| 367 | Openly admits to times of struggle over own personal faith. | 2.39 | 2.64 | 2.90 | | | |

		avg. lay rating	avg. Luth. rating	avg. pro. rating	very true	somewhat true	not true
354	Talks openly about own experiences of faith and doubt.	2.50	2.62	2.75			
376	Doesn't try to hide the fact that he or she worries.	2.02	2.14	2.25			
395	Actively tries to change the traditional shape of ministry to fit the future better.	1.55	1.86	2.17			
375	Seeks the thinking of other Christians as one way of knowing God's will.	2.17	2.30	2.43			
362	Acknowledges there are times when he or she gives in to temptation.	2.69	2.92	3.15			
372	Admits privately that the ministry has its disappointments.	1.38	1.73	2.08			

Characteristic 47
Community Bridge Building 2.18 2.31 2.43

Ability to gain the cooperation and trust of a community for improving services to people with special needs.

134	Provides community leadership in ways that awaken trust.	2.42	2.45	2.48			
150	Works to improve community services to such persons as mentally retarded, emotionally disturbed, aged, etc.	2.46	2.54	2.62			
132	Builds bridges between groups within the community and facilitates cooperation among them.	2.12	2.24	2.37			
125	Actively supports efforts to improve public schools in the community.	1.76	1.94	2.12			
149	Stands behind community efforts to fight for justice for all people.	2.16	2.36	2.56			

Characteristic 48
Integrative Ministry 2.08 2.30 2.51

	avg. lay rating	avg. Luth. rating	avg. pro. rating	very true	somewhat true	not true

Integrating people of varying racial, cultural, and socio-economic backgrounds into the congregation and community.

136 Works toward racial integration in the community.	1.83	2.11	2.40			
156 Works for racially integrated congregations.	1.45	1.80	2.14			
135 Encourages all classes of people to join the congregation.	3.04	3.12	3.21			
168 Integrates people of varying educational, ethnic, and cultural backgrounds into the congregation.	1.96	2.25	2.54			
133 Ministers to prisoners and their families, whether members of the congregation or not.	2.13	2.19	2.25			

Characteristic 49
Equipping for Community Service   2.02   2.30   2.57

A concept and manifestation of ministry in which one equips members attitudinally and theologically to enter with understanding into community activities as a Christian ministry.

171 Helps people identify and evaluate the adequacy of their goals and values.	2.31	2.51	2.70			
173 Views ministry to the needs of persons and to the needs of the community as complementary, rather than contrasting, ministries.	2.07	2.35	2.63			
179 Believes the pastor's special responsibility is for encouraging, training, and equipping the laity for their ministry in the community.	2.28	2.64	3.00			
172 Alerts members to their need for learning from Christians in other parts of the world.	1.99	2.19	2.38			

	avg. lay rating	avg. Luth. rating	avg. pro. rating	very true	somewhat true	not true
181 Assures his or her people that God works through structures of economics, health, welfare, police, courts, and family to accomplish his purpose.	1.99	2.19	2.39			
170 Relates to nonchurched people within the community in a nonjudgmental and nonpatronizing way.	1.78	2.22	2.67			
177 Demonstrates understanding of the impact of social, economic, and political forces.	1.40	1.78	2.16			
148 Makes members aware of how the congregation is ministering to the community.	2.33	2.46	2.59			
157 Locates people to whom to refer individuals not helped by community agencies.	2.07	2.34	2.60			
152 Gives public expression to own concern for the well-being of the whole community.	1.98	2.26	2.55			

Characteristic 51
Prophetic Concern for the Oppressed 2.00 2.25 2.49

Demonstrating theologically alert concern and compassion for those who are different or oppressed, through ministries sponsored by the congregation.

	avg. lay rating	avg. Luth. rating	avg. pro. rating	very true	somewhat true	not true
122 Shows concern for liberation of oppressed people.	2.20	2.42	2.64			
155 Shows compassion and understanding of people usually condemned by society.	2.39	2.64	2.88			
180 Develops educational ministries with persons of other races and cultures.	1.64	1.75	1.87			
128 Asserts that the congregation is the place where prophetic leadership should emerge and move throughout society.	1.77	2.07	2.36			

	avg. lay rating	avg. Luth. rating	avg. pro. rating	very true	somewhat true	not true
294 Explores theological issues underlying current social movements.	2.00	2.35	2.71			
Characteristic 54 **Broad Intellectual Stimulation**	2.13	2.19	2.24			

Seeking the stimulation and knowledge to be found in a variety of experiences both in and outside the profession, that may evidence some commitment to professional growth.

	avg. lay rating	avg. Luth. rating	avg. pro. rating			
346 Is familiar with the principles of all major schools of practice in the field of counseling.	1.91	1.74	1.58			
309 Regularly views a wide variety of movies, plays, or television programs.	1.15	1.42	1.68			
350 Participates in educational retreats, workshops, and seminars to increase own effectiveness.	2.87	2.93	3.00			
308 Shows confidence in own intellectual ability.	2.51	2.43	2.34			
336 Works with members of other professions as colleagues.	2.16	2.43	2.70			
342 Makes constructive suggestions to national, local, and regional church leaders.	2.20	2.17	2.14			
Characteristic 55 **Co-Ministry to the Distressed and Alienated**	2.07	2.16	2.25			

Utilization of congregational groups in ministering to persons with a wide variety of special needs and offering personal assistance to estranged individuals and families.

	avg. lay rating	avg. Luth. rating	avg. pro. rating			
286 Shows congregations how to extend a ministry to single parents.	1.96	2.03	2.09			

		avg. lay rating	avg. Luth. rating	avg. pro. rating	very true	somewhat true	not true
287	Leads a care group of people who are all under stress.	1.48	1.56	1.65			
288	Provides supportive ministry to unmarried fathers and mothers and their parents.	2.10	2.20	2.31			
279	Makes contacts to locate work opportunities for jobless persons.	1.49	1.67	1.86			
274	Helps members both anticipate and adjust to retirement.	1.88	2.10	2.32			
265	Sees that groups are trained to carry out specialized ministries (rehabilitation, crisis intervention, legal and medical aid, financial counsel, etc.).	1.70	1.86	2.02			
253	Is an active member of a suicide prevention team.	1.32	1.34	1.35			
276	Involves more isolated persons (divorced, widowed, singles, migrants, etc.) in the life of the congregation.	2.47	2.57	2.68			
268	Helps organize members ready to help others in times of illness and trouble.	2.56	2.61	2.67			
254	Assists persons working through problems before and after divorce.	2.55	2.67	2.80			
278	Provides parental counseling for youth or students out of touch with parents.	2.89	2.79	2.68			
270	Establishes communication between estranged couples.	2.43	2.52	2.61			

Characteristic 56
Active Concern for the Oppressed   1.82   2.09   2.36

Sensitivity and concern for the welfare and future of oppressed peoples shown by efforts to combat smugness and racism in congregation and community with authoritative information.

		avg. lay rating	avg. Luth. rating	avg. pro. rating	very true	somewhat true	not true
141	Makes individuals aware of their possible part in causing world poverty.	1.67	1.92	2.17			
142	Uses authoritative information and facts to meet racism and prejudice in congregation and community.	1.87	2.08	2.29			
138	Acquaints self with the history and aspirations of minority groups and other oppressed people.	1.75	1.97	2.19			
139	Raises the awareness of church members regarding happenings, needs, and issues within the community.	2.12	2.27	2.43			
145	Raises members' level of sensitivity to injustice and denial of opportunity.	1.68	2.19	2.70			

Characteristic 58
Ecumenical Openness   1.87   1.96   2.05

A cooperative, open stance that
welcomes activities involving new
groups, experimental new forms, and
the testing of new ideas.

83	Participates in ecumenical projects with ministers of other denominations.	1.90	1.79	1.67			
111	Does not attempt to keep own congregation "apart" from congregations of other denominations.	2.20	2.12	2.03			
67	Fosters cooperative activities within a cluster of Lutheran congregations.	1.95	2.04	2.14			
107	At times, leads contemporary, experimental forms of worship.	1.64	1.83	2.03			
66	Supports responsible persons trying new educational methods or ideas.	2.16	2.33	2.49			
120	Encourages members to express their faith through the fine arts						

	avg. lay rating	avg. Luth. rating	avg. pro. rating	very true	somewhat true	not true
(such as painting, sculpture, poetry, drama, music).	1.40	1.66	1.92			

Characteristic 60
Balanced Acceptance of Theological
Diversity — 1.96 1.89 1.81

Advocacy and acknowledgment of the legitimacy of theological diversity whether involving the church's mission, ecumenicity, or pentecostalism.

311 Advocates balance between preaching the gospel and working to improve the material well-being of people.	1.71	1.79	1.87			
295 Appears on public platforms with clergy of other religious denominations where acts of worship are involved.	1.89	1.60	1.31			
337 Is open to pentecostal charismatic renewal in the congregation.	1.33	1.08	0.84			
328 Encourages members to acknowledge one another as belonging to the body of Christ, even when they hold divergent theological views.	2.91	3.06	3.21			

Characteristic 62
Assertive Civic Leadership — 0.97 1.31 1.65

Informed and vigorous personal participation and encouragement of the church's involvement in the struggle for social justice.

161 Declares a willingness to run for public office in the community.	−0.34	−0.04	0.25			
163 Asserts that the pastor is as free to participate in community activities as any other citizen.	1.57	1.69	1.80			

		avg. lay rating	avg. Luth. rating	avg. pro. rating	very true	somewhat true	not true
165	Takes an informed position on controversial community issues.	1.30	1.79	2.27			
178	Participates in movements to correct unfair and unjust public policy.	0.93	1.32	1.71			
167	Insists that political matters are rightful concerns of the church.	0.60	1.18	1.76			
176	Organizes action/reflection groups in congregation to discuss public affairs.	0.49	0.97	1.44			
169	Pressures public officials on behalf of the oppressed.	0.59	1.03	1.47			
164	Involves professionals from the community in congregational programs, services, or activities.	1.72	2.01	2.29			
175	Works to make sure that all people are free to secure housing in areas of their choice.	0.72	1.09	1.48			
129	Participates vigorously in community services as a private citizen.	1.51	1.72	1.94			
154	Organizes groups to change civil laws which seem in the light of Scripture to be morally wrong.	1.11	1.34	1.56			
123	Uses principles and methods of community organization for social change.	1.37	1.62	1.87			

Characteristic 64
Openness to Civil Disobedience   0.63   0.93   1.22

Willingness to disobey civil laws in order to protest social wrongs or to change laws that are unjust or morally wrong.

| 124 | Is willing to risk arrest to protest social wrongs. | 0.35 | 0.65 | 0.95 | | | |
| 154 | Organizes groups to change civil laws which seem in the light of Scripture to be morally wrong. | 1.11 | 1.34 | 1.56 | | | |

	avg. lay rating	avg. Luth. rating	avg. pro. rating	very true	somewhat true	not true
126 Disobeys unjust laws unhesitatingly when the gospel or concrete situation dictates.	0.45	0.81	1.17			

Area VIII
Informed Leadership
of Liturgical Worship
(Chapter 10)

	avg. lay rating	avg. Luth. rating	avg. pro. rating	very true	somewhat true	not true
Characteristic 33 **Effective Speaking**	2.96	2.73	2.50			

In speaking situations, commanding and holding attention by means of effective delivery and theologically meaningful substance.

	avg. lay rating	avg. Luth. rating	avg. pro. rating			
93 Reads aloud clearly and distinctly.	3.09	2.91	2.73			
113 Has a strong speaking voice.	2.72	2.45	2.18			
70 When preaching, holds the interest and attention of all hearers.	3.22	3.00	2.78			
94 Leads prayer and devotional times as one familiar with the theological and liturgical foundations of prayer.	2.81	2.56	2.31			

	avg. lay rating	avg. Luth. rating	avg. pro. rating			
Characteristic 52 **Balanced Liturgical Judgment**	2.41	2.25	2.09			

Leading worship in a dignified yet personal manner, including appreciative and competent use of suitable music and traditions of the church year.

	avg. lay rating	avg. Luth. rating	avg. pro. rating			
54 Observes the traditions of the church year in worship.	2.46	2.19	1.92			
55 Handles disturbances during						

	avg. lay rating	avg. Luth. rating	avg. pro. rating	very true	somewhat true	not true
worship in ways that both maintain the dignity of the service and minister to needs.	2.42	2.30	2.19			
95 Demonstrates an appreciation for music and hymns which are liturgically and pastorally suitable.	2.36	2.26	2.17			

Characteristic 63
Liturgical Orientation   1.45   1.14   0.84

A stance toward worship that places a high priority on the proper and effective observance of traditional liturgical practices and the use of paraments.

114	Places considerable emphasis on altar hangings and vestments that are symbolic of the church year.	1.70	1.40	1.11
63	Is primarily worship oriented— sees self as first and foremost a liturgist.	0.98	0.75	0.52
117	Chants clearly and pleasantly.	1.69	1.26	0.84

Area IX
Not Wanted:
Dominating Influence
(Chapter 4)

Characteristic 61
Extreme Adherence to Scriptural
Authority   2.00   1.37   0.74

Dogmatic and somewhat legalistic adherence to verbal inspiration, historicity, literal interpretation, and ubiquitous applicability of the Bible as authority in matters of daily living.

	avg. lay rating	avg. Luth. rating	avg. pro. rating	very true	somewhat true	not true
303 Teaches that God directly supplied the words used in writing the Bible, including those referring to historical, geographical, and scientific matters.	2.29	1.11	--0.06			
351 Tends to give authoritative answers based on specific Bible verses.	2.24	1.35	0.46			
334 Insists that Adam, Eve, and Jonah are historical figures.	1.20	0.72	0.25			
348 Reinforces advice on ethical decisions with specific verses from Scripture.	2.32	1.90	1.49			
319 Acknowledges the presence and activity of a personal devil (Satan).	2.51	2.23	1.94			
310 Gives answers on doctrinal issues that do not allow any other position.	0.76	0.30	−0.16			
338 Preaches sermons which accent people's need to work at gaining faith in God.	2.72	1.74	0.76			
344 Distinguishes between the genuineness of faith and holiness of life.	1.97	1.59	1.22			

Characteristic 65
Spiritual Talk — 1.23 / 0.81 / 0.39

A conversational vocabulary that frequently includes the phrase, "born again," references to God's personal help, and at times the claims of having experienced the gift of tongues.

	avg. lay rating	avg. Luth. rating	avg. pro. rating
374 Refers to self as a "born again" Christian.	1.90	1.26	0.62
394 In social conversation, talks about what the Lord has done recently in own life.	1.73	1.45	1.16
384 Claims to have experienced the gift of tongues.	0.07	−0.27	−0.61

	avg. lay rating	avg. Luth. rating	avg. pro. rating	very true	somewhat true	not true
Characteristic 66 **Exclusive Devotion to Congregational** **Concerns**	0.27	−0.10	−0.46			
Avoidance of involvement in community action in order to concentrate on identifiably religious (or Christian) ministries within the congregation.						
160 Insists that clergy should stick to religion and not concern themselves with social, economic, and political questions.	0.21	−0.32	−0.86			
147 Remains generally uninvolved in civic (government) activities.	0.60	0.12	−0.36			
130 Shows little concern for individuals outside the congregation.	−0.79	−1.10	−1.41			
162 Priorities in use of time indicate the belief that the one and only way to build an ideal world society is to convert everyone to Christianity.	1.14	0.73	0.32			
174 Frequently approaches strangers to ask about the condition of their souls.	0.17	0.08	0.00			
Characteristic 67 **Law unto Self**	−0.43	−0.84	−1.25			
A style of leadership that assumes total responsibility for all activities and their outcomes whether these activities involve discussions, specific tasks, congregational decisions, or programming.						
697 Dominates group discussions.	−0.31	−0.79	−1.27			
728 Gives impression that if a job is to be done right, he or she must do it.	−0.66	1.09	−1.52			

	avg. lay rating	avg. Luth. rating	avg. pro. rating	very true	somewhat true	not true
724 Seeks to be viewed as the ultimate authority in the congregation.	−0.14	−0.62	−1.10			
704 Acts as though planning is less necessary in the church than in other institutions.	−0.67	−0.90	−1.14			
707 Relies primarily on charisma and intuition in planning parish activities.	0.05	−0.27	−0.59			
712 Cannot let go of details and delegate responsibility.	−0.32	−0.78	−1.24			
701 Commits congregation to a program without consulting governing boards.	−0.98	−1.43	−1.88			

Characteristic 68
Spiritual Superiority   −0.55   −1.08   −1.61

An attitude of spiritual superiority
evidenced by a tendency to
discount both the competence of lay
persons in religious matters and
the contribution of formal theological
training.

339 Preaches the priesthood of believers, but treats nonordained Christians as second-class citizens in the kingdom.	−0.88	−1.54	−2.20			
352 Does not want lay persons to teach Bible classes.	−1.20	−1.66	−2.12			
343 Questions the need for lengthy and formal theological training.	0.43	−0.03	−0.50			

Characteristic 69
Unbusinesslike Leadership   −1.01   −1.28   −1.54

A lack of leadership and a careless
disregard for one's responsibilities
as demonstrated through failure
to plan, procrastination, indecision,

	avg. lay rating	avg. Luth. rating	avg. pro. rating	very true	somewhat true	not true

incompletion, belittling of others, and superficial measures of success.

725 Plans projects without consider- ing financial requirements.	−1.10	−1.33	−1.54			
732 Shows a pattern of procrastina- tion (e.g., unmet deadlines, late reports or incomplete records, postponed decisions).	−1.07	−1.44	−1.79			
677 Fails to provide leadership at times when congregation is looking for direction.	−0.79	−0.93	−1.06			
737 Often belittles a person in front of others.	−1.95	−2.20	−2.43			
743 Measures success by size of budgets, buildings, and membership.	−0.16	−0.52	−0.87			

Area X
Not Wanted:
Ministry-Defeating Behaviors
(Chapter 5)

Characteristic 70 **Secular Life-Style**	−2.33	−2.15	−1.96			

Personal behavior that is offensive to many because it violates social norms of behavior for clergy or bears the marks of rebellious or undisciplined behavior.

509 Occasionally tells jokes that hearers consider dirty.	−2.72	−2.41	−2.11			
531 Displays mannerisms commonly associated with members of the opposite sex.	−2.59	−2.46	−2.32			
526 Enjoys visiting cocktail lounges.	−2.31	−1.85	−1.38			
505 Wears casual clothes even for professional activities.	−1.55	−1.44	−1.34			

	avg. lay rating	avg. Luth. rating	avg. pro. rating	very true	somewhat true	not true
530 Is unable to get along with spouse.	−2.78	−2.85	−2.91			
519 Has the reputation of a fast, and often careless, driver.	−1.99	−1.86	−1.73			

Characteristic 71
Self-Centered Isolation | −2.19 | −2.22 | −2.24

A preoccupation with self that prevents deep relationships with associates and family including deep feelings of insecurity.

524 Seldom talks about own family, spouse, or children.	−1.34	−1.40	−1.46			
525 Gives the impression of being always busy or in a hurry.	−1.96	−1.95	−1.95			
517 Worries excessively about what others think of him or her.	−2.20	−2.31	−2.43			
514 Tends to be a loner in relation to other pastors.	−2.24	−2.14	−2.04			
523 Takes criticism of parish programs personally.	−2.19	−2.27	−2.35			
534 Tends to be pessimistic and negative in own attitudes.	−2.69	−2.67	−2.64			
521 Is jealous of other staff members' popularity with parishioners.	−2.74	−2.72	−2.71			

Characteristic 72
Evidences of Insecurity | −2.21 | −2.29 | −2.36

Display of need for constant reassurance that he or she is right, is in control, is in authority, and is universally approved.

502 Seeks constant reassurance that he or she is doing a good job.	−1.93	−1.96	−2.00			
503 Sets up meetings in such a way that he or she is sure to be in control.	−2.12	−2.29	−2.45			
501 Questions the motives of anyone who opposes him or her.	−2.27	−2.48	−2.70			

		avg. lay rating	avg. Luth. rating	avg. pro. rating	very true	somewhat true	not true
499	Strongly seeks public acclaim for what the congregation accomplishes.	-2.03	-2.07	-2.10			
508	Under pressure is likely to violate own principles and conform to expectations of congregation.	-2.51	-2.50	-2.50			
500	Uses the pulpit to express personal irritations.	-2.80	-2.87	-2.94			
507	Appears humiliated over mistakes made in public.	-1.79	-1.82	-1.86			

Characteristic 73
Instability   -2.48   -2.37   -2.25

Lack of stability in commitment to ministry, in decision making, and in financial judgment.

515	Wonders in conversation with members whether he or she should be in the ministry.	-2.50	-2.24	-1.99			
516	Makes impulsive decisions.	-2.26	-2.17	-2.08			
511	Complains publicly about own low salary.	-2.63	-2.46	-2.29			
538	Lives beyond personal means.	-2.53	-2.58	-2.63			

Characteristic 74
Self-Isolating Behavior   -2.67   -2.66   -2.65

Behaving in ways that isolate from others through demonstration of impatience, extreme expectations, and inability to forgive oneself.

545	Talks as though unable to forgive self.	-2.62	-2.69	-2.75			
546	Views self as ultimate authority in matters of taste.	-2.65	-2.64	-2.63			
542	Tends to be abrupt and impatient when talking with people.	-2.87	-2.77	-2.68			
520	Publicly shows impatience with people who resist change.	-2.30	-2.20	-2.10			

		avg. lay rating	avg. Luth. rating	avg. pro. rating	very true	somewhat true	not true
504	Pouts publicly when things don't go own way.	−3.09	−3.12	−3.15			
498	Rarely lets anyone get to know him or her.	−2.51	−2.56	−2.60			

Characteristic 75
Insecure Authoritarianism   −2.81   −2.85   −2.88

An insecure authoritarianism which is generally domineering and bossy, but at times deferent to or completely intimidated by persons of influence.

529	Acts as boss, second only to God.	−3.03	−3.12	−3.20			
527	Acts as though there is only one right way to do most things.	−2.32	−2.41	−2.51			
528	Can be completely intimidated by some one person of influence.	−2.80	−2.82	−2.84			
532	Appears to believe own opinion as a minister should be accepted without question.	−2.77	−2.85	−2.92			
537	Uses sermons to attack certain members in the congregation or community.	−3.21	−3.31	−3.40			
540	Uses ministerial role to maintain a sense of superiority.	−2.91	−2.97	−3.04			
539	Is quick to condemn people whose words or actions seem questionable to him or her.	−2.89	−2.88	−2.87			
535	Looks for another call or appointment the moment things do not go well.	−2.91	−2.86	−2.80			
513	Frequently shows favoritism.	−2.56	−2.62	−2.68			
533	Pays less attention to the thinking of women than the thinking of men.	−2.64	−2.58	−2.52			

Characteristic 76
Undisciplined Living   −3.20   −3.10   −3.00

	avg. lay rating	avg. Luth. rating	avg. pro. rating	very true	somewhat true	not true

*Questionable or immoral behavior
that irritates, shocks, and offends.*

541 Is occasionally intoxicated.	−3.19	−3.04	−2.89			
544 Occasionally gambles.	−2.83	−2.67	−2.50			
543 Occasionally involved in extra-marital affairs or illicit sexual relationships.	−3.58	−3.60	−3.62			

**Characteristic 77
Impersonalness Without Trust** −3.04 −3.10 −3.16

*Lack of commitment to the welfare of
the people one serves and inability
to commit one's life and work to
God's care.*

506 Tends to be cold and impersonal.	−3.04	−3.00	−2.96			
522 Discusses with members of the congregation what has been said in confidence.	−3.43	−3.56	−3.69			
510 Life and work are not committed to care of God.	−3.30	−3.32	−3.33			
512 Is insensitive to feelings of people who are closest to him or her (immediate family, relatives, co-workers).	−2.81	−2.93	−3.05			
536 People are afraid to come to him or her for counseling on problems and problem situations.	−3.04	−3.06	−3.08			
518 Seems oblivious to people because of being engrossed in "higher things."	−2.61	−2.72	−2.84			